Getting Familiar with the Levels Tool

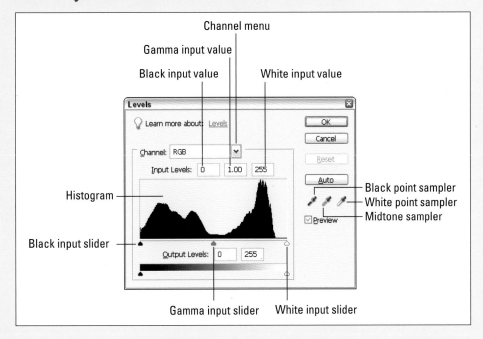

Channel menu

Gamma input value

Black input value · White input value

Histogram

Black input slider

Black point sampler
White point sampler
Midtone sampler

Gamma input slider · White input slider

- ✔ Open an image in Elements Full Edit mode (Standard Edit mode on the Mac in Elements 4.0).
- ✔ Press Ctrl/⌘ + L to open the Levels dialog box.
- ✔ View the histogram to see where the data in the image appears.
- ✔ Move the Black slider to reset the black point. (Press Alt/Option when moving the slider to see the first appearance of black in the image.)
- ✔ Move the White slider to reset the white point. (Press Alt/Option when moving the slider to see the first appearance of white in the image.)
- ✔ Move the Gamma slider left to lighten the overall image or right to darken the overall image.
- ✔ Click the Midtone sampler and click on a neutral gray in the photo.

Color Management for Digital Photographers for DUMMIES

Cheat Sheet

Keyboard Shortcuts for Tone and Color Corrections

	Windows	Macintosh
Auto Smart Fix	Alt+Ctrl+M	Option+⌘+M
Auto Levels	Alt+Ctrl+L	Option+⌘+L
Auto Contrast	Alt+Shift+Ctrl+L	Option+Shift+⌘+L
Auto Color Correction	Shift+Ctrl+B	Shift+⌘+B
Auto Red Eye Fix	Shift+Ctrl+M	Shift+⌘+M
Levels	Ctrl+L	⌘+L
Adjust Hue/Saturation	Ctrl+U	⌘+U
Remove Color	Shift+Ctrl+U	Shift+⌘+U
Convert to Black and White	Alt+Ctrl+B	N/A*
Image Size	Alt+Ctrl+I	Option+⌘+I
When the Levels dialog box is open		
Red Channel	Ctrl+1	⌘+1
Green Channel	Ctrl+2	⌘+2
Blue Channel	Ctrl+3	⌘+3
Composite Channel	Ctrl+~ (tilde)	⌘+~ (tilde)

*Not available on Mac in version 4 of Elements.

For Dummies: Bestselling Book Series for Beginners

Color Management for Digital Photographers

FOR

DUMMIES®

by Ted Padova and Don Mason

BICENTENNIAL
1807
WILEY
2007
BICENTENNIAL

Wiley Publishing, Inc.

Color Management for Digital Photographers For Dummies®

Published by
Wiley Publishing, Inc.
111 River Street
Hoboken, NJ 07030-5774
www.wiley.com

WILEY

About the Authors

Ted Padova first began his interest in amateur photography as a Peace Corps volunteer in Venezuela. He toured five Latin American countries, collecting shoeboxes of slides he hopefully will one day sort out. Upon completion of his two-year Peace Corps tour, he attended the New York Institute of Photography in Manhattan when it was a resident school, earning a diploma in Commercial Photography.

In 2004, he retired from his Digital Imaging Service Bureau and Custom Photo Finishing Lab after 15 years of owning and operating three facilities. He has authored over 25 computer books on Adobe Acrobat, Adobe Photoshop, Adobe Photoshop Elements, and Adobe Illustrator. Today, he spends his time writing and speaking nationally and internationally on Acrobat PDF and digital imaging.

Don Mason is a graduate of Brooks Institute of Photography in Santa Barbara, California. He has been a professional photographer for more than three decades and works in virtually every aspect of commercial photography. Don first started using a computer in 1999, when he didn't believe that digital imaging would ever replace his wing lynch system used for processing all his E-6 film and his darkroom where he made his own C-prints. After 4 years of intensive work in Adobe Photoshop, he abandoned his analog film lab and went completely digital. Today, he divides his time shooting professional commercial photography and printing art prints for a wide range of clients on his two, oversized Epson inkjet printers.

Dedication

Ted Padova: For Arnie

Don Mason: For Jim, Joe, and Wes

Authors' Acknowledgments

Our sincere thanks to the following people who graciously allowed us to use photos of their delightful children: Claire Lahorgue and her children, Michael and Sarah; and Jennifer Randle and her children, Cody, Calico, and Becky.

We'd also like to thank Courtney Creasy, Joel Berkovitz, Karen Krulikowsky, Lisle Gates, Carole Murray, Dan Mancini, Mark Young, Cheri Zadarski, Nicole Saint-John, and Kortney Penrose.

To the AOL Photo Chat gang — your input helped keep it real.

Publisher's Acknowledgments

We're proud of this book; please send us your comments through our online registration form located at www.dummies.com/register/.

Some of the people who helped bring this book to market include the following:

Acquisitions, Editorial, and Media Development

Project Editor: Rebecca Huehls

Sr. Acquisitions Editor: Bob Woerner

Copy Editors: Laura Miller, Heidi Unger

Technical Editor: Michael Sullivan

Editorial Manager: Leah P. Cameron

Media Development Specialists: Angela Denny, Kate Jenkins, Steven Kudirka, Kit Malone

Media Development Coordinator: Laura Atkinson

Media Project Supervisor: Laura Moss

Media Development Manager: Laura VanWinkle

Editorial Assistant: Amanda Foxworth

Sr. Editorial Assistant: Cherie Case

Cartoons: Rich Tennant (www.the5thwave.com)

Composition Services

Project Coordinator: Patrick Redmond

Layout and Graphics: Denny Hager, Heather Ryan

Proofreaders: Laura Albert, Betty Kish

Indexer: Palmer Publishing Services

Anniversary Logo Design: Richard Pacifico

Publishing and Editorial for Technology Dummies

Richard Swadley, Vice President and Executive Group Publisher

Andy Cummings, Vice President and Publisher

Mary Bednarek, Executive Acquisitions Director

Mary C. Corder, Editorial Director

Publishing for Consumer Dummies

Diane Graves Steele, Vice President and Publisher

Joyce Pepple, Acquisitions Director

Composition Services

Gerry Fahey, Vice President of Production Services

Debbie Stailey, Director of Composition Services

Contents at a Glance

Table of Contents

Introduction

*Y*ou rarely find a photo you can take with a digital camera or scan on a desktop scanner that doesn't need some kind of brightness, contrast, or color correction. Taking pictures with your camera is only half of your job when you want to print pictures or host them on the Web. The other half of your job is editing in your digital darkroom.

In this book, you can find out how to get color just right by setting up a digital darkroom in your home (or wherever you work on your digital photos) and using the plentiful and robust tools in Photoshop Elements to correct tone and color.

About This Book

In this book, we try to provide a comprehensive view of tone and color correction, using the tools available in Photoshop Elements versions 4 and 5. We stick to what Elements provides you in the application without using third-party products designed to overcome limitations in the program. What Elements offers off-the-shelf is all you need to create the pictures you want with proper brightness, contrast, and color.

Who This Book Is For

If you've had problems getting brightness and color correct on your pictures, this book is for you. This book is also meant for Photoshop Elements users.

If you're a Macintosh user, you'll find this book equally as helpful as Windows users do. We use screen shots from the newest release of Photoshop Elements, which is available only in Windows, as of this writing. However, just about all the techniques, the dialog boxes, and almost all tools are the same in a Mac's Photoshop Elements 4 as those found in Window's Photoshop Elements 5.

If you're a Photoshop user, we recommend our book *Color Correction For Digital Photographers Only* (Wiley Publishing) rather than this one because in this book, we limit the coverage of color correction to working with Photoshop Elements.

Conventions Used in This Book

We point you to menus where you'll frequently access commands throughout the book. You need to know how to decipher the references for where to go when we detail steps in a procedure. First off, you need to know how we show accessing a menu command. You might see something like this:

Enhance⇨Adjust Color⇨Adjust Color for Skin Tones

When you see commands such as these, we're asking you to click the Enhance menu to open that menu, then click the menu command labeled Adjust Color to open a submenu. In the submenu, select the Adjust Color for Skin Tones command. Many of the menu commands we talk about then open a dialog box where you perform your editing.

Another convention we use relates to using keystrokes on your keyboard. When we mention some keys that you need to press on your keyboard, the text looks like this:

Shift+Ctrl+M (Shift+⌘+M on Macs)

In this case, you need to press the Shift key, the Control key in Windows (the ⌘ key on a Mac), and the M key at the same time. This keyboard shortcut opens the Adjust Smart Fix dialog box.

How This Book Is Organized

This book is divided into logical chunks (parts). Chapters that discuss related topics are grouped together in five different parts.

Part I: The Basics of Color Editing

The first three chapters in the book are devoted to understanding color, calibration, and the essentials you need to do to prepare your color editing environment. We talk about terms and concepts you need to know for any kind of color correction and tonal editing. Be certain you understand the concepts in these three chapters and, in particular, make sure you get your monitor calibrated for proper color viewing.

Part II: Image Brightness and Contrast Corrections

In almost all cases, color correction begins with tonal corrections. In the three chapters in this part, we talk about all the methods you have available in Photoshop Elements to get the proper brightness and contrast in your pictures. As you can discover for yourself, doing these corrections first makes the job of color correction much easier.

Part III: Color Corrections

This part relates exclusively to color correction, and it's by far the largest part in the book. We cover color correction techniques for a wide variety of image problems related to color reproduction. You can find out all that Elements has to offer for professional color-correction methods, and we avoid using menu commands and tools that just don't measure up when you want to create quality images.

Part IV: Finishing Work

This part is limited to color printing. We talk about what you need to do to get your output to look like your monitor and how to print your pictures with color profiles. We cover several, common, consumer-grade printers and how you print your files to these printers.

Part V: The Part of Tens

We wrap up the book with the Part of Tens chapters, where you can find tips for better tone and color corrections. After you gain experience with Elements and the techniques in this book, if you become curious about upgrading to Photoshop, we provide a chapter that offers an overview of Photoshop's additional features for correcting brightness and color.

Icons Used in This Book

In the margins throughout this book, you see icons next to key paragraphs. These icons indicate some important information in the text they accompany. Here are the icons and their meanings:

Tips tell you how to use an alternate method for a procedure, shortcut, or workaround, or they give you other helpful information related to working on tasks in the sections in which they appear.

Pay particular attention when you see the Warning icon. This information tells you when you may have some problems performing your work and how to avoid those problems.

This icon gives you a heads-up about something you may want to commit to memory. Usually, it informs you of a shortcut or a repetitive task, where remembering a procedure can save you time.

No matter how hard we try to simplify our explanations of features, we can't entirely avoid the technical. If we think something is complex, we use this icon to alert you that we're moving into a scary, technical subject. You won't see many of these icons in the book because we try our best to give you the details in nontechnical terms.

When you see this icon, the text it's next to includes a reference to a file on the companion Web site for the *Color Management for Digital Photographers For Dummies* book. Log on to www.dummies.com/colormanagement, and you can download files that we uploaded to help you follow some important steps. If you have a little time, visit the Web site and download all the files so that you have them ready to use when you see this icon in a chapter.

Where to Go from Here

The first part of this book involves the basics of color, and it's the foundation for all the remaining chapters. Try to spend a little time going through the first three chapters in Part I. Next, be sure to thoroughly review Part II. You need to become familiar with tone and brightness corrections before moving on to color correction. After reviewing Part II, feel free to jump around the color correction chapters.

If you have some questions, comments, suggestions, or complaints, send your comments to customer@wiley.com.

As an additional source of information, feel free to contact us, the authors, directly with any questions you have related to the book contents. You can reach Ted at ted@west.net, and you can contact Don at DMason5849@aol.com.

We wish you much success and enjoyment in using Adobe Photoshop Elements for tone and color corrections, and we sincerely hope that the information in this book helps you produce better pictures.

Part I
The Basics of
Color Editing

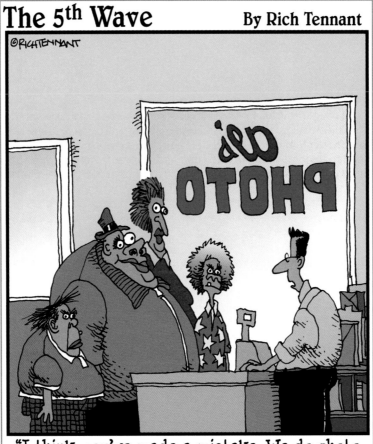

In this part . . .

*Y*ou need to walk before you can run. In Photoshop Elements terms, you need to know some basics about color and calibration before you can start color correcting photos.

In this first part, we talk about some essentials to help you fully understand all the parts ahead. Chapter 1 gives you some basic understanding of color, how Photoshop Elements sees color, and some fundamental principles to follow in all your color work. You can find out how to best set up your workspace's light for image viewing in Chapter 2. Chapter 3 focuses on color calibrating your monitor — the most critical step for you to perform when preparing for color editing. In Chapter 4, we move on to managing color, and we also look at color profiling and how you use profiles.

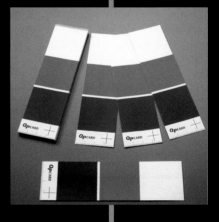

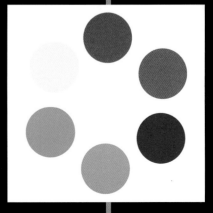

1

Understanding Color

*I*n order to manage and correct color photos, you need to understand a few things about how your digital camera, your computer, and your printer handle color. The tools you use to create your photos capture and display color in a consistent manner. Although not the most exciting aspect of correcting an image for proper color viewing, the basics of color and how your devices deal with color is an essential ingredient to producing better color photos. In this chapter, we cover some essentials of color that you need to know as you work through all the other chapters in this book.

Understanding Calibration Basics

Throughout this book, we talk about working in a good color-management workflow. Developing such a workflow begins with the essentials — setting up your work environment, getting your monitor in shape, and using your color desktop printer properly.

In this book, we talk about some sophisticated measures to help you best view, edit, and print color images. In some cases, you may think that some recommendations and tips we offer are a bit more than you want to do when you edit your own pictures. If you're not ready to change your work environment, you need to make some decisions about what you can realistically do to prepare your environment and your computer as best you can to effectively edit photos.

One thing to keep in mind is that the more preparation steps you cut out of your color-management workflow, the farther you move away from accurate color reproduction. Therefore, you may decide to eliminate some things that we consider critical to preparing your work environment; but realize that you can't expect to achieve the most accurate color in your photos.

We tried to write this book in such a way that you don't need to read it cover to cover, but even so, you do need to work through some essentials in order to dive into Elements' Standard Edit mode and begin editing your pictures. You can't avoid these essentials — you need to address them before you begin image editing. To prepare your work environment and set up your computer for good color management, you need to do some preliminary tasks:

- **Controlled lighting:** One of the most commonly overlooked areas related to good color-viewing conditions is carefully setting up your viewing environment. If you work on a super professional color monitor, have your monitor tweaked with a $5,000 color calibrator, and use the most sophisticated color profiles, you're only halfway to managing color. If light coming through your window and from your overhead light fixtures results in a colorcast on your monitor, you're not working in an optimum viewing environment. The first consideration you need to make is controlling the lighting of your workplace. We cover setting up lighting in Chapter 2.

- **Monitor calibration:** You've heard it all before, and we repeat it here — you need to be certain your viewing device reflects the best possible brightness and gray balance that you can get. On the low end, you can purchase some inexpensive calibration equipment; on the high end, you can purchase some very sophisticated calibration tools. At some point, you need to use a device to get your monitor to display the best it can, in terms of brightness and gray balance, as we explain in Chapter 3.

- **Color profiles:** You may have heard the term color profiles before. A *color profile* is a small computer file that contains all the settings that give you the best color capture, view, and/or print. If you don't use color profiles, your reproduction efforts are like taking a shot in the dark.

Color profiles are created through the process of calibration. Therefore, you need to first get familiar with some of the steps used for calibration: Color profiles are ultimately created from your calibration adjustments. In many cases, you acquire color profiles with your hardware equipment — especially color printers. You need to know when and how to create a color profile and how to use color profiles supplied by hardware developers. We cover color profiles more in Chapter 3.

There you have it. Your first steps in color correction involve controlling lighting, calibrating your monitor, and having all the color profiles you need for editing images and outputting them either for Web hosting or printing. After you have these essentials in place, you can begin the task of color correction.

Getting to Know the Language of Color

Color terms and definitions can be very confusing, but for this book, we use the same terms and concepts that Adobe Photoshop Elements uses and avoid all the fancy scientific stuff you really don't need to know to edit your images.

Color is defined by just three terms: hue, saturation, and brightness. In order to make the concept of correcting color much easier to understand later in the book, we also give you the definition of a complementary color, which means the exact opposite (on the color wheel) of the color you're looking at.

Stay awake because the following sections are really important.

Hue

Hue is the term used to name the actual color you're looking at. Your eyes perceive only three pure colors, but those three colors mix in your brain to give you all the colors you actually see.

The human eye has special receptors called *cones.* Cones come in three different kinds, each sensitive to a narrow portion of the light spectrum humans can see. One cone type responds to short wavelength light and sees blue. One cone type responds to middle wavelength light and sees green. The last cone type responds to the longest wavelengths and sees red. Our eyes' three-color cone design is why your monitor can show you millions of colors, even though it projects light in just three pure hues: red, green, and blue. These colors are known as the *additive model.*

Photoshop Elements works with color by mixing (adding) red, green, and blue. You need to identify these hues in the same way that Photoshop Elements does. Take a look at the color wheel in Figure 1-1.

Figure 1-1 shows a standard, simplified color wheel. The colors are as close to the real monitor hues as we can show you in this book because of ink limitations.

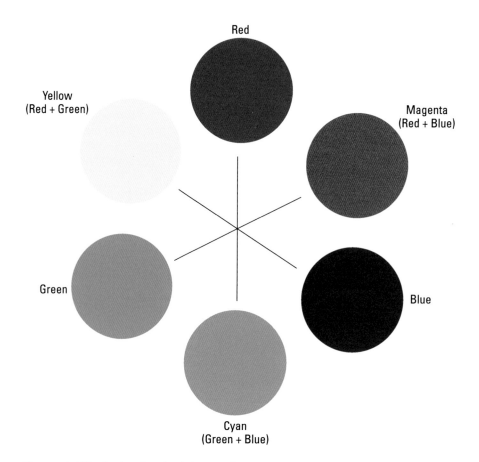

Figure 1-1: This simple color wheel shows red, green, and blue hues.

The first thing you might question is the yellow patch, made from green plus red. Keep in mind that you're mixing light, not paint. Mix equal parts of red and green light, and you get yellow. No, we're not making this up! Your eyes see yellow when something you're looking at emits equal parts of green and red light.

Still doubt us? Well, paint a yellow patch on your monitor in an Elements file, then zoom in and look very closely at the monitor. The only colors you see are little, glowing pixels of green and red. It's counter-intuitive, but green and red light make yellow.

The next color that might confuse you is blue. It looks purple, you say? You also might think that the cyan patch should really be called blue. Remember, you're mixing light, not paint.

Your kindergarten teacher is probably to blame for the confusion. Back when you mixed paints in those long-ago classes, she showed you that blue and yellow mixed together made green, and you probably had a pot of paint called purple that looked like the blue patch on our color wheel.

Mixing paints to get different colors uses subtractive primaries. The subtractive primaries are cyan, magenta, and yellow. Your teacher probably called them blue, red, and yellow. It made naming the paints a lot easier, but it wasn't really correct.

Equally mixing the red, green, and blue primaries create cyan, magenta, and yellow on your monitor, as shown on the color wheel in Figure 1-1. Just remember that you need the basic hues of red, green, and blue to make a full range of hues (or colors) on the computer.

Colors exactly opposite of each other on the wheel are called *complementary colors*. Mix the complementary colors together on the monitor in equal parts, and you get a shade of gray, light gray, or white. The complementary colors cancel each other out. We talk more about this concept of colors canceling each other out in Chapter 8, where we show you how to correct the color on a bad image file.

Saturation

The term *saturation* defines the purity of a hue. Saturation is pretty easy to understand if you look at a few examples, such as the ones shown in Figure 1-2. The green patch in Example A is a highly saturated hue. In Example B, the patch is the same hue but less saturated. In Example C, the patch is desaturated more than B. Finally, in Example D, you see the same hue completely desaturated and therefore devoid of color.

Saturation defines the vividness of the hue in question. Think of a desaturated color as one with white, gray, or black mixed in. Gray represents a fully desaturated tone — no color at all.

Brightness

Brightness means what it says: It's the term used for how light or dark is the hue in question. Keep in mind that a hue can be bright without being saturated. Here's an example: The three cyan patches in Figure 1-3 are equal in saturation, but they vary in brightness.

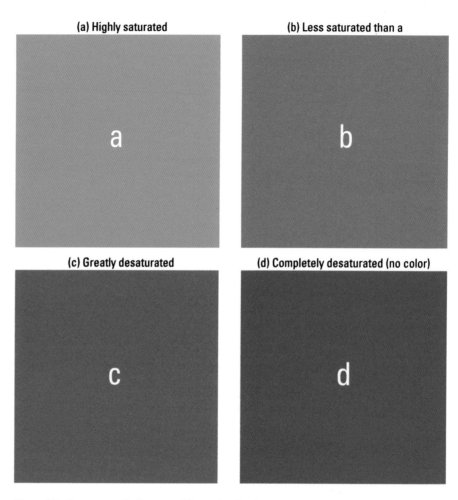

(a) Highly saturated

(b) Less saturated than a

a

b

(c) Greatly desaturated

(d) Completely desaturated (no color)

c

d

Figure 1-2: A green patch shown at different levels of saturation.

Figure 1-3: These three cyan color patches vary in brightness values, from least bright on the left to brightest on the right.

We repeat these color concepts a great deal in this book as we work our way through color management. Editing a file to change overall color, brightness, and contrast often affects the hue, saturation, and brightness of the colors in your file. Understanding how to define those changes can make the rest of the book far easier to understand.

Color space

Throughout this book, we continually refer to the term *color space. Color space* is a way to numerically describe color on computers. Color space is also often referred to as a *color model.* RGB (Red, Green, and Blue) is a color space. CMYK (Cyan, Magenta, Yellow, and blacK) is a different color space. HSB (Hue, Saturation, and Brightness) is a color space that describes color as we define it in the preceding sections.

For most purposes, because Elements is limited in the number of color spaces that you can view, we pretty much stick with the RGB color space throughout this book.

Color gamut

Another term you find frequently used in this book is color gamut. *Color gamut* is simply the entire range of color within a given color space. We might use a phrase such as "outside the color gamut," which simply means that a particular color isn't contained within the range of color for a particular color space. As a result, you can't see the color on your monitor, and you can't print the color on your printer.

You might have a color visible on your monitor because it fits within the monitor color gamut, but the color may not print on your color desktop printer. The color isn't within the printer's color gamut.

Clipping

Quite often, we talk about colors or tones being *clipped,* which means that the value is cut off. A color that's clipped, for example, won't print. When Elements prints a photo that has some color clipped, the print shows you the closest color to the clipped value. Beyond that value, the clipped colors aren't printed.

Clipping also relates to image tones (or grays). If we say that a very light or dark tone is clipped, for example, the print appears with some whites and blacks lost. This loss of tone results in a loss of detail in highlights (whites) and shadows (blacks).

Suppose you took a picture in which the foreground subject is in the sun. In the background, your eyes see a beautiful range of shaded trees. When you print your photo, the leaves on the trees aren't completely visible. They look dark and don't have much detail. The dark tones were clipped (cut off) from the image.

Mixing Colors

Your computer monitor is capable of displaying a total of 16.7 million distinct and individual colors. The monitor is capable of showing you all these colors by mixing the primary hues of red, green, and blue together. Understanding how your monitor mixes the colors ultimately helps you understand how to edit your pictures for color correction.

Imagine a diaphragm similar to your camera's diaphragm. You can turn the f-stop ring to open or close the diaphragm. As you open the diaphragm, you let more light pass through the lens. If you could close a diaphragm all the way on a lens, you would block all light from passing through the lens.

When your monitor displays a color, it allows certain amounts of light to pass through the RGB color phosphors in a similar fashion to a camera lens. The monitor can control the amount of light that passes through the phosphors in 256 individual steps. It's like having a ring on your camera lens with 256 separate adjustments.

In computer terms, 0 (zero) is a number; therefore, the 256 value is really measured from 0 (zero) to 255. If you assign 255 to the red hue and 0 (zero) to the green and blue hues, you see a fully saturated red color on your monitor. To test this theory, follow these steps:

1. **Open any file in Standard Edit mode.**

2. **Double-click the mouse cursor on the Foreground color swatch in the Tools palette.**

   The Color Picker dialog box opens.

3. **Set the color to a fully saturated Red.**

   Type **255** in the R text box in the Color Picker. Type **0** (zero) in the G and B text boxes, as shown in Figure 1-4. These numbers mean that you open the diaphragm all the way for the Red channel and close it all the way for the Green and Blue channels. The result is a fully saturated red color. (For more on channels, see the section "Understanding channels," later in this chapter.)

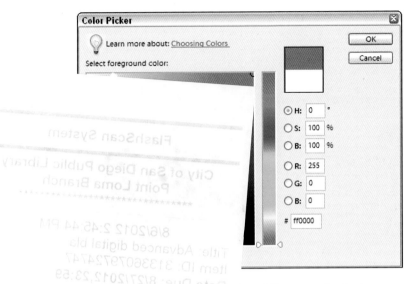

...ies a fully saturated red color.

...ngs you have for color mixing are commonly
...the computer monitor doesn't have a diaphragm,
...controlling the amount of light that passes
...e RGB phosphors.

...e of glass. If you paint the glass solid black and
...ack glass, zero light passes through it. If you then
...ent gray, some light passes through the glass. As
...y to smaller percentages, more light passes
...g in more saturated color.

...ients terms, you have 256 levels of gray that permit
...se the saturation on the three individual hues.
...that your computer monitor can display 16.7 million
...his number by multiplying the maximum number of
grays for each hue together (256 × 256 × 256 = 16.7 million). This number
really means that you have 16.7 million combinations of levels of gray with
which you can create colors.

Understanding channels

In Photoshop Elements terms, the three hues your monitor displays (red, green, and blue) are called *channels*. You can easily see the three channels by opening an RGB color image in Standard Edit mode and opening the Levels dialog box. Select Enhance➪Adjust Lighting➪Levels or simply press Ctrl+L (⌘+L for Macs). When the Levels dialog box opens, click the RGB menu (the down-pointing arrow), and you see the three channels, as shown in Figure 1-5.

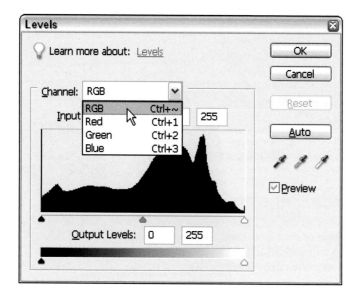

Figure 1-5: In the Levels dialog box, you can access the three RGB channels.

We commonly refer to the RGB channel as the *composite channel* because it's a mix of the different gray levels in all three channels. If you make an adjustment to this channel, all three RGB channels are adjusted together. However, you can also individually make adjustments to the Red, Green, and Blue channels.

When we refer to making adjustments to either the composite channel or the individual channels, we're really talking about painting that imaginary glass darker or lighter to allow more or less light to pass through, resulting in more or less saturated color.

As you work through the chapters in this book, we continually reference tone levels (represented by the 256 levels of gray) and channels. A slight edit to the tone levels in either the composite channel or any one of the individual channels can greatly affect image brightness and color.

Why are there 256 levels?

This 256 number comes up a lot when talking about image modes. What makes it so special?

Reproducing tone on paper or a monitor requires a minimum of about 200 tone levels to give smooth results without *banding* (or making sharp transitions between) the tones in smooth gradient image areas. Some images can get along with far fewer levels of tone, such as highly textured images or those that don't really contain any smooth tones.

 Two hundred tone levels is a kind of minimum benchmark for good results. So why 256 levels and not exactly 200? It has to do with the way computers calculate. Computers use binary math, and 8-bit encoding allows exactly 256 tone levels. Seven-bit would result in just 128 tone levels. So, 8-bit mode became the minimum standard for full tonal range image files.

The 256 tone levels of 8-bit mode also allow a little headroom for file editing. Image editing always causes some amount of information loss, and as a direct result, an edited 8-bit file always has less than 256 real tone levels remaining. The extra 56 levels allow more editing before any tone banding problems become visible.

Understanding Color Modes

A *color mode* is a fancy term for the method Elements uses to display and print your image. Elements allows you a choice of four different color modes. And although Elements doesn't support the CMYK mode, it can convert a CMYK-mode file to a mode it does support.

RGB

You'll probably use RGB, Elements' standard default mode, 99 percent of the time. This mode uses three channels (Red, Green, and Blue) to describe color and tone. This mode is the most versatile and gives you access to all the editing tools and filters in your Elements application. RGB files allow embedded color profiles (which we talk about in Chapter 4).

Index color

This is an ancient color mode in the computer world. Unlike RGB 24-bit mode, with 16.7 million possible colors, index color allows only 256 colors. This mode was originally created back in the old days as a means to keep color file sizes as small as possible. Computers couldn't display 16.7 million colors back then, so monitors that showed images in only 8-bit mode used index color.

Web pages still use index color today, in the form of GIF-format files that are limited to 256 colors. The Save for Web option in Elements allows you to save files in the GIF format, if you want.

The main advantage to the GIF format is the ability to keep graphic elements clean and sharp on Web pages, unlike JPEG files, which can add distracting visual artifacts to graphics when the JPEG files use high compression settings. But index color doesn't allow the use of color profiles.

Grayscale

You can think of grayscale as the black-and-white image mode, in terms of black-and-white photos. Just a single channel is used to describe image tone without color information. Grayscale has 256 distinct gray levels supported in 8-bit mode and more than 40,000 gray levels in 16-bit mode.

Grayscale mode has advantages if you like to work with classic black-and-white photography. Grayscale files are just one-third the size of an RGB file, so you get much faster computer performance and can store more files on your hard drive.

If you want to tone, paint, or tint a grayscale creation, you must convert to RGB mode to do so.

Grayscale supports embedding special profiles to indicate the display Gamma used and also for dot gain if the file is for traditional press use.

Bitmap

Bitmap is a 1-bit file format. *One bit* means that only two tone values are supported — just white and black with no grays. Bitmap can simulate gray values by using a display we call *dithering,* which places the black and white pixels in a pattern to visually appear as grays.

Elements users should probably see bitmap as more of an image appearance than as a standard file format to use. The main advantage to this mode is the small final file size, compared to grayscale mode. Convert a grayscale file to bitmap, play with the options available for conversion, and you might find a visual style that you like.

CMYK

You can't edit in this mode, but Elements does allow you to open a CMYK color mode file that Elements converts upon opening to RGB mode so that you can work with the image.

CMYK is the color mode used for traditional printing press reproduction of color images. For example, this book was printed from CMYK-mode files.

Printing presses need to use four separate ink plates to reproduce full color images on paper. The press plate colors are cyan, magenta, yellow, and black, so it's called CMYK mode. (Black is abbreviated K because, a long time ago, people were afraid that using B for black might be confused with blue.)

CMYK supports embedded color profiles. (We talk about color profiles in detail in Chapter 4.)

Converting Color Modes

In some situations, you need or want to convert one image mode to another. You may need to convert a grayscale or bitmap file to RGB so you can colorize, paint, or tint the image for output to a color printer. If your file's in bitmap mode, you must convert first to grayscale and then to RGB mode. You can make these conversions by selecting Image⇨Mode and then selecting a color mode from choices in the submenu that appears.

In other situations, you may need to convert from RGB mode to index color mode for Web use. Sometimes, you need to make a mode conversion from index color to RGB so you can edit the file for color or tone, before converting it back to index color mode.

Follow these tips when you make image mode conversions for editing:

- ✔ To allow full editing capabilities for an index color file, convert the file to RGB mode, edit it, and convert it back to index color mode.

- ✔ If you plan to create multiple images for use in index color mode, keep your original files in RGB mode and convert duplicates. You can't recover the information you lose when you convert RGB mode to index color mode.

- ✔ You have to convert bitmap mode to grayscale mode in order to edit the tones of the image. You can convert back to bitmap when you finish editing in grayscale mode.

✔ Grayscale mode has far more editing options than bitmap mode. It's best to keep master files in grayscale mode and convert to bitmap mode as a final step before viewing or printing the file.

✔ If you want to convert RGB to grayscale, always convert a duplicate file. All the color information is lost when you convert a file to grayscale mode.

2

Controlling Lighting

*C*orrecting color in digital images requires you to optimize your working conditions for the best possible viewing environment, as well as make sure all your equipment is calibrated properly. Getting color precise with absolutely no discernible differences isn't completely possible when viewing color images on monitors and printing photos on a wide range of output devices. Therefore, what we strive for is to control the variables as much as possible to bring our color viewing and printing together as close as we can. If you skip one variable in the process, you move just a little farther away from an ideal color-matching system.

In this chapter, you take the first step toward controlling those variables — creating the optimal lighting in your workspace. Accurate and consistent color editing requires full-spectrum lighting, with a color temperature reasonably matched to the monitor color temperature setting so that both the viewing area and monitor view are consistent with one another.

Most quality, full-spectrum lighting used today involves fluorescent-type lighting fixtures that use special lamps with a sophisticated phosphor mix that yields a full, white-light spectrum.

We realize that the average amateur photographer who takes occasional snapshots of the kids and makes a few prints after holidays and special occasions is not likely to turn the bedroom into a color work studio. The results you want depend on how much you want to invest some money and energy in creating a solid workplace designed for color-correction work. We give you the whole nine yards here and in Chapters 3 and 4, where we cover monitor calibration and color profiles, and you can pick and choose what changes you want to make in your workplace. Hopefully, you know that if you cut a lot of corners and you expect to do quality color work, you're not likely to achieve the best possible results.

Understanding Color Temperature

We could have titled this section *"What Color Are Your Whites?"* In the computer world, white is a relative value.

Your eyes and brain are constantly at work adjusting what you see to let you perceive a pure white when you find it. This is why you can move from a department store to the great outdoors and not notice the change in lighting color from one place to another.

Unlike a camera, we tend to see colors as normal no matter what kind of light is illuminating a scene. Set your camera to daylight balance, however, and that department store interior most likely photographs with a strong, yellow-green colorcast from the indoor fluorescent lighting. Your eyes see no cast at all. That's because your brain figures out a real white point and adjusts your internal white balance in an instant — pretty amazing.

This property of your eyes is very important when it comes to editing images on a monitor and viewing the resulting print outputs. You see, your eyes can adjust to only one viewing environment at a time. Why is this important?

Well, if you have a monitor set to one white balance and your viewing area has a different white balance, images on them *look different* to your eyes because your brain can adjust for only one situation at a time. We have to try our best to match the monitor whites to our viewing area whites. If we don't, a perfect printer output looks like a mismatch to the monitor.

The term used to define white balance is called *color temperature.* In simple terms, average daylight has a color temperature of around 5,000 degrees Kelvin. The term has to do with the color of light from very hot objects like the sun. That's why 5000K is a kind of standard for neutral white.

However, as we said, white is relative.

When determining a white point for a monitor, the final setting you use depends on trying different, white-point monitor settings in the actual place you'll be using the monitor. As the color temperature increases, the white tends to look bluer. Set your monitor white point to 6500K, and then to 5000K, and you'll notice right away that 5000K looks much more yellow than 6500K.

However, remember that the lighting of the room impacts the way you perceive color on your monitor, too — which is why it's important to start setting up your color-management work area by making the room's lighting as close to daylight as possible before moving on to calibrating your monitor, which we explain in Chapter 3.

The best possible lighting for viewing should be *daylight balanced,* which requires lights in the 5000K to 6000K color temperature range.

Using Balanced Lighting

Balancing lighting is an attempt to make the quality of your indoor light as close to natural daylight as possible. With different light bulbs in studios and homes, the balance of your ambient light varies farther away from natural daylight, although the extent of this variation depends on the light sources influencing your environment.

 The color quality of light is rated as the *CRI* (color rendering index) in percentage values. A CRI of 100 percent is a perfect match to natural daylight, although the best lamps available are rated around CRI 98 percent — a very close match to natural daylight. A standard, cool-white, fluorescent lamp has extremely poor color quality and is rated at about CRI 60 percent. Full-spectrum lights fit in standard fluorescent fixtures and are also available in the new Spiralux form that fits in a standard light bulb fixture. By checking this rating when you shop for light bulbs, you'll have a better idea what bulbs can help create an environment that's as close as possible to natural daylight.

Ideally, the *Kelvin rating* (color of the lamp) should match closely to your monitor's color temperature setting. A 5000K lamp (daylight balance) should, ideally, be used with a 5000K monitor setting. We find that the lamps seem a bit cooler (bluer) in color than the same monitor setting, at least on a CRT monitor, so we use 5000K lamps with a 5500K monitor setting. Your mileage might vary depending on your monitor and available natural light in your studio.

Prices for these lamps are usually about three times or more higher than prices for inexpensive, cool-white lamps. The good news is that they last for years, and some are very reasonably priced. Don's studio uses standard, 96-inch fluorescent fixtures that are fitted with Sylvania Sun Stick lamps that are rated at 5000K and a CRI of 92. Cost is about $8 per tube. You can find Sun Stick lamps at your local home improvement store. The homemade viewing booth, shown in Figure 2-1, uses a pair of 48-inch Triten 50 full-spectrum tubes. Color temperature is 5000K, with an awesome CRI of 98 percent. Cost per tube is $6. To purchase the Triten 50 full-spectrum tubes, visit `www.1000bulbs.com`. This vendor also stocks Spiralux full-spectrum lamps. Just look for `Full Spectrum` links on the vendor Web site.

Figure 2-1: A homemade, color-correction workplace.

Keeping the lighting consistent is important. The lighting in a room with large windows varies a great deal during the day. For viewing purposes, a windowed room should have good curtains or shades to keep ambient light levels consistent at all times. Visual monitor calibration is based on the viewing environment. In a windowed room without shades, monitor calibration is like a broken clock — it's always correct once a day!

Going for Neutral Gray

All the nice, balanced lights you purchase don't mean much if you put your monitor against a bright, yellow-and-orange wall. What you need is an area encased in a neutral gray environment. To make this happen, you have a number of options. If you're serious about color management and have space dedicated to the task, we suggest creating your own viewing booth. However, if you need a more makeshift solution, check out the "Employing viewing booth alternatives" section a little later in this chapter.

Building a viewing booth

For a makeshift viewing booth, follow these steps:

1. **Purchase an 18 percent gray card.**

   You can find 18 percent gray cards at photo suppliers. Just ask a sales person for a gray card or shop online at photo suppliers. A good online source for all your photographic needs is www.calumetphoto.com.

   You can also use a QPcard like the one shown in Figure 2-2. These cards have a neutral gray as well as a black and white patch you can use when photographing scenes. You can purchase the cards at Calumet Photographic as well.

2. **Purchase a paint that matches the color of the gray card.**

   Take your 18 percent gray card to your local paint store and ask for a flat paint that matches the color of your gray card when the paint dries. Most hardware and commercial paint stores are happy to provide exactly what you need.

Figure 2-2: The center patch on a QPcard is an 18 percent gray.

3. **Construct your booth.**

   Using particle board or unfinished plywood, construct the booth so that it surrounds the viewing space around your monitor. You might paint the unfinished wood or particle board before assembly.

4. **Touch up the paint.**

   It's not a piece of fine furniture, but you might spruce it up a little with some touchup paint if you paint the material before assembly.

5. **Set up your monitor.**

   If you have a *CRT monitor* (which is a television-type of monitor), you can cut a hole in the back of the booth (see Figure 2-3) and push the monitor back to provide more surface area for your keyboard.

Figure 2-3: A monitor's viewing booth with space for a CRT monitor.

Get rid of the swimming fishes

When you open a program like Photoshop Elements, you'll notice the default background color in the Elements window is a neutral gray. Software engineers set this color as a default intentionally because neutral gray is the best color to minimize any colorcasting problems and visual perception anomalies when viewing your color photos.

If you use a desktop color or image, you infect your viewing environment with extraneous color. This is most obvious when you minimize the Elements window and see the desktop pattern in the background.

If you're serious about color correction, resist the temptation to change your background from anything other than a boring, neutral gray. It doesn't look as snappy as watching multicolored fish floating across your screen, but it does go a long way in helping you keep your visual perception of color at an optimum.

Employing viewing booth alternatives

A viewing booth is ideal for photo editing, but here are some tips for your viewing environment if you feel a viewing booth is overkill for your needs.

- Get a piece of gray foam core board and place it behind your monitor in your viewing area. Having a neutral value in your field of vision helps a great deal. You can store the gray board when you're not using it.

- Cover your working surface with a neutral material, especially if your desk surface is a bright color. It doesn't have to be gray, although gray is best. A white tablecloth is fine for this. You can even place a second piece of gray foam core board on the viewing surface.

- Add some daylight-balanced Spiralux lamps to your existing light fixtures.

Just remember that keeping your viewing area devoid of competing color makes image editing much easier.

Calibrating Your Monitor

Calibrating your monitor is the second phase of setting up your color-management environment, after you take steps to control lighting, which we explain in Chapter 2. By calibrating your monitor, you ensure the color temperature is as close to daylight as possible, not only so you see colors more accurately, but also to ensure that the color temperature of your monitor is balanced with your room.

What Is Monitor Calibration?

Your monitor needs to be calibrated so that it accurately displays the colors contained in any given image. You calibrate your monitor by adjusting a number of different variables, which may include the following, depending on your monitor and the tools you use to calibrate:

↣ **The balance of colors on your monitor:** This balance corrects any color tints or colorcasts.

↣ **Brightness:** The brightness control historically adjusts the black point, which is the darkest point on the monitor.

↣ **Contrast:** Adjusting contrast used to mean adjusting the *white point,* which is the lightest point on the monitor. As you calibrate your monitor, you need to experiment with different monitor white-point settings until the white of the monitor looks as pure as possible.

- **Gamma:** *Gamma* is the brightness of mid-level tones in an image.

  In technical terms, Gamma is a parameter that describes the shape of the transfer function for one or more stages in an imaging pipeline.

- **White balance:** You adjust the white balance setting to try to get the brightness as close to natural daylight as you can.

You have a few choices for what tool you can use to adjust your monitor brightness:

- Expensive calibration equipment that can cost $3,000 or more

- A low-cost hardware device priced at less than $300

- Software tools provided by Adobe (or your OS developer) to set up your monitor

We discuss how you use low-cost hardware devices and software tools in the sections "Calibrating with Hardware Devices" and "Adjusting Hardware Controls on an LCD Display," later in this chapter.

Working with CRT versus LCD Monitors

Computer monitors come in two flavors — CRT (cathode ray tube) and LCD (liquid crystal display). The CRT monitors look much like old TV sets, and the LCDs offer a sleeker, thinner look. Each type has its pros and cons when it comes to monitor calibration.

LCD monitors, although now more prolific and newer in the marketplace, just don't match the color clarity you find in CRT monitors. In addition to improved color clarity, CRT monitors also cost much less than LCDs. As of this writing, a Dell Trinitron 21-inch display sells for less than $200 at online reseller outlets — try www.tigerdirect.com. CRTs have their downside, however. In addition to their large size, overall bulkiness, increased power consumption, and the excess heat they produce, they're becoming increasingly scarce. Many CRT manufacturers have discontinued entire lines of CRTs in favor of the newer LCD technology.

If you find a good value on a CRT monitor, find out when the monitor was made. If you purchase an older, used monitor, it may have exceeded its useful life. You can expect to get about three to five good years out of a CRT before it starts losing definition and color clarity. We can't give you a magic formula, however, because monitors vary greatly in fidelity and life expectancy. You can easily check the date a monitor was manufactured by looking at the label affixed to the back of the monitor.

Because of the popularity of LCD monitors and the anomalies associated with calibrating LCD displays, we thought we'd point out some real problems you may encounter when trying to calibrate an LCD display with the visual (software) calibration utilities for both Windows and the Mac.

The visual calibrators were designed with CRT displays in mind. LCDs differ from CRTs in two fundamental ways:

- ✏ **LCDs are much brighter than CRTs and have a much higher overall contrast.** Setting picture contrast to the highest setting on an LCD, as instructed by the calibration utility, usually makes the picture far too bright for the calibration utility to work properly.

- ✏ **The LCD monitor controls work differently than CRT controls.** CRT brightness and contrast controls are part of the monitor hardware, just like a CRT television set. The brightness control adjusts the black point, and the contrast control adjusts the white point by varying the output of the electron guns. The same is true of the color adjustments.

  An LCD (unless it's a very expensive professional model) varies the brightness and contrast by changing the internal monitor color Look Up Tables (LUT) to change the monitor image. The backlight is always bright — very different from a CRT.

We worked long and hard to create a foolproof way to visually calibrate an LCD monitor. If you decide to use a visual calibration tool, check out the section "Adjusting Hardware Controls on an LCD Display," later in this chapter, and you should get a result that matches your print outputs much more closely than the monitor default settings. Just keep in mind that you need to use a hardware calibration device for the very best results.

An LCD monitor that's calibrated for print work always looks darker and warmer in tone than with the factory default settings.

If you have an LCD monitor now, keep your eye on product reviews and current literature. The LCD technology is new and continually advancing. Computer CRT monitors have been around for more than 25 years, with 25 years of continued research, development, and improvement. As time goes on, we expect LCD monitors to advance and ultimately render even better color clarity than the best CRTs of years past.

Calibrating with Hardware Devices

We skip the high-end costly devices and suggest that, at the very least, you should make one valuable purchase for creating a monitor profile — a hardware profiling system. (See Chapter 4 for more on monitor profiling.)

On the low end, you have some very affordable devices that go a long way in helping you adjust your monitor brightness and color balance:

- ✏ **ColorVision Spyder2express:** This calibration system is one of the newer devices on the market. For as low as $69, you can purchase an easy-to-use, three-step device that balances the color on your monitor and adjusts it for optimum brightness (for both Macs and PCs). This device is receiving five-star ratings at online resellers, including www.amazon.com.

- ✏ **Pantone Huey Monitor Color Correction system:** This new, low-cost calibration system can calibrate both CRTs and LCDs (and supports both Macs and Windows). This unit retails for $88 and sells for $74.95 at Amazon.com, as of this writing.

- ✏ **GretagMacbeth Eye-One Display 2:** For a little more money, you can order this low-end calibration device with superb capabilities from GretagMacbeth (www.gretagmacbeth.com) — a company that has long been a leader in sophisticated hardware equipment for creating calibrations and color profiles. This device costs $249, as of this writing.

  Eye-One Display 2 is an easy-to-use profiling tool that works with CRT displays, LCDs, and laptop computers. You attach the suction cup that comes with your Eye-One Display 2 to your monitor (see Figure 3-1), click a few buttons in the software application accompanying the hardware, and Eye-One Display 2 eventually prompts you to save a monitor profile. Your operating system automatically uses the profile you create when you start up your computer. When the profile kicks in, your monitor is balanced, using the settings determined when the device performed the calibration.

If you decide to purchase the Pantone Huey or the ColorVision Spyder2express, either device will give you the best possible result on an LCD monitor if you do a rough visual calibration for monitor brightness and contrast before using it. Look over our tips for visually calibrating an LCD monitor for brightness and contrast with the built-in monitor controls (see the section "Calibrating LCD monitors that have brightness and contrast controls," later in this chapter) and at least get your LCD monitor in the ballpark first.

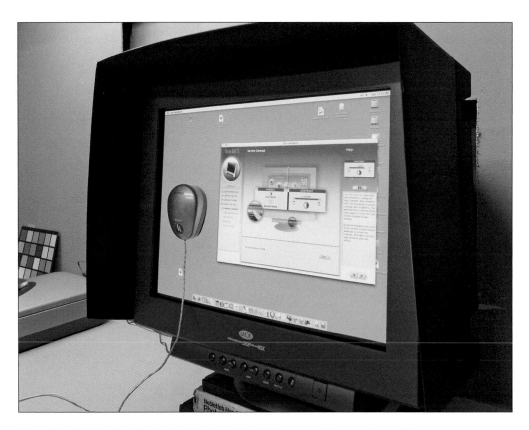

Figure 3-1: The Eye-One Display 2 calibration device helps you create a monitor profile.

Adjusting Hardware Controls on an LCD Display

What do we mean by visual calibration? If you don't purchase at least a low-cost hardware calibration device, such as those discussed in the preceding section, or you need to quickly color correct some photos of the family reunion before your device arrives, you can use a software utility already available on your computer.

On the Macintosh, the Mac OS X software Preferences provides you with a calibration utility called the Display Calibrator Assistant. On Windows, Adobe provides you with the Adobe Gamma control panel when you install Photoshop Elements. These software tools allow you to make visual monitor settings as you work through steps in a wizard window.

Before you can use the visual calibration tools on a Windows machine or a Mac, you need to do a little work making some hardware adjustments. Without making some hardware corrections, your software calibration tools won't get your monitor to closely match your printed output for color and brightness.

LCD monitor controls vary a great deal. Some LCDs have full control of brightness, contrast, white point, and color balance (using individual red, green, and blue controls). Others have some combination of these controls, and some offer only color-balance presets for the red, green, and blue controls. In the following sections, we try to explain the best methods to use when making hardware adjustments, in spite of the lack of consistency among LCD-monitor makers.

We ran across a couple of Dell LCDs with just preset and *RGB-slider controls* (that is, sliders that adjust the levels of red, green, and blue). Because a Dell monitor of this type is a popular brand, we'll start here. Many other LCD monitors are limited to just these controls, too, so try to apply our example of adjusting a Dell monitor to your brand. Here are the steps to follow:

1. **Open the hardware adjustment controls on your monitor, and you're presented with something like you see in Figure 3-2.**

   The monitor has no brightness or contrast controls! Developers continually rely on auto-brightness and -contrast adjustments, and many are eliminating these manual controls on LCD displays.

2. **On the Dell monitor, navigate to the Color Settings option and open the adjustment settings.**

   You find options like those you see in Figure 3-3.

   On an LCD, you may have to navigate through the controls on your remote control device or on the monitor.

Figure 3-2: You can adjust settings on a Dell monitor by using these hardware controls.

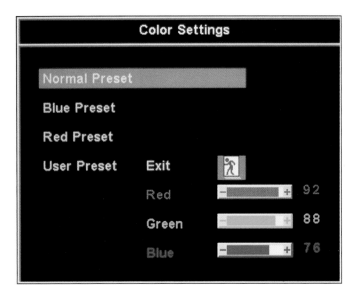

Figure 3-3: You can make adjustments to the Color Settings on a Dell monitor.

The Color adjustment contains a limited series of presets and a user preset with RGB controls. You don't have a Color Temperature option on this monitor. (For an introduction to color temperature, see Chapter 2.)

The Normal Preset monitor setting is a generic setting that seems to adjust for the normal blue color bias of an LCD monitor.

3. Make note of the settings and close the Color Settings panel.

To get close to a proper gray balance, we need to mix less blue than green and less green than red. Our monitor has a slight blue cast and is much too bright at the default settings.

4. In Photoshop Elements, open the `MonitorCalibrationFile.tif` file (shown in Figure 3-4) in Standard Edit mode.

We provide this monitor calibration file, `MonitorCalibrationFile.tif`, in the Chapter 3 folder on the Wiley companion Web site for you to download. (See the Introduction for details about the Web site.)

5. Size the image to about one-fourth of your monitor size by pressing Ctrl+– (minus) to zoom out.

You want to make it easy to see but small enough to move around as needed.

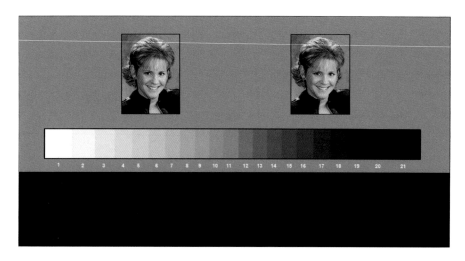

Figure 3-4: You can use our Monitor Calibration File to get your monitor looking just right.

6. **Open the monitor Color Settings control (one of the LCD monitor control buttons).**

7. **Select User Preset and reduce the Red output to 75 percent.**

   We start with this setting because we need to cut overall brightness to make sure the monitor's appearance matches images you print from your computer.

8. **Using only the Green and Blue sliders, adjust the color settings to obtain the best neutral gray that you can on the test file and Photoshop Elements' neutral gray background.**

   Placing a standard photographic gray card next to the monitor can really help you determine a true neutral gray.

   After you have the best gray, you're now ready to use the visual software calibration tool. If you have a PC, see the following section, "Using Adobe Gamma." If you're using a Mac, jump to the section "Calibrating with just RGB controls on a Mac," later in this chapter, instead.

Using Calibration Software

After you adjust hardware presets, or if you have a monitor without hardware controls, you can use software available from Adobe (installed with Elements in Windows) or software installed as part of the Macintosh operating system to calibrate your monitor. But remember, a hardware tool specifically designed for calibrating your monitor is the best solution. However, if you don't have a hardware calibration device, using a software tool to calibrate your monitor is the next best thing to getting the monitor brightness correct.

Using Adobe Gamma

The Adobe Gamma application has been around for some time. It was discontinued on the Mac version of Elements when the Mac OS X operating system was introduced. However, on the Windows version of Elements, it remains the software utility to use. Like the Macintosh Display Calibrator Assistant (which we describe in the section "Calibrating with just RGB controls on a Mac," later in this chapter), Adobe Gamma enables you to figure out proper monitor adjustments that you can eventually save as a monitor profile.

To use the Adobe Gamma control panel device, follow these steps:

1. **Open your Control Panel by clicking the Start menu and choosing Settings⇨Control Panel.**

2. **Double-click Adobe Gamma in the Control Panel folder.**

   The Adobe Gamma dialog box appears.

3. **Select the Step-by-Step (Wizard) radio button and click Next. (See Figure 3-5.)**

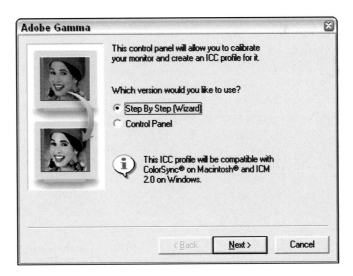

Figure 3-5: Select the Step By Step (Wizard) radio button and click Next to begin the calibration.

4. **Type a name for your profile and click Next.**

5. **Adjust the brightness and contrast controls on your monitor (see Figure 3-6) and click Next.**

   Follow the description in the wizard to make your monitor adjustments.

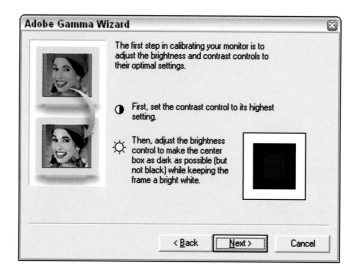

Figure 3-6: The Adobe Gamma Wizard helps you adjust brightness and contrast controls on your monitor.

6. **On the pane that asks you to select the Phosphors for your monitor from a menu, Custom appears as the default choice. Leave this setting alone and click the Next button.**

   By default, Adobe Gamma supplies the Custom choice taken from the default monitor profile.

7. **On the Gamma settings pane, deselect the View Single Gamma Only check box.**

   The pane displays individual Gamma adjustments that you can make for Red, Green, and Blue. (See Figure 3-7.)

8. **Place each slider in the exact center under each box, as shown in Figure 3-7.**

9. **Return to the single Gamma view by selecting the View Single Gamma Only check box.**

   Disregard the Red, Green, and Blue Gamma boxes that appear.

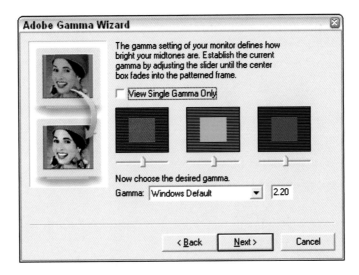

Figure 3-7: Place each slider in the exact center below each of the RGB boxes.

10. **Place the Adobe Gamma dialog box next to the open monitor calibration file, so you can easily view both at once.**

11. **Select a Gamma choice from the Gamma menu. Select Windows Default 2.20 for the Gamma, then click Next.**

    You arrive at a pane in which the Hardware White Point check box is selected. This setting defines the general colorcast on your monitor. You can choose a setting anywhere between 5,000 degrees Kelvin (which gives your image a slight red cast) and 9,300 degrees Kelvin (which produces a cooler blue colorcast).

12. **Set the Adjusted White Point to 5500K for now.**

    The monitor view becomes slightly warmer than the 6500K setting that we normally use to match natural daylight. This setting relates to color temperature, which we introduce in Chapter 2.

13. **Click the Back button in the wizard to return to the Gamma adjustment pane.**

    The test file and the Adobe Gamma Control Panel should both be visible, as you can see in Figure 3-8.

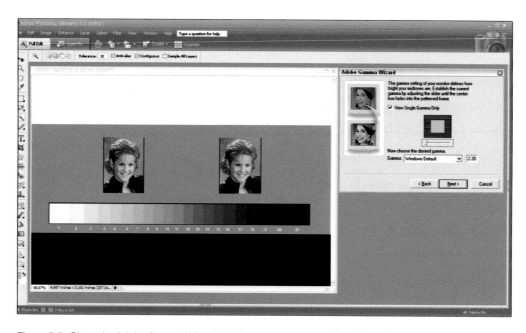

Figure 3-8: Place the Adobe Gamma Wizard window next to the test file while you're making the Gamma adjustment.

14. **Now, adjust the single Gamma slider in Adobe Gamma until the little square above the slider seems to match the surrounding gray (be certain the box for View Single Gamma Only is selected).**

    Slightly squint your eyes as you move the slider back and forth if that helps you distinguish shades of gray. If the monitor controls are near the correct setting, the Gamma slider will wind up fairly close to center, but place it where it needs to be to match the little gray square to the grid.

    Look at the step tablet below the portrait images in the test file (the grayscale gradient). Can you see all the steps from white to black? The dark step to the left of the black step should separate from that blackest step and look slightly lighter than black. All steps toward white should be visible, with no steps merged together toward white. The portrait images should have a normal brightness. The big gray patch in the middle should look gray. In Figure 3-9, a monitor adjustment appears too light on the left, too dark in the middle, and properly corrected on the right side of the figure.

15. **Click Next and Next again to arrive at an option to change the white point for your working conditions from your hardware white point. Leave the white point set to Same as Hardware and click Next.**

Too light	Too dark	Proper brightness adjustment

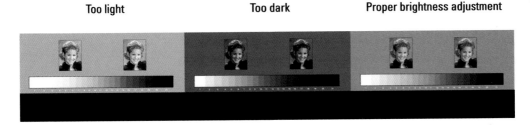

Figure 3-9: A monitor adjustment, too light (on the left), too dark (in the middle), and just right (on the right).

16. Click Finish in the last pane, and the profile is created.

The profile is automatically set to make the adjustment to this profile each time you start your computer.

Unless you get really lucky in the preceding steps, your monitor display still doesn't look quite right. You need to do some more work to bring the overall brightness of an LCD monitor within a close approximation of your printed output. Follow these steps to make the final adjustments:

1. Examine a test file on your monitor.

Ask yourself, is the final result too light or too dark?

If the black patches in the step tablet are merging together and the faces on the test file look a little dark, you need to brighten the monitor.

2. Open the monitor RGB controls on your monitor and navigate to the User Preset.

Menus and controls on your monitor may have different names, but you should be able to poke around a little and find the right setting to make the adjustments we outline in this list.

Don't use the Red slider to adjust color balance. You have to use the Red slider as your brightness control.

3. If your monitor calibration is too dark, begin by brightening the Red slider. If the test file appears too light, you can darken the monitor settings by moving the Red slider in the monitor controls 10 or 15 percent toward darken.

Our Red slider was at 75, so we moved it to 85.

4. To maintain gray balance as much as possible, move the Green and Blue sliders equal amounts.

We moved the Red slider to brighten by 10 percent (from 75 to 85 on our monitor). Just add 10 to both the Green and Blue sliders to maintain an equal balance. If you're darkening the monitor, subtract an equal amount from the sliders, instead.

5. **Open the Adobe Gamma dialog box (you can find Adobe Gamma in the Control Panel) and move to the Gamma pane by clicking the Next button until you arrive at the Gamma adjustment. Readjust the Gamma slider to match the solid square above the slider to the gray surrounding it.**

   Reexamine the test file. Does it look better? Hopefully, you say yes.

6. **Click Next through the panes and click the Finish button to save your changes in the Adobe Gamma dialog box.**

   If the monitor brightness is still too dark, start by changing the Red slider setting toward lighten (the test file turns pinkish) and match the change on the Green and Blue sliders. The gray balance should return or at least be very close. You can make adjustments in a similar way (just reverse the directions you move the sliders) to darken.

7. **Make your final fine adjustments to the color balance by using just the Green and Blue sliders. Do your best to match brightness to the gray card.**

   After you finish with your final color balance settings, you can make a *small* final adjustment to screen brightness with the Gamma slider, even if the little square doesn't quite match the grid. Being able to see all of the light steps toward white is most important of all.

8. **After you finish adjusting the monitor controls for best gray balance, check the big white patch on the test file.**

   Does the white look like a neutral, pure white, or does the white patch have a blue or yellow cast? If you think the white doesn't look quite right, try resetting the Adjusted White Point in the Adobe Gamma utility to a higher value, such as 6500K, for a cooler white or to a lower value, such as 5000K, for a warmer white. Use whatever setting gives you the best, cleanest white.

9. **Save your monitor profile in the Adobe Gamma dialog box.**

   After you complete this process, don't mess with the monitor adjustment controls. Your profile is valid only with the monitor settings you used to create it. You might want to make note of those settings, in case the gamer in your family turns the monitor back to full brightness.

Calibrating with just RGB controls on a Mac

On the Mac, you use the Display Calibrator Assistant to calibrate your monitor. To use this tool, follow these steps:

1. **In Photoshop Elements, open the `MonitorCalibrationFile.tif` that you can download from the Chapter 3 folder on the Wiley companion Web site and size the image to about one-fourth of your monitor size.**

   You want to make it easy to see but small enough to move around as needed.

2. **To open the Display Calibrator Assistant, click the System Preferences in the Dock, click Displays in the Preferences window, click the Color option at the top of the dialog box, and then click the Calibrate button.**

3. **Click the Expert Mode check box, as you see in Figure 3-10. Click Continue to move to the next pane.**

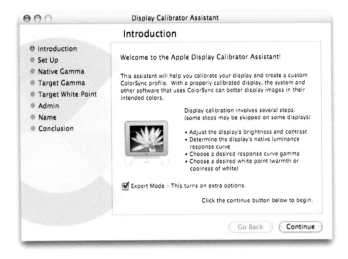

Figure 3-10: In the Display Calibrator Assistant, select Expert Mode.

4. **Compare the test file to the display adjustment.**

   On the monitor display, place the open test file and the dialog box so that you can easily view both at the same time. Ignore the instruction to turn up monitor contrast and observe the black-point test chart. At the same time, check the dark end of the step tablet on the test file.

   The circle in the black-point reference window should look like a dark ellipse, and you should see a slight separation in tone between the test file's step-tablet black patch and the dark gray patch to the right of it. Depending on your monitor brand and viewing conditions, you might see a slight separation in tone of the two background patches surrounding the Apple when the darkest gray patch to the right of the black patch in the test file shows a slight separation. (See Figure 3-11.) If in doubt, use the test file as the final reference.

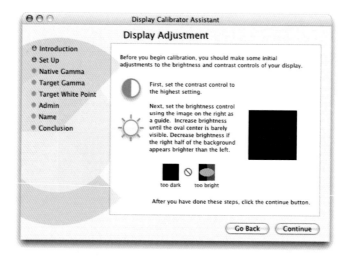

Figure 3-11: Verify the elliptical circle is visible in the Display Adjustment dialog box.

5. **Adjust for the black point.**

    You need to get this setting (black point) just right. If the black-point setting is too dark or too light, follow the adjustment instructions we use for Windows platforms with similar monitor controls in the section "Using Adobe Gamma," earlier in this chapter, until you have the best black-point adjustment you can achieve. If you have to err, slightly too dark is better than too light.

6. **Set the monitor brightness with the Red slider control.**

7. **Carefully readjust monitor gray balance with the Green and Blue sliders.**

    Okay, you have your monitor-view black point adjusted, and the gray balance is correct. The rest is easy.

8. **Click the Continue button, and you're presented with the first of five dialog boxes that say Determine Your Display's Native Response. (See Figure 3-12.)**

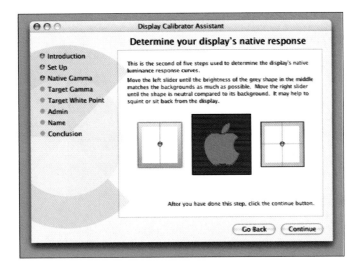

Figure 3-12: Adjust the left slider until the Apple appears in the center of the grid.

This totally cool feature is unique to Macs. It allows the computer to provide very accurate tonal rendering of your file on the monitor.

9. **Adjust the left-side Gamma slider until the Apple in the middle matches the surrounding square as closely as you can get it.**

   Don't change the setting of the right-hand Gamma box in any way in all five of the native response dialog boxes!

10. **In each of the dialog boxes, set the left-side Gamma as accurately as you can and then click Continue.**

11. **In the dialog box that appears, called Select a Target Gamma, simply select the Use Native Gamma check box (see Figure 3-13) and click Continue to open the next pane.**

   The native Gamma of your LCD is probably in the 2.20 range anyway, so leave it at the default.

12. **In the dialog box that appears, select a Target White Point and deselect the Native White Point check box.**

   Observe the big white patch on the test file. The white in the dialog box is a good reference, also.

13. **Move the Color Temperature slider until the whites on the monitor look neutral — not bluish or yellowish. A good starting point on the slider is 5500K, as shown in Figure 3-14.**

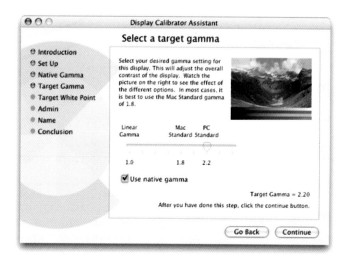

Figure 3-13: Select the Use Native Gamma check box to leave the native Gamma as the default.

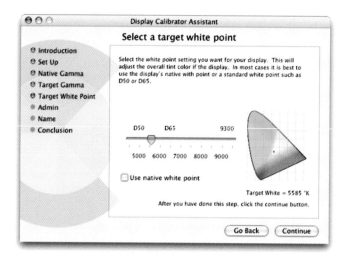

Figure 3-14: Set the white point to 5500K.

Step back a bit from the monitor if you're not sure whether the setting is correct. Having a piece of pure white printer paper near the monitor can sometimes help to see a pure white setting.

14. **Click the Continue button after you finish with the white-point adjustment.**

    The Administration Options dialog box appears.

15. **Click Allow Other Users To Use This Calibration to set Administration privileges and click Continue.**

    The last pane appears, in which you supply a name for your profile.

16. **Type a name different from the original monitor profile, as shown in Figure 3-15, and click Continue to save the new profile.**

    Make note of your final monitor RGB settings, just in case they're changed at a later time.

Figure 3-15: To save your profile, type a name and click Continue.

Calibrating LCD monitors that have brightness and contrast controls

Some LCD monitors have built-in contrast and brightness controls. These controls make calibration far easier than it is with just RGB slider controls. You can adjust black point, white point, and overall image contrast independently from the monitor color balance.

This type of LCD monitor also usually includes a number of presets for overall monitor color balance. In many cases, one of the presets comes very close to a neutral color balance with good gray rendering. You just have to experiment a little with the settings and see what you find. If the presets don't work, you need to try a more fine-grained adjustment with the various sets of sliders. The following sections step you through the process.

Starting with the presets

ViewSonic monitors have the kind of preset controls that often come with this type of monitor, and we use ViewSonic as an example here for how to make hardware adjustments. If you have similar controls on your monitor, you can follow along closely. Follow the steps below to make your hardware adjustments for color temperature:

1. **Open the test file `MonitorCalibrationFile.tif`, which you can download from the Chapter 3 folder on the companion Web site, with Elements. Size the image onscreen to about one-fourth of the monitor view so you can easily view it and move it around if needed.**

2. **Open your monitor control menu and select Color controls.**

   In Figure 3-16, you can see the controls we found on an inexpensive ViewSonic LCD monitor. This low-end monitor has a nice range of controls.

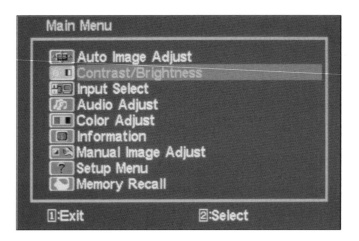

Figure 3-16: Low-end monitors, such as View Sonics, have a nice range of hardware controls.

3. **Choose sRGB, if you have the option.**

The ViewSonic offers a number of options, including a mode called sRGB. After we tried out all the other color presets, the sRGB preset (Figure 3-17) came very close to a perfect neutral gray!

As a rule, an sRGB or 6500K preset tends to hit the closest to neutral gray, but you might as well try them all while you're at it.

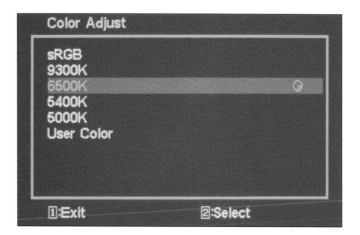

Figure 3-17: sRGB on the ViewSonic is very close to neutral gray.

sRGB is actually a color-space profile, not a specific profile for a particular monitor. When you find this setting on a monitor, it's usually a good idea to try it out before you try any other settings. The sRGB preset is an attempt to set the monitor up for a 6500K white point and a decent gray balance. In other words, if it looks good, use it!

If one of the monitor color presets gets you close to a neutral gray, proceed to the following section. If none of the presets produce a good gray balance, you have to use the User Color controls.

Adjusting the brightness and contrast

In your Monitor Color Control dialog box, the individual red, green, and blue color controls can have many different names, such as Custom, RGB, User, and so on. Look around until you find them. The custom color control may be just a white-balance adjustment, sometimes called the Color Temperature adjustment. If you have a monitor with only custom presets and a white-balance adjustment, do the following:

1. **Adjust the white balance.**

   Find the preset with the best overall gray balance and then fine-tune it as best you can by using the White Balance slider. Moves toward higher color temperatures add blue, and moves to lower values add yellow.

2. **If your monitor has RGB sliders, look at these settings and make note of the positions.**

   In Figure 3-18, you can see the individual controls for R, G, and B on the ViewSonic monitor.

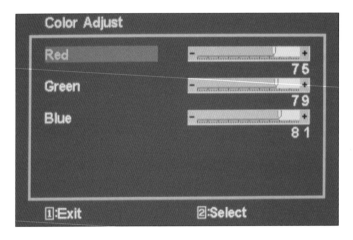

Figure 3-18: Make note of the default settings for Red, Green, and Blue.

Monitors vary when you select this option. Sometimes, opening the option makes the screen turn bluish because all the sliders are set to 100 percent. On some monitors, some kind of preset is in place when you open the dialog box, and less change happens onscreen.

3. **Adjust the R, G, and B sliders to obtain the best overall gray balance that you can.**

   As a rule, you want to adjust by using just two of the sliders to avoid chasing your tail. We advise moving just the G and B sliders to make the adjustment. You can move the R slider slightly at the end for a final color tweak, if needed. See the section "Adjusting Hardware Controls on an LCD Display," earlier in this chapter, where we talk about adjusting two color values.

   Using a photo gray card as a gray reference is a big help here. Place it near the monitor and try to match the gray as best you can.

After you have a good gray balance, you need to set brightness and contrast.

4. **With the test file open, set brightness and contrast to 50 percent.**

In Figure 3-19, you can see the brightness and contrast adjustments we made to our example ViewSonic monitor.

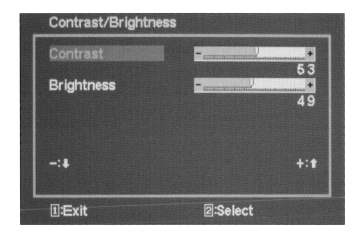

Figure 3-19: Some monitors provide you with hardware adjustments for brightness and contrast.

5. **Examine the image for brightness.**

Does the step tablet show all 21 steps, from white to black? Do the portrait images seem to be a normal brightness?

Note: Your LCD has far more relative visual contrast than the paper example in this book, but the tonal relationships should be similar.

Closely observe the last two dark steps in the gray scale. If the last two (or more) steps are solid black, you need to turn up the brightness control. Turn it up until step 20 on the test file looks just the slightest bit brighter than the full black at step 21.

6. **Examine the light side of the gray scale (the contrast).**

Can you see all the steps to white? If step 2 on the test file (or more) is merged with the white step 1, you need to turn down the contrast control. Turn it down until you can see all the white steps clearly, but not so much that the portrait image looks too dark.

7. **Recheck the blackest steps. If steps 20 and 21 are merged again, turn up the brightness a little bit until they just barely separate again.**

   Note: We're not trying to drive you nuts, it's just that the brightness and contrast controls affect each other. Make fine adjustments until you can resolve all the grayscale steps and the portrait has a normal density.

   Some lower-quality LCDs have a hard time separating the last two black steps when the white steps and portrait look normal. If five or ten minutes of adjusting attempts still can't resolve those two pesky dark steps when everything else looks normal, that's probably as good as you can visually calibrate your LCD monitor.

8. **Readjust gray balance.**

   Make one last visual check of the gray balance. A few LCDs vary a little in color balance after you make large adjustments to the brightness and contrast controls. Readjust the gray balance, if needed. If you have access to only a Color Temperature slider for this adjustment, just do the best you can.

Calibrating monitors that have white-balance, brightness, and contrast controls in Windows

For Windows users, you use the Adobe Gamma utility after you adjust a monitor that has controls for white balance, brightness, and contrast. For this kind of calibration, follow these steps:

1. **Open Adobe Gamma (which you can find in the Control Panel) and set the Phosphors.**

   Set the Phosphors box to Custom if it's not set to that already. Your monitor values are preloaded to Custom by the generic profile that came with your monitor.

2. **Adjust the Gamma.**

   Set the Gamma to Windows Default 2.20

   Now, carefully adjust the Gamma slider so that the little gray box in the center matches the surrounding gray box. Squint and lean back from the monitor if it helps you distinguish the shades of gray.

3. **Set the white point.**

   Set the hardware white point to 6500K. That's the native white point of your monitor.

   Set the adjusted white point to 6500K. If the test file white patch seems a bit too cool (blue), try the 5500K setting. Use whichever setting gives you a white closest to neutral white.

4. **Type a new name for your monitor profile in the final Adobe Gamma pane and click Save.**

   You're now ready to work on your photos in Elements!

Calibrating monitors with just white-balance controls in Windows

If you have only white-balance controls on your monitor to control color balance, and if your test file seems to be a little off from neutral gray, you can use Adobe Gamma to adjust for proper gray balance. Just follow these steps:

1. **Open Adobe Gamma (which you can find in the Control Panel) and set the Phosphors to Custom if it's not set to that already.**

   Your monitor values are preloaded to Custom by the generic profile that came with your monitor.

2. **Set the Gamma to Windows Default 2.20.**

3. **Set the hardware white point to 6500K.**

   That's the native white point of your monitor.

4. **Set the adjusted white point to 6500K.**

5. **Carefully adjust the Gamma slider so that the little gray box in the center matches the surrounding gray box.**

   Squint and lean back from the monitor if it helps you distinguish the grays.

6. **Deselect the Single Gamma View check box, and you're presented with Red, Green, and Blue Gamma boxes.**

   The boxes are very close to the proper adjustment already, but you can use them to get your monitor grays just right.

7. **For the Red and Green boxes, do your best to merge the center color boxes with the surrounding boxes by moving the sliders below the respective colors.**

   Very small moves make very visible changes to the gray balance of the test file.

8. **Adjust the Blue slider by watching the test-file gray patch and adjusting for the best possible gray.**

   If the test-file gray patch still seems a little off after you set the Blue slider to the best adjustment you can determine, you can play with the Red and Green slider settings a little more — just make very small moves. Be patient and work until you have the best gray you can get.

If you get the RGB sliders completely messed up, just revert back to the single Gamma view, reset the Gamma adjustment there, deselect Single Gamma View, and start over.

9. **Check the white patch on the test file. If the white seems too cool (blue), try the 5500K setting on the adjusted White Point option. If the test file looks better, use that setting. If not, use the 6500K setting.**

10. **Type a new name for your monitor profile in the final pane and click Finish to save the profile.**

Calibrating Mac monitors that have white-point adjustments

Follow the steps in the section "Calibrating with just RGB controls on a Mac," earlier in this chapter, to calibrate a Mac monitor. After you make your hardware adjustments, follow the steps to work through all the panes in the Display Calibrator Assistant.

Color Profiles and File Formats

*I*n a nutshell, *color management* means keeping color consistent from the image that you capture (on a digital camera, for example) to how that image looks on your monitor and then to how it looks when you finally print it. In practice, you can achieve consistent color by changing the image data in a controlled way to keep the perceived color the same at all steps in the digital photographic process. If it all works correctly, the scene you photographed appears correctly on your computer monitor, and the print you make looks just like the monitor view.

The key to this color consistency working correctly is monitor calibration (adjusting monitor brightness and color for correct viewing) and the use of color profiles for each device that you use to view or print images. We cover the details of calibrating your monitor in Chapter 3, and in this chapter, you can find out the basics you need to know in order to add profiles to your color-management workflow.

What's a Color Profile?

A *color profile* is a little data set that tells the computer what color the data numbers really mean. A computer doesn't know what color really is. The computer just reads numbers. For example, say you have a color you know as orange displayed on the monitor screen. The monitor doesn't have any orange-colored phosphors or dyes in it, just red, green, and blue. To make orange, the monitor has to light up a lot of red, a little green, and maybe even a tiny bit of blue (if the orange you see isn't super saturated). The monitor needs to use even more blue and green if you're looking at a pastel orange.

Color profiles are commonly referred to as *ICC profiles*. ICC stands for the International Color Consortium. ICC is a standards committee that regulates standards related to color. Color profiles are supplied to users and created with color profiling equipment that meets standards set forth by the ICC committee.

So, the computer defines a particular shade of orange as certain Levels (amounts) of red, green, and blue. To the computer, this orange color might be: Red = 214 (bright); Green = 133 (medium); and Blue = 40 (dim). Figure 4-1 shows the orange color that these Red, Green, and Blue measurements define.

Figure 4-1: You get this orange color with the values R=214, G=133, and B=40.

The problem is, the computer has no clue what the actual colors of the monitor's primary colors really are. The computer also doesn't know how you've adjusted the monitor for color and brightness. These same numbers sent to a different monitor might look like Figure 4-2. Both patches are orange, but they look very different.

This difference is easy to understand if you visit your local TV megastore. Find ten different TVs tuned to the same station, and they all display colors differently, even though they're all receiving the exact same color numbers.

Figure 4-2: This orange has the same RGB values as Figure 4-1, but it's viewed on a different monitor.

The color data needs an authority to make the final call on what the color numbers really mean. That authority is the color profile. If two different kinds of monitors are accurately calibrated, and if each has its own custom profile, the computer for each monitor changes the input data to make the color match, using the color profile as the final authority. Therefore, two completely different monitors, hooked to two different computers, can each display that orange patch exactly the same, from the original computer file, if they're color managed with color profiles.

Understanding the Different Types of Profiles

As you put profiles to work, you might find it helpful to understand that you use color profiles for three different sources. These sources are

- Monitor profiles
- Workspace profiles
- Output profiles

If there's a monkey wrench in the color-management process, it's differentiating between a monitor color profile and a color working profile. In the sections that follow, you can find out the basic purpose of each type of profile.

Monitor profiles

You get your monitor color profile by calibrating your monitor to remove any colorcasts and obtain the optimum brightness on your monitor. We explain creating a monitor profile in Chapter 3. The monitor profile is automatically loaded by your operating system when you start your computer. You may see a sudden change in your monitor brightness during your computer's startup. That's because the brightness settings that you create in your monitor profile may differ from the default settings.

Don't be confused about loading a monitor color profile in Elements. You see your monitor color profile among the other color profiles when you print files. Don't select the monitor color profile for any kind of viewing or printing. It's automatic, and your computer loads it at startup.

Workspace profiles

Your color workspace profile is a profile you choose when editing your images. Color workspace profiles define how your image color translates between different color monitors and viewing conditions. If, for example, you want to exchange a file with another user, you *embed* (or save) your color workspace profile in the file. The recipient of your file may use another color workspace, in which case, he or she might convert your image from your color workspace to his or her workspace. Through this conversion, you (and the person you send the file to) maintain as much of the same color from your original workspace to the converted color workspace.

Photoshop Elements, the image-editing program we focus on in this book, offers two options for a color workspace profile: sRGB or Adobe RGB (1998). (Other editing programs might offer more or different options.) Before you choose an option, it's helpful to know that the workspace provides you a view of the optimum *color gamut* (color range). The Adobe RGB (1998) color profile shows you a larger color gamut than sRGB (meaning more colors are visible when you use this profile), but specific desktop printers and service centers may prefer sRGB. We talk more about using sRGB over Adobe RGB (1998) in the section "Working with Workspace Profiles in Elements," later in this chapter.

Output profiles

You use output profiles with printing equipment. When you print a file, a color conversion takes place. The conversion is made from your workspace color to the colors that your printer can reproduce. In essence, this conversion attempts to convert all the color you see in your photo to as close a match as your printer can reproduce.

You can manually or automatically select these profiles for your desktop printer and the paper you print to, or you can get profiles that are custom created by either you or a profile creation service. For the details on working with output profiles, see the section "Managing Print Colors with Output Profiles," later in this chapter.

Working with Workspace Profiles in Elements

An embedded profile is simply the authority that tells the computer what colors the file data really represent. *Embedding* a profile means saving the profile along with the image that you save to your hard drive.

Unfortunately, Photoshop Elements affords you only two options for profile embedding — sRGB or Adobe RGB (1998). You can embed profiles in an image file only when you select certain file format options. In addition, you need to define your color workspace prior to saving the file so that the profile is recognized in the Save/Save As dialog box.

In the sections that follow, you can find out the basics of choosing your color workspace profile and embedding it in an image.

Defining your color workspace

Photoshop Elements provides you with two primary color workspaces when you install the program. To choose a color workspace, follow these steps:

1. **Launch Photoshop Elements, and in the Adobe Photoshop Elements Start Up Window that appears, click Edit and Enhance Photos to enter Standard Edit mode.**

   For all our color correction work, we use the Standard Edit mode.

2. **Select Edit⇨Color Settings to open the Color Settings dialog box.**

   In the Color Settings dialog box, you have four choices, as shown in Figure 4-3. Your choices include the following:

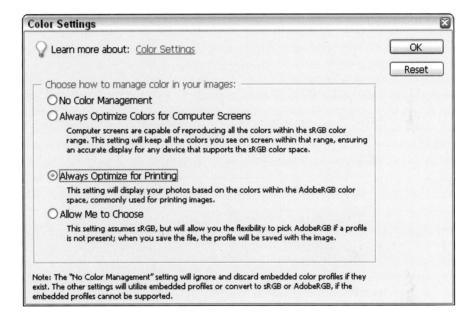

Figure 4-3: You can choose how to manage your images' colors in the Color Settings window.

- **No Color Management:** Be certain to *not* select this option. Clicking the radio button turns off all color management.

- **Always Optimize Colors for Computer Screens:** This option uses the sRGB color profile that Microsoft created as a general color profile to display consistent color across computer monitors. Typically, you use this profile for Web and screen graphics. However, our tests show that the sRGB profile works best for most desktop color printers. See Chapter 13 for more on color profiles and printing.

- **Always Optimize for Printing:** This option suggests that you should choose it for all printing. This profile contains more colors than the sRGB color profile and works well with a number of printers. However, if you're working in Photoshop Elements and printing to a typical desktop printer, the sRGB profile is better suited for printing. Most desktop color printers can't reproduce all the colors in this workspace.

- **Allow Me to Choose:** Clicking this option means that a dialog box opens when you open photos that have a different profile than your chosen sRGB or Adobe RGB (1998) color workspace. In the dialog box, you can choose to convert color to your workspace or preserve the workspace that was saved with the file. For example, if your workspace is sRGB and you open a photo that was saved with the Adobe RGB (1998) color workspace, you can choose to convert Adobe RGB (1998) to sRGB or to leave the photo in the Adobe RGB (1998) workspace. We suggest that you don't select this radio button until you fully understand what color conversion is all about, as we explain in the section "Converting color," later in this chapter.

3. **If you want to follow many of the lists of steps in this book, we recommend selecting the Always Optimize Colors for Computer Screens radio button.**

4. **Click OK to exit the dialog box.**

Embedding the workspace profile

After identifying the color workspace (which we cover in the preceding section), follow these steps to embed the workspace profile in your photo:

1. **Open an image in Photoshop Elements in Standard Edit mode.**

2. **Select File⇨Save As to open the Save As dialog box, shown in Figure 4-4.**

3. **From the Format menu, select a file format that supports embedding a color profile.**

   Most of the time, you'll choose .psd, .tiff, or .jpg. See the section "Choosing and Changing File Formats," later in this chapter, for more details on using color profiles with different types of files.

4. **Select the Color ICC Profile check box.**

   If the format you select supports profile embedding, the Color check box becomes active. Select the box, and the profile you use for your workspace appears to the right of ICC Profile, as shown in Figure 4-4.

5. Click Save.

The file is saved with the profile embedded in the image. If you exchange the photo with a user who works with a different color workspace profile, the user can choose to preserve the profile in the photo or convert the color from your profile to his or her color workspace.

Figure 4-4: You can choose in what format you want to save your image in the Save As dialog box.

Managing Print Colors with Output Profiles

When it comes time to print your photos, part of your color-management workflow involves using the right output profiles (also called *device profiles*). In the following sections, we help you weigh your options as you decide whether to opt for developer profiles or take a more customized (and more expensive) approach to profiles.

With your profile on your computer, you then need to install it and make sure your printer gets the right profile information when you select your print options. You can find an overview of how to use profiles in this chapter, and Part IV explains in detail how you can incorporate profiles in the printing and image-proofing process.

Acquiring device profiles

If you send your photos to a commercial photo lab or print vendor, you can often find color profiles available on the vendor's Web site specifically created for the output equipment and papers that vendor uses. For your own personal desktop printers, you can sometimes find output profiles available on developer Web sites or on the CD that shipped with your printer. Paper manufacturers may also provide profiles for printing to the different types of paper they offer.

You may be wondering if the profiles you acquire from developer sites (also known as *canned profiles*) are well suited to your printer and the paper you use. Unfortunately, most canned profiles fall short of printing accurate color.

You may find that your printer does a very good job of printing to papers supplied by your printer manufacturer. For example, the Epson line of printers does an excellent job when printing to Epson papers, such as Premium Photo Glossy and a number of other stocks. Epson has done a fine job in creating accurate profiles that get the color very close to what you see on your monitor in a well-managed, color-management workflow.

But what happens when you want to print on a type of paper developed by a manufacturer other than your printer manufacturer? For example, suppose you use a Canon printer, and you want to print on Epson paper. Typically, the paper manufacturer creates color profiles for the papers they produce, and often, you can find profiles created for a particular paper when it's used with a number of different printers.

To understand how things can go awry, take a look at Figure 4-5. Both images in this figure represent the results of printing on a Kodak Semi Matte paper by using an Epson 4000 inkjet printer. Kodak's own profile was used to create the print on the right. The differences in the color transitions are very obvious, and you can see the many awkward color shifts. On the left, you see the results of our custom-developed profile that we created with a hardware color-profile device. In this image, the colors transition smoothly, creating a pleasing flow of color.

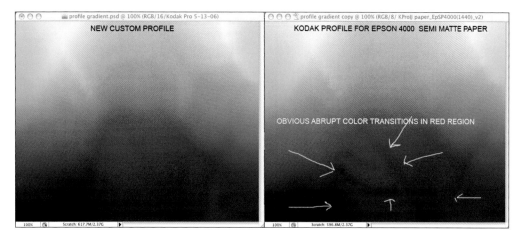

Figure 4-5: A print with a custom color profile (on the left) looks much smoother than a print that used a canned profile (on the right).

The only solution you have for such disparities in printing is to either buy a hardware device capable of creating printer profiles or use a profiling service. If you're a professional or semi-professional photographer, you should probably purchase equipment that enables you to develop custom profiles for all your printers and papers.

If you like to use a particular printer and type of paper, and you use them regularly, then by all means, use an online profiling service and have a custom profile created for you. For between $25 and $50, you end up saving in the long run when you measure your costs against consumables you use to make test prints to get the color right. We talk more about profiling services in the following section.

If you find that the printer and paper you use with a canned profile provides a good representation of your onscreen color images, stay with that canned profile and the papers that work with your printer.

Getting profiles from a custom profile service

If you have a desktop color printer or large-format printer and you want to have a profile created, you can use a custom service that creates the profile for you. Rather than spend a lot of money on a calibration device you may use for only a few printers, you can commission a provider that offers custom profiling services for a fee.

Understanding CMYK color

CMYK color is commonly referred to as *process color* and represents the four colors of Cyan, Magenta, Yellow, and blacK. Print shops use CMYK color for offset printing.

Some desktop color printers use four separate inks — one for each of the CMYK colors. You may also find five, six, seven, or more inks that include variations of CMYK inks, such as Magenta, Light Magenta, Cyan, Light Cyan, and so on.

When you print a file to a color printer that uses CMYK inks, you print your RGB file to the printer. You don't need to make a color conversion from an RGB to a CMYK color mode. It's just as well that you don't have to convert color modes from RGB to CMYK because Photoshop Elements doesn't support the CMYK color mode. (Other imaging software programs, such as Adobe Photoshop, do support the CMYK color mode, though.)

To prepare files for offset printing, you need to submit your RGB files to your printer and have the print shop convert your photos from RGB to CMYK color. If you want to find out more about CMYK color and programs supporting that color mode, see Chapter 16.

Providers, such as inkjetart.com (`www.inkjetart.com/custom_profiles`) and Dry Creek Photo (`www.drycreekphoto.com`), charge from $25 to $50 to create a custom ICC profile for you, for each paper stock you use. At Dry Creek Photo, you can get a year's worth of support and free upgrades for $99.

Just log on to a provider Web site and download a target file. Then print the target file, using no color management, on the paper type for which you want to create the profile. Send the printed piece back to the provider, and they'll e-mail you a file attachment that you can copy to the folder where you save your profiles.

For information on printing files without color management, see Chapter 13.

Getting profiles from a custom profile device

In a best-case scenario, you'd use a high-end device costing between $1,500 and $3,000 to create printer profiles for all your output devices. These custom profile devices enable you to create custom profiles from test prints you output to your printer.

A test page containing an array of colors is measured by the device's spectrometer, which you drag across rows and columns of printed color swatches. After completing the color assessment, the device creates a profile for that specific printer and paper.

GretagMacbeth (www.gretagmacbeth.com) offers the Eye-One Photo system, a low-cost solution for a profile-creation system that includes calibration equipment and software to calibrate your monitors, RGB and CMYK output devices, digital cameras, scanners, and digital projectors for screen displays. You can get this system for a list price of $1,695, as of this writing. If you want to knock out digital cameras from the equipment support, you can purchase the Eye-One Proof system for a suggested list price of $1,495.

If you decide to purchase a calibration system for your output device, be careful to purchase the right system for the kind of output you produce. Some devices are designed to create profiles for CMYK-only printers. That's fine for some inkjets and prepress proofing systems; however, devices such as mini-photo labs and most of the desktop color inkjets are RGB output devices and won't benefit from a CMYK profiling system. See the nearby sidebar "Understanding CMYK color" for more on RGB versus CMYK color.

Installing profiles on your computer

If you see a list of profiles in the Elements Print dialog box for your printer and various types of papers after you install a printer driver on your computer, your printer installation added the profiles automatically to the proper folder on your hard drive.

On the other hand, you may acquire a printer profile from a desktop printer developer, or you may have a custom profile created for your printer and a certain type of paper. If this is the case, you may need to manually install a profile to the location on your hard drive where all your output profiles are stored. The Photoshop Elements Print dialog box lists all output profiles stored in a specific folder on your hard drive.

The folder names and directory paths differ between Macintosh and Windows. Look over the following sections to see where profiles are stored on your system.

On a Mac

Follow these steps to install a profile on a Mac:

1. **On the hard drive, select Library⇨ColorSync⇨Profiles.**

   The complete directory path is Macintosh HD/Library/ColorSync/ Profiles. If you don't have Administrative privileges on your computer, open your User folder and follow the path User/Library/ColorSync/ Profiles.

2. Copy your profile to one of the Profile folders.

When you print files in Photoshop Elements, Elements looks to this folder, which lets you easily select a printer profile. In Figure 4-6, you can see all the profiles we have stored in our Profiles folder.

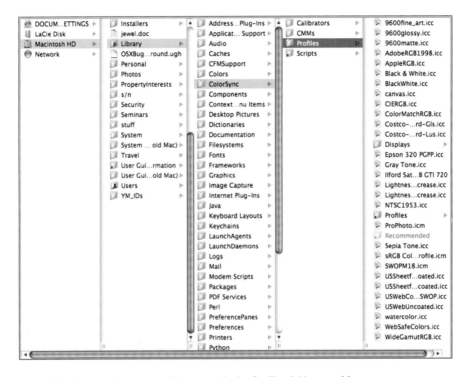

Figure 4-6: You can find color profiles stored in the Profiles folder on a Mac.

In Windows

To install a profile in Windows XP, follow these steps:

1. Navigate to the Color folder on your hard drive, using the following path: C:\Windows\system32\spool\drivers\color.

2. Copy your profiles to the color folder (shown in Figure 4-7).

The output profiles are logically grouped together when you open a menu to select a profile.

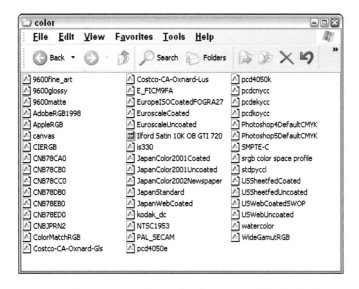

Figure 4-7: You can store color profiles in the color folder in Windows.

Using output profiles when printing

After you acquire or create an output color profile, you need to use that profile when you print to your desktop printer, or you need to somehow get the color profile embedded in the image before sending that image file to a commercial photo lab. You have two options for printing with color profiles, if you're using your own printer:

✔ Select the profile at print time.

✔ Convert color and embed the output color profile in your image.

If you send your images to a commercial lab for printing, the lab may provide you instructions for saving your files as sRGB or Adobe RGB (1998), and they perform the profile conversion when they print to their commercial equipment. Ask a service what they prefer before you submit files.

Selecting a profile at print time

You select output color profiles at print time. After you perform all your color and tonal corrections, select File➪Print to print your image. Selecting this command opens the Print Preview dialog box. In the Print Preview dialog box, shown in Figure 4-8, you can choose a printer profile from the Printer Profile menu.

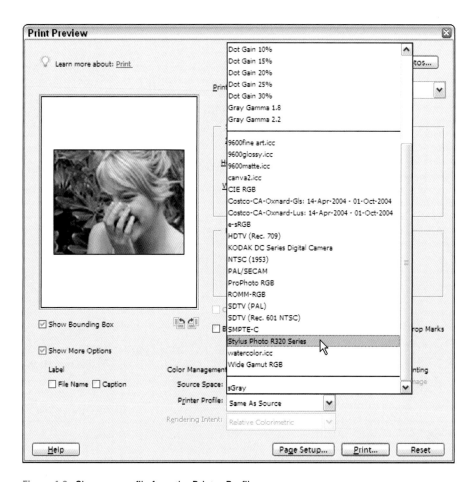

Figure 4-8: Choose a profile from the Printer Profile menu.

The Printer Profile menu is visible only when you select the Show More Options check box in the lower left-corner of the Print Preview dialog box.

Ideally, you want to use the profile for the type of paper you're printing on. If no profile appears for your paper type in the Printer Profile menu, choose your printer type from the menu. You can select the paper type later in the Printer Properties. Selecting a profile and clicking the Print button then converts your color workspace profile to the printer profile. This conversion is automatic — you don't have to do anything.

For specific details about printing photos, see Chapter 13.

Converting color

When you print a photo, the color workspace you use (either sRGB or Adobe RGB [1998]) is converted to the color your printer uses. During the printing process, the color workspace profile is converted to the printer color profile. Typically, printer color profiles are installed on your computer when you install a new desktop color printer.

Printer profiles are developed for each paper you use to print your pictures. If, for example, you use a glossy photo stock, you should have a matching printer color profile for that glossy photo stock.

One great limitation you have in Photoshop Elements is the lack of an option to convert color within Elements. You have no menu command for converting color from your workspace to your printer color. This limitation prevents you from previewing onscreen the color as it will appear on the paper you use to print your image. The color conversion happens at print time, and you get your only proof of whether the color is correct from the final output, the printed image.

We do have a workaround for converting color so that you can preview your prints onscreen, and you can find much more detail on how to perform color conversions in Chapter 14.

Choosing and Changing File Formats

To color manage your files, you need to know which file formats support color management. In the following sections, you can find out which file formats in Elements to use and which ones to avoid. You can also find out how to convert a file from one format to another and still maintain its embedded profile.

Which formats support profiles?

Not all file formats support embedding color profiles. Photoshop Elements offers you a number of different file formats in which you can save your pictures. Look over Table 4-1 and note the file formats that support profile embedding.

Table 4-1	File Formats Supporting Profile Embedding	
Format	*File Attributes*	*Supports Profile Embedding*
Photoshop (.PSD; .PDD)	As you work on images, use this format to preserve layers and edits until you save the final file for output.	Yes
BMP (.BMP; .RLE; .DIB)	Don't use this format for images you're color correcting.	No
CompuServe GIF (.GIF)	Use this format for Web graphics.	No
Photoshop EPS (.EPS)	As a general rule, don't use this format for printing to desktop color printers.	Yes
JPEG (.JPG; .JPEG; .JPE)	If you're sending files to a photo lab, the lab may prefer this format.	Yes
JPEG2000 (.JPF; .JPX; .JP2; .J2C; .J2K; .JPC)	This newer JPEG format doesn't lose data when the file is compressed.	Yes
PCX	Don't use this format for images you're color correcting and printing.	No
Photoshop PDF (.PDF)	Use PDF to embed text and images in layouts. You typically don't use this format for photos you plan to print.	Yes
Photoshop RAW	Don't use this format for images you're color correcting and printing.	No
PICT File (.PCT; .PICT)	Don't use this format for images you're color correcting and printing.	No
Pixar (.PXR)	Don't use this format for images you're color correcting and printing.	No
PNG (.PNG)	Don't use this format for images you're color correcting and printing.	No
Scitex CT (.SCT)	Don't use this format for images you're color correcting and printing to desktop printers or photo labs.	No
Targa (.TGA; .VDA; .ICB; .VST)	Don't use this format for images you're color correcting and printing.	No
TIFF (.TIF; .TIFF)	This is one of the best all-around file formats for exchanging and printing files.	Yes

With the number of file formats available, you may find deciding which format to choose when working on photos and submitting them for printing confusing. Fortunately, you can reduce the list of formats to just a few when you find out what formats your own desktop color printer or the professional photo lab to which you send your images supports.

The formats you're most likely to use for color correction and printing include

- **Photoshop (.PSD; .PDD):** Many people use this format when editing photos. If you have to save a photo and return to it later to perform more edits, save it as a .psd file, and the file is saved without compression. Before you submit the file to a photo lab, you can choose another format in which to save the final file. When printing to your own desktop color printer, you can print the file saved in this format — no need to convert.

- **JPEG (.JPG; .JPEG; .JPE):** Your digital camera saves your photos in JPEG format. Some cameras also support the camera raw format. JPEG is a *lossy compression format,* which means you experience some data loss each time you save the file as a JPEG. While working on a file, open a JPEG image and choose another format, such as Photoshop .psd or TIFF, to prevent further data loss. If you submit photos to a photo lab, the lab may request a JPEG file. Use the JPEG format as the final step in your editing process just before you send files to the lab.

- **TIFF (.TIF; .TIFF):** TIFF format is like the Photoshop .psd format, in which the file is saved without lossy compression. Use this format when saving files for output and when you need to integrate files in designs that use other software programs.

When can you change a file format?

Because Photoshop Elements offers you only two choices for profile embedding, you may be concerned about changing a file format from something like TIFF to JPEG or vice versa. For example, say you save a file as a TIFF so that you can use a profile converter to soft proof colors. Then, after doing a final check of the file, you need to prepare the file for an output service, which requires you to save your file as a JPEG. Services such as the Costco Photo Labs require files in JPEG format. Fortunately, after you embed a profile in a photo, Photoshop Elements does permit you to preserve an embedded profile.

If you need to save the file in another format after you've embedded a profile in your image, follow these steps:

1. **Open the image in Photoshop Elements Standard Edit mode.**

2. **Select File⇨Save As.**

3. **In the Save As dialog box, select the output format you want.**

   In this example, we open a TIFF file and choose JPEG as our Format, as shown in Figure 4-9. The ICC Profile section of the Save As dialog box shows you the color profile embedded (saved) in the file. If you leave the ICC Profile alone, that profile is preserved when you save the file in a different format.

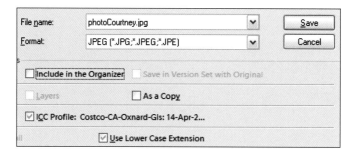

Figure 4-9: Choose the file format you want to apply to your file from the Format menu.

4. **Click the Save button.**

5. **In the dialog box that appears, select the appropriate options.**

   If you select JPEG as your format in Step 3, the JPEG Options dialog box opens. Be certain to move the slider to Large File (12 and Maximum appear above the slider), as shown in Figure 4-10. This setting minimizes data loss when saving a file as a JPEG.

6. **Click OK, and your file is saved in the new format while preserving the embedded profile.**

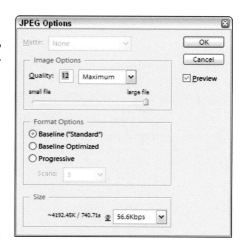

Figure 4-10: Select the Maximum Quality when saving your image as a JPEG.

Only some file formats can embed color profiles. For the complete list of file formats that support color profiles, see the preceding section.

Understanding Bit Depth

As we explain in Chapter 1, RGB color images are represented in three channels. Each of these channels contains a level of gray to express any given color. Essentially, the gray values block out or hold back light. A level of 0 in each channel means no light passes through any channel, resulting in a black image. Conversely, a level of 255 is wide open and lets all light pass through, resulting in a pure white image. The number 255 is a figure you want to remember. Because 0 (zero) is also a number in the computer color world, you have a total of 256 levels of gray in an 8-bit image.

When you work with 256 levels of gray for each channel, you're working on an 8-bit image. If you multiply $256 \times 256 \times 256$, you get a number in excess of 16 million, which is the total number of colors in the RGB color space. When it comes time to reproduce your images on a printer, the printer outputs your file from 8-bit images in an effort to reproduce as many of those possible 16.7 million colors as it can.

If you use a digital camera capable of capturing camera raw images, your camera sensors are likely to capture 12-bit or higher images — the most common higher bit is 16 bit. A 16-bit image has 4096 levels of gray per channel. This extra data allows you to decide which 256 levels of gray you ultimately want to use on your final printed piece. In Figure 4-11, for example, you can see the Levels dialog box (Image⇨Adjust Lighting⇨ Levels) for an 8-bit image. The left side of the histogram shows no data, which means the darker areas of the image have no detail.

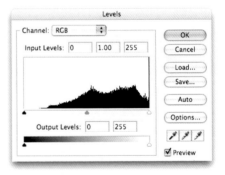

Figure 4-11: The Levels dialog box shows data distribution in an 8-bit image.

Because your printer can print only 8-bit images, the extra image data from a higher bit-mode file are tossed during printing. However, when you edit an image for brightness and color correction, you want to perform as much of your editing as you can while in a higher bit mode. Having the extra data in an image lets you decide, when you print the image, which 256 levels of gray you want to use from the 4096 levels you have.

Figure 4-12 shows the Levels dialog box for a 16-bit image with data across all 256 levels of gray. You can skew the input sliders on this image to the left or right to pick up a little more detail in either the highlights or shadows. In essence, you're telling Photoshop Elements which levels of gray you want to reproduce.

Photoshop Elements provides you a means to convert 16-bit images to 8-bit images by using the Image➪Mode➪8 Bits/Channel menu command. If the menu command

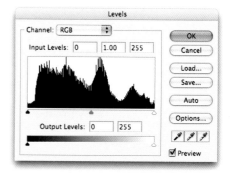

Figure 4-12: The Levels dialog box shows data distribution in a 16-bit image.

appears grayed out, as shown in Figure 4-13, you're already working with an 8-bit image. If the menu command isn't grayed out, you can select it to perform operations such as saving the file in JPEG format.

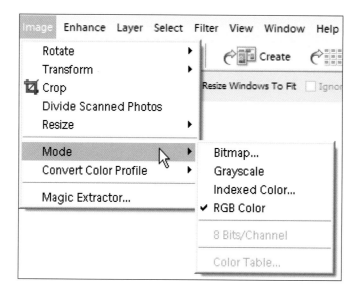

Figure 4-13: If the 8 Bits/Channel command is grayed out, the file is already in 8-bit mode.

Understanding dynamic range

Dynamic range is the measure of capturing data in the highlights and shadows. If your images are *clipped* (showing no data on either end of a histogram), the dynamic range is much less than a photo in which you see a histogram containing data at both ends and all through the midtone areas. In Figure 4-11, you can see an absence of data on the left side of the histogram, indicating a loss of detail in the highlights.

Input devices, such as cameras and scanners, are categorized in terms of dynamic range, just as output devices are. Looking at a digital camera, you can find many point-and-shoot models that boast more than 7 or 8 megapixels and cost less than $500. You can also find digital cameras in the 4- to 6-megapixel range that cost more than $2,000. One of the primary differences between the cameras is the dynamic range of the sensors. Obviously, the more costly cameras provide you a greater dynamic range, which means you see much more detail in the shadows and highlights.

16-bit images generally provide you more dynamic range, so you clearly notice more detail in shadows and highlights.

Where you get 16-bit images

In Photoshop Elements, you're stuck with 8-bit images if your camera can capture only JPEG files. Unfortunately, you don't have an option for converting 8-bit to 16-bit, which would be ideal for adjusting brightness, tones, and color. If you have a camera that captures images in the camera raw format, your images are captured in 16-bit mode. Perform all your brightness and color corrections on higher bit images before you change the mode to 8-bit for final printing.

For more information on camera raw, see Chapter 12. To find out more about adjusting brightness on 8-bit and 16-bit images, see Chapter 11.

Part II
Image Brightness and Contrast Corrections

The 5th Wave   By Rich Tennant

"I've got some new image-editing software, so I took the liberty of erasing some of the smudges that kept showing up around the clouds. No need to thank me."

In this part . . .

As we continually repeat throughout this book, you need to bring your photos into proper tonal balance for brightness and contrast before you do any color-correction work. This part is divided into three chapters to help simplify tone corrections.

We use different kinds of images to show how one method may work better than others when you're adjusting brightness and contrast. We cover the essential tools you need to use in Elements, and we avoid talking about tools that won't produce the best results.

Chapter 5 covers how to make tonal and brightness corrections to your image files, and Chapter 6 talks about how to fix contrast. Finally, you can discover the joys of adjustment layers in Chapter 7.

5

Making Tonal and Brightness Corrections

In This Chapter

▷ Using brightness and tone corrections

▷ Correcting images with the Levels dialog box

▷ Setting black and white points

▷ Knowing when to bend (or break) the rules

*T*he single most frequently used feature of a program like Photoshop Elements is the ability to make brightness and color adjustments. If you shoot pictures with a digital camera and want to print your photos, you probably want to darken up some of the light images and brighten up some of the dark ones. If skin tones don't look right, you need to make some adjustment to color. Shooting a picture and being able to print a perfect copy without needing to make any brightness or color corrections is a rarity.

One thing that you need to remember when correcting pictures for color is that you should always begin by correcting brightness and contrast first. Sometimes, a simple tweak of brightness and contrast can also balance the color in your pictures. On the other hand, if you begin by adjusting color and then work on brightness and contrast, the color can get thrown out of whack.

In this chapter, we talk about using the tools Elements provides you for making brightness and tonal corrections. We add in a few workarounds for getting around the limitations of the program, and we also tell you when to break the rules. We discuss adjusting for contrast in Chapter 6 and cover using adjustment layers for contrast edits in Chapter 7. To get the most out of this Part, start here, in Chapter 5, and then read through the following two chapters, as well.

Checking Out Your Images

Almost every photo you'll ever shoot will need some tonal and brightness corrections. Even the best digital camera metering systems are really just making a best guess for the brightness and contrast needed for an acceptable final result.

The exposure metering system doesn't know what you have in mind when you capture an image, and the internal image processing of your camera then tries its best to generate a file based on a few assumptions. In general, these assumptions are

✔ The image will have a slight amount of full black and pure white tones.

✔ All the tones mixed together will equal a medium gray.

These assumptions that your camera metering and processing systems make are the cause of most exposure errors. Fortunately, Photoshop Elements has some powerful tools to correct most of the problems.

The computer in your digital camera makes another assumption when creating the JPEG file that's stored on your camera memory card. The camera computer looks at the brightness range captured and selects a certain brightness range based on the entire capture to create a normal contrast range.

This brightness range is about 6½ f-stops from full white to full black. The range happens to be the same as a good quality glossy photo paper. A photo with a natural brightness range will look real to the viewer, so a 6½ f-stop brightness range is the default for the camera processor. Professional photographers spend years figuring out how to always make this magic range fit the photo paper for a natural-looking result.

Sometimes, the captured range fits nicely, and the JPEG file has a full range of tones. An example of a photo with a full range of tones appears in Figure 5-1. In this photo, a pure white, a rich black, and a smooth transition of tones in the midtone area appear.

Figure 5-1: A photo with a full range of tones.

Fixing Tone Problems

To illustrate how to correct tone problems, we picked out some images that have a fair color balance and don't need color correction. For more on understanding how to correct color, turn to Part III. In this section, we work on correcting the brightness and contrast in images. Most files have some degree of color problems, too, but just worry about tone corrections for now.

If the captured range of brightness is too wide, the camera computer clips off some of the tones, resulting in either blank white highlights or full black shadows (and sometimes both). So what does it really mean to have a too-wide range of brightness? Camera chips capture a range of light. If the light is too bright, the light areas (called *highlights*) are clipped. *Clipping* means that some of the tones are cut off or lost.

On the other side of the tone curve, the camera chip might not capture enough light, which results in clipping the dark areas, called the *shadows*. When you look at a photo that has clipping in the highlights and shadows, the picture appears washed out or too dark. You can't completely fix these kinds of problems after you actually take the picture, but you can edit the file for best results with the data you have to work with.

Several kinds of image problems can occur when your camera sensor doesn't capture a full range of tones: too much or too little contrast, too much or too little exposure, or a combination of contrast and exposure problems. As an example, look at Figure 5-2. This photo has too much contrast.

Figure 5-2: A photo with too much contrast.

An image capture of a low-contrast scene looks muddy and lifeless with an assumed 6½ f-stop brightness range, in most cases; but at least all the data are there in the file, and Elements allows you to easily fix the problem after the fact. In Figure 5-3, you can see a good example of a *flat* file — one with little contrast — that you can effectively correct in Photoshop Elements.

An image that's underexposed looks too dark all over, and overexposed images look too bright and washed out. The image shown in Figure 5-4, where you see an overexposed picture, and the image in Figure 5-5, where you see an underexposed picture, are more difficult to correct than the images with contrast problems, shown in Figure 5-2 and Figure 5-3.

Figure 5-3: A photo with too little contrast appears flat and lifeless.

Figure 5-4: An overexposed image.

Figure 5-5: An underexposed image.

Using the Levels Dialog Box

Levels is perhaps a tool with a strange name — no, it doesn't have anything to do with checking the tilt of a picture frame. Levels got its name from the 256 levels of image tone we talk about in Chapter 1. Yes, it does display all those image tones, but it does far more than that. It's the best single tool in Photoshop Elements (especially considering the crummy Color Curves option that's been added to Elements 5).

Levels allows you to set the black and white points, change overall image brightness, and correct color casts. In this section, we take a look at the Levels dialog box to help you completely understand the tool you have to work with. It might seem a little bewildering at first, but you can master it in no time.

Choose Enhance➪Adjust Lighting and, from the submenu that appears, select Levels to open the Levels dialog box, shown in Figure 5-6. Alternatively, press Ctrl+L (⌘+L for Macs).

The most prominent feature of the Levels dialog box is the histogram. A *histogram* is just a bar chart, a sort of a graph that shows proportions. The chart has 256 bars, and they all look blended together most of the time. Black is far left, and white is far right. Gray is in the exact center. The higher the bars on any given level, the more pixels of that tone are present. For example, if the far-left black point has a high spike, your picture has areas that show a pure black tone.

As shown in Figure 5-6, the graph appears like a bell curve. We drew a gradient across the bottom to show you how the tone, when blended with the same tone level for all points, should appear.

The most important keyboard shortcut when you're editing images for tone and color corrections is Ctrl+L (⌘+L on a Mac) to open the Levels dialog box. As you work through this chapter, and most of the chapters ahead, we continually return to the Levels dialog box.

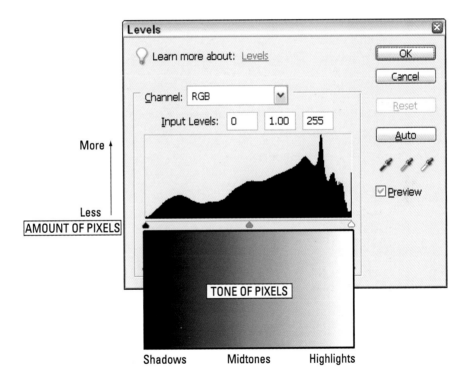

Figure 5-6: The Levels histogram.

To help you visualize what an image might look like when you view a histogram, check out the toned view shown in Figure 5-7. As you look at the histogram, you can see this altered view that shows the gradual move from black on the left to white on the right.

The default Levels dialog box in Photoshop Elements shows the graph as pure black simply to make the whole thing easier to see.

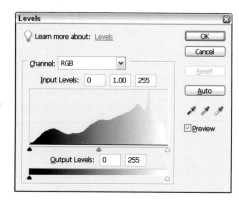

Figure 5-7: A tone histogram artificially created to show the effect of the frequencies of the tone points.

You may have noticed that you also have available in Elements a Histogram palette that you can access by selecting Window➪Histogram. The histogram graph is identical to the Levels histogram. We prefer to use Levels to view a histogram while tone editing because you can easily access the Levels dialog box with a keyboard shortcut — something you can't do with the Histogram palette. In addition, you can always make an edit in the Levels dialog box, whereas the Histogram palette offers no editing options.

To understand how a histogram represents a photograph, check out these examples. Some of these examples are intentional exaggerations for the purpose of clarity. Most of your own images will probably be easier to deal with than these examples. We simply want to show you that the histogram is easy to understand, even if you're not a math wiz. Most of your images will have one of five basic histogram shapes:

- **A skew to the left:** Underexposed images don't have a true white point.

- **A skew to the right:** These histograms have no rich blacks and are generally the result of an overexposed image.

- **No data on both ends:** These histograms are quite often the result of a low-contrast image with no true blacks or whites.

- **A bell curve:** When the tone points reach the ends of the graph, you're likely to find a properly exposed image.

- **An inversed bell curve:** These kinds of histograms come from high-contrast images resulting from direct sunlight. These kinds of images are the most difficult to make tone corrections to.

After you understand these shapes and know what they mean in terms of your image data, you begin to have an idea about what corrections you need to make.

The histogram shown in Figure 5-8 appears when you open the Levels dialog box (Ctrl+L for PCs, ⌘+L for Macs) on the photo shown in Figure 5-1.

The image has slightly more light values (levels) than gray or dark values, so the histogram hill is piled up a bit on the right. The image has a full tonal range from white to black, so the histogram runs the entire length of the box.

The histogram for the underexposed photo in Figure 5-5 (shown in Figure 5-9) never reaches the right side because the photo has no white values. The huge hill on the left represents all the dark values in the image. The quantity of dark values far exceeds the light values, as shown by the low height of the rest of the histogram.

As you might expect, the histogram for the overexposed photo in Figure 5-4 is just the opposite of the underexposed photo. In Figure 5-10, all the image data are piled toward the right side, where light values reside. The image lacks any full black tones, so the histogram displays an absence of image data long before it gets to the left side. Almost the entire histogram is to the right of middle gray.

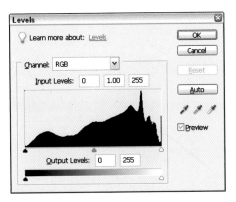

Figure 5-8: The Levels histogram for the image in Figure 5-1.

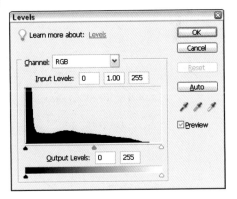

Figure 5-9: The Levels histogram for an underexposed photo.

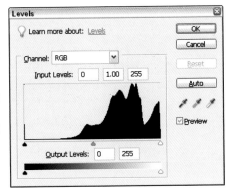

Figure 5-10: The Levels histogram for an overexposed photo.

The flat image shown in Figure 5-3 lacks both black and white. As you might suspect, the tone data for this flat image appear in the center of the histogram, as shown in Figure 5-11. The result is an image with very low contrast. The histogram reflects the lack of black or white tones because the histogram doesn't reach the black and white endpoints in the dialog box.

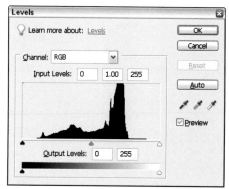

Figure 5-11: The Levels histogram for an image with little contrast.

As a final view of histograms from different kinds of images, Figure 5-12 shows the histogram for the high-contrast image shown in Figure 5-2. This image is off the scale with excessive contrast. Shooting into the sun was far beyond the brightness range of the camera. Much of the sky is blown out to pure white values, and the tree trunks are full black with no detail. The histogram is piled high on both the left and right side, confirming the loss of shadow and highlight detail. The center of the histogram dips low, showing the lack of normal middle tones.

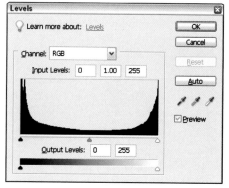

Figure 5-12: The Levels histogram for a high-contrast image.

All image editing should begin with the Levels dialog box. Optimizing your image file with Levels allows the rest of the correction tools to work properly and saves you time and frustration in the long run. There are times when Levels isn't the best choice to use first, but we do our best later in the book in Part III to show you the special problem files where this is the case. Otherwise, always examine and edit your file first with Levels.

Getting to Black and White

Setting a black-and-white point for your image is the single most frequently used feature of the Levels dialog box. Most images require a small amount of full black and white pixels to achieve a full tonal range and a pleasing sense of brilliance in the final edited file. Some files need more black and white adjustments.

If you work with JPEG files taken with your digital camera, the internal camera processing has probably already made a guess at the proper black-and-white point, and the histogram somewhat resembles the normal version shown in Figure 5-13. Exposure errors or unusual lighting situations yield histograms similar to the problem files we show you in the section "Using the Levels Dialog Box," earlier in this chapter.

You still always want to check the histogram and make any needed adjustments.

Adjusting Gamma levels

The Levels dialog box has three adjustment sliders (black point, white point, and Gamma) that you use to adjust the brightness values. You can see these sliders in Figure 5-13. Think of the Gamma adjustment in Levels (the center slider) as the Brightness control. It's just as important as the black-and-white point settings when you're editing your files. Moving the Gamma adjustment controls how the light and dark tonal values are biased. Moving the Gamma adjustment slider to the left lightens the image, and moves to the right darken the image.

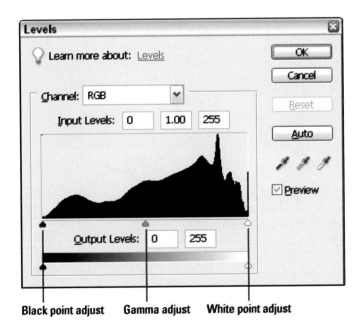

Black point adjust   Gamma adjust   White point adjust

Figure 5-13: You use the three sliders to adjust brightness values.

The Gamma adjustment works by changing the proportions of the light and dark tones. Here's an example, using an image with a grayscale, to show what the Gamma slider really does. To see the effects of the Gamma slider, check out Figure 5-14, which is an unedited image before we make any Gamma adjustments.

Figure 5-14: An unedited image.

Moving the Gamma slider re-proportions the image tones, resulting in a lighter or darker image. Think of it as moving the middle gray value right or left on the histogram — Elements then compresses or stretches the rest of the tones to fit from white to black.

Moving the slider to the right shifts middle gray toward black. The dark tones are stretched to fit, and the image darkens overall as a result, as you can see in the left image in Figure 5-15. The shadow tones gain contrast, and the light tones lose contrast. The light tones are smashed together, and the shadow tones are spread out.

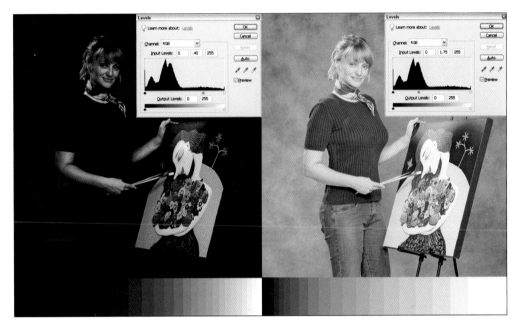

Figure 5-15: Moving the Gamma slider right darkens an image (left). Moving the slider left lightens an image (right).

In Figure 5-15, you can see the results of moving the Gamma slider left to 1.75 on the right side of the image. Moving the slider to the left shifts middle gray toward black. The light tones are stretched to fit, causing the image to lighten up overall. The result has more contrast in the light portions of the file and less in the dark tones.

This re-proportioning of the image tones is why you sometimes need to read-just the white and black points after a big Gamma slider adjustment.

Correcting a low-contrast file

Take a look at the low-contrast file shown in Figure 5-3. The overall brightness is about right, but the image needs to be edited to add a touch of real white and black tones.

To make corrections to this file, download `tooFlat.jpg` from the Chapter 5 folder of the Wiley companion Web site.

With the Levels dialog box open (Ctrl+L for PCs, ⌘+L for Macs), move the black and white sliders until they just touch the beginning of the histogram hill on each side. This slider positioning controls where full black and white tones should begin. Elements then remaps the available tones to stretch across all 256 Levels. You end up with a much snappier-looking image, as shown in Figure 5-16.

Figure 5-16: A too-flat image after black and white tone correction.

If you reopen the Levels dialog box again after the edit, you can see that the remapped tones now create a normal-looking histogram, with a full 256 image tone levels (see Figure 5-17). The large hill to the right represents all the bright tones in the sky area.

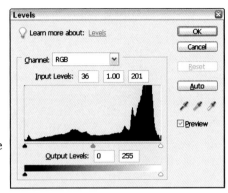

That was an easy fix. After setting the black and white points, the overall image brightness seemed fairly normal. Sometimes, that's all you need to do.

Figure 5-17: Returning to the Levels dialog box shows the tone curve remapped.

Correcting an underexposed file

To make corrections to the image file shown in Figure 5-5, download `flowers.jpg` from the Chapter 5 folder of the Wiley companion Web site.

In Figure 5-5, the tones are just too dark overall, and the image has no bright highlights to give it some sparkle. In the Levels dialog box, start by making a big Gamma slider move to the left to lighten up the overall image tones. Next, move the white-point slider to the left until you just touch the histogram, as shown in Figure 5-18. Leave the black slider in place because the histogram shows that you already have full black tones in the file.

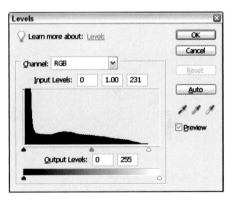

Figure 5-18: For this underexposed image, move the white-point slider to the beginning of the histogram

The result after clicking OK in the Levels dialog box shows a nicely recovered underexposed photo, as shown in Figure 5-19.

Figure 5-19: After making a single Levels adjustment, the image brightness is corrected.

Correcting an overexposed file

An overexposed photo, such as the one in Figure 5-4, has the opposite problem of an underexposed image. Most of the tones are brighter than middle gray, and the image looks washed out. To fix the problem, start with a large Gamma slider move to the right to darken the light tone values. Move the black slider to the start of the histogram hill on the left to insure that it maintains a full tonal range in the resulting file. Leave the white point slider at the default position because the histogram indicates plenty of full white tones.

To make corrections to this file yourself, download duck.jpg from the Chapter 5 folder on the Wiley companion Web site.

You should have an idea for the view of the histogram in the Levels dialog box after moving the black-point slider to the beginning of the histogram hill. The result in the image appears as shown in Figure 5-20. Compare this image with the original in Figure 5-4.

Figure 5-20: After moving the black slider, the image brightness is corrected.

Correcting a high contrast file

You can't really repair a file with excessive contrast by using the Levels command, but Elements has provided some advanced tools that can improve a contrasty file a great deal. To find out more about correcting images with high contrast problems, see Chapter 6.

Finding the first real black and white pixels

For the editing examples in this chapter, we play a little fast and loose with our black-and-white point settings. It's perfectly all right to set black-and-white point by bumping the sliders into each side of the visible histogram, but to obtain the very best final quality from a file, you may need to know exactly where the first white and black pixels are located and the exact slider position you need to find them.

With most image files, only a tiny percentage of the image pixels should be full white or black. Overdoing the edit can cause *posterization* (the replacement of subtle gradations of color with patchy, abruptly-changing colors) and lack highlight and shadow detail. This over-editing can make tonal edits with other Elements tools more difficult or prevent the best final result.

You can see posterization in images when you spread out the pixels, leaving gaps in the tone curve that are visually apparent in the histogram. The pixels are then clumped together at the nearest tone points and produce a muddy gray color in areas of your photo.

When in doubt, be conservative with the black-and-white point settings. You can always go back and clip off a few more tones later, but you can never recover tones lost after a bad edit.

As an example, take a look at a file that requires a precise setting of black and white points. The file in Figure 5-21 has normal contrast but lacks full white and black tones. As a result, the image just doesn't pop off the page like it should. We want to correct the file, but we need to do it very carefully.

To make corrections on the same file, download `girl.jpg` from the Chapter 5 folder of the Wiley companion Web site.

Figure 5-21: This image needs a subtle fix to its black and white tones.

The Levels black-and-white preview option

The Levels dialog box has a nifty option for viewing the pixels you select when you use the black and white sliders. This Levels viewing option comes in very handy on an image such as Figure 5-21. To use this option, follow these steps:

1. **Open the file you want to edit and open the Levels dialog box (Ctrl+L for PCs, ⌘+L for Macs).**

2. **Set the black point.**

   Place the cursor on the black-point slider, hold down the mouse button, and press Alt/Option on your keyboard. If your file has no black pixels, the image window turns completely white. That's normal. The window is telling you that the black slider needs to move to the right to create some black pixels.

   Slowly move the black slider while holding down the Alt/Option key until the first real black pixel tones show up in the image window. As our example shows, some colored pixels appear in the window along with a few black pixels. (See Figure 5-22.)

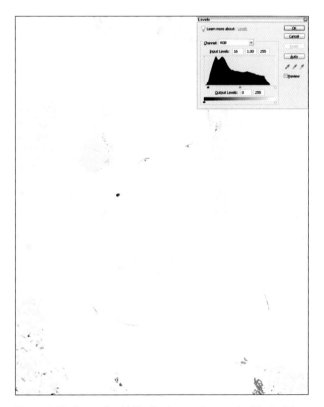

Figure 5-22: Press the Alt/Option key and move the black slider until you see black appear in the image.

As a general rule, move the black slider until you can see just a few black pixels. Release the Alt/Option key, and your image returns, showing the result of the black slider move.

3. **Set the white point.**

Hold down the Alt/Option key again and use the cursor to move the white-point slider to the left. The image window becomes full black if the file has no white pixels. Move the white point slider left until the first visible pixels begin to light up on the dark background. (See Figure 5-23.)

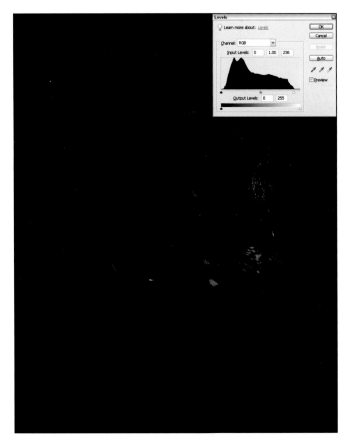

Figure 5-23: Press the Alt/Option key and move the white slider until you see white appear in the image.

Use a little caution when setting a white point. A lot of red pixels appear before the first real white pixel becomes visible. Those red pixels show up first because the red-channel pixels are being clipped first.

The underlying image is of the little girl's blond hair, and the color is highly saturated. The red channel's pixel values are the brightest in that area and reach a tone value of 255 before any other pixels in the file.

Red and green make yellow, and the hue of blond hair needs a little more red than green to look normal.

As a general rule, you probably want to set the white point based on the first pixels that become visible onscreen, regardless of the color, to avoid loss of highlight detail in bright-colored areas of the file. You especially want to follow this rule if the file also needs moderate to heavy color correction.

In Figure 5-24, the file is shown after a custom setting of black and white points, using the Levels preview method.

Figure 5-24: After the Levels adjustments are made, the image brightness is corrected.

In Figure 5-25, the black and white points have been over-corrected. Notice the harsh posterization of the bright highlights and loss of highlight detail. The darkest shadows are blocked up and lacking detail. Be careful — after you clip off the highlight and shadow tones with Levels, they're gone forever.

Figure 5-25: Over-correction can lead to bright highlights and posterization.

Breaking the Rules of Editing

In this chapter, we tell you all the rules for tone editing your images with the Levels dialog box. But hey, sometimes you have to break the rules! Knowing when to break the rules depends on the image content and the final result you're after.

We refer to moving the sliders to the beginning of the histogram hill on either side of the histogram as *standard edits*. These standard edits work when you're editing images that need brightness adjustments to the backgrounds and foregrounds equally, and the results render a pure white and a rich black.

Sometimes, however, an overall adjustment doesn't bring the most important part of your photos into a suitable brightness and contrast view. You might want to weight the adjustment to emphasize the foreground subject matter or the background contrast and brightness, or you may need to adjust both separately. For these kinds of edits, you need to break the rules of standard editing for the Levels tool.

Knowing when to break the rules

To determine whether you should break the rules or follow more conventional editing guidelines, follow these steps:

1. **Examine your image.**

   The first step in any editing process is to study your photo after opening it in Full Edit mode (Standard Edit mode on the Mac in Elements 4). Know what problems exist and what you need to correct. Determine whether the photo has a good pure white and a rich black. In some images, a very small portion of your photo or just a few pixels may be pure white or rich black. Finding the white and black points in a photo by moving the Levels slider remaps the histogram and recalculates the tone curve so the tonal transitions ultimately appear much better.

2. **Test a standard edit.**

   Open the Levels dialog box and move the sliders to the beginning of the histogram hill on both sides of the histogram. Click the title bar on the dialog box and drag the dialog box out of the way so you can see the preview for the adjustment. (Make sure that the Preview check box in the dialog box is selected.)

   At this point, ask yourself whether the highlights contain a pure white and the shadows have a rich black. If they do, you can click OK, and you're finished with editing for tonal brightness. If the answer is no, you need to break the rules. While in the Levels dialog box, press the Alt/Option key, and the Cancel button changes to Reset. Click the Reset button, and you can start your editing by using the methods we describe in the following sections.

3. **Determine the most important part of the photo.**

   If you need to break the rules, look over the photo and determine what content is the most important part. Is it the foreground or the background, highlights or shadows? Camera chips quite often don't capture a full range of tones from white to black under many different lighting conditions. You can improve many photos by making edits to the most important areas of the image. After you determine what's important, knowing which direction to proceed with your edits becomes much easier.

Breaking the rules for white-point adjustments

A good example of a photo where breaking the rules works well is when you have different lighting for foreground and background areas. In most cases, a single adjustment in the Levels dialog box can't completely correct the brightness in the photo.

If you don't have such an image, you can use the file `cat.jpg` in the Chapter 5 folder on the companion Web site.

Follow these steps on photos in which the background appears with bright backlighting and the foreground appears darker in a shaded area:

1. **Open a file with uneven lighting, such as a photo that has a dark foreground and bright background.**

   Figure 5-26 is a snapshot of a family cat taken on a shaded porch. The original file is too dark because the camera meter was fooled by the bright spots in the sunny background.

Figure 5-26: A photo shot under shade with bright backlighting.

2. **Open the Levels dialog box by pressing Ctrl+L (⌘+L for Macs), shown in Figure 5-27.**

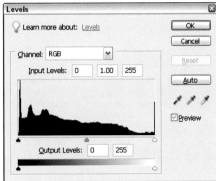

   After opening Levels, you can see that many pixels are already a full white tone because the histogram slams up against the right side of the window. In this image, all the full-white (or near-white) pixels are in the bright background. With a photo such as this, the background doesn't matter; we want to see the kitty!

3. **Keeping the black point at the default position, move the Gamma slider to the left (to about 1.50) to brighten the image.**

Figure 5-27: The histogram shows more tone levels in the black with a strong decline in the light area of the photo.

   Click OK and review the results. A single Gamma adjustment leaves you with a very dreary, low-contrast image of the kitty, as you can see in Figure 5-28.

   Because you want the viewer's attention on the kitty, edit for the kitty and ignore the background.

4. **Select Edit⇨Undo or press Ctrl+Z (⌘+Z for Macs) to undo the last edit.**

Figure 5-28: Adjusting the midtones by moving the Gamma slider lightens the foreground but leaves you with a flat, dreary image.

5. Find the white point in the foreground.

Open Levels again (Ctrl+L for PCs, ⌘+L for Macs). After you open Levels, hold down the Alt/Option key, ignore the background, and move the white-point slider until you see the first pixels of the kitty. The background is blooming in the preview, but you're editing for the cat only, so ignore the background. The cat isn't pure white, so after you see the first kitty pixels, back off the adjustment — move the slider back toward the right a little. In this photo, we rest the white-point slider at 205, as shown in Figure 5-29.

6. Move the black slider to the right slightly to insure a full black in the cat part of the image.

Yes, it's well into the black side of the histogram, but the cat part of the image looks best with that setting. Our final black point adjustment rests at 10.

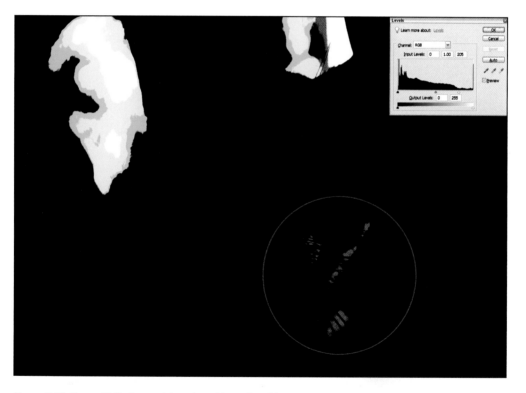

Figure 5-29: Press Alt/Option and drag the white-point slider until you see some white pixels and then move back slightly to the right.

7. **Make a Gamma slider adjustment left to lighten the image and click OK.**

   The final edits in the Levels dialog box appear, as shown in Figure 5-30.

8. **Click OK in the Levels dialog box and look over the final edited image, shown in Figure 5-31.**

   The resulting file has better tonal separation on the cat, and the resulting highlight clipping and loss of detail on the background doesn't really detract from the image.

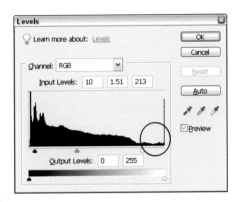

Figure 5-30: Adjusting the midtones by moving the Gamma slider lightens the foreground.

Figure 5-31: Hello, kitty! The final edits show a proper brightness correction on the foreground subject.

Breaking the rules for black-point adjustments

Do you find that some of your snapshots don't snap — they just don't look like they have the right contrast? Do blacks in the photo appear flat without a rich black look? This flat appearance is common for many photos taken with indoor flash and in low lighting conditions. For this kind of photo, a simple Levels adjustment doesn't put the punch in the image, so you may need to break the rules to adjust the brightness. The solution is to intentionally over-edit the black point.

If you like, use the file `couple.jpg` in the Chapter 5 folder on the companion Web site.

To add a crisper look by over-editing the black point in photos that need a rich black, follow these steps:

1. **Open the photo in Full Edit mode (Standard Edit mode on the Mac, using Elements 4).**

   Figure 5-32 is a typical kind of snapshot for which you need to break the rules. This snapshot was lit by the in-camera flashgun, and the background received far less overall illumination. The background isn't really important in a photo such as this, so you want to devote your attention to the foreground subjects. Overall, the photo is a little underexposed.

Figure 5-32: An underexposed photo lacking contrast and a rich black.

2. **Open the Levels dialog box (Ctrl+L on PCs, ⌘+L on Macs) and move the white-point slider to the beginning of the histogram hill, as shown in Figure 5-33.**

3. **Click OK in the Levels dialog box and examine the edited image.**

As you can see in Figure 5-34, a standard edit following the standard rules gives this photo a visually dull result. The overall adjustment sets the black point to the background, whereas the main foreground subject (the

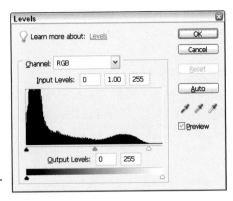

Figure 5-33: A standard rule of thumb is to move the white (and black) points to the beginning of the histogram hill.

most important part of this photo) lacks any true black tones.

With this kind of file, you need to use the foreground main subject as your reference for the black-and-white point, rather than the entire image.

Figure 5-34: A standard edit results in a flat and lifeless photo.

4. **Press Ctrl+Z (⌘+Z for Macs) to undo the edit and return to the original unedited image.**

5. **Find the black point on the foreground subjects.**

   You need to know where black begins in the most important area of the photo and ignore the least important part, which is the background area.

   Open the Levels dialog box (Ctrl+L for PCs, ⌘+L for Macs). Press the Alt/Option key and drag the black-point slider to the right. In this example, we move the black slider to level 28.

6. **Adjust the white point.**

   Still in the Levels dialog box, use the white-point slider to find the first white pixels in the foreground subject. The foreground subject has the brightest image tones, so you do the edit by using the standard procedure. Press the Alt/Option key and move the white-point slider until a few bright pixels become visible. The results of both slider adjustments are shown in Figure 5-35.

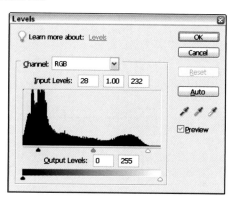

Figure 5-35: Adjusted black and white points.

   As you can see, much of the background has reached full black as you begin to see the first black pixels in the foreground subject. As shown in Figure 5-35, the black-point slider has moved well into the left side of the histogram. The portion to the left of the slider represents pixels in the unneeded background tones. When you move the Levels dialog box out of the way of the image behind it, you can see the effect on the photo, as shown in Figure 5-36. Note that you need to select the Preview check box in the Levels dialog box to view results in the image window while the Levels dialog is open.

7. **Adjust the Gamma.**

   The photo is obviously much too dark, but you have the correct black-and-white point adjustments. Therefore, you only need to adjust the overall brightness. For this adjustment, use the Gamma slider. Move the middle slider to the left. (We moved it to about 1.56 for the image in Figure 5-37.)

8. **Click OK in the Levels dialog box.**

When you compare the original image to the final edited image, shown in Figure 5-37, the edited image is a much better quality than the original. Breaking the rules and pushing the black point limit well into the histogram didn't harm the image. In fact, the edit produced what we were after when we captured the original image. Even though the black limit was set well into the histogram, the edited image preserved the important shadow detail of the subject matter.

Figure 5-36: Photo as it appears after the black-and-white point adjustments.

It's okay to break the rules, as long as you get the results you need.

Figure 5-37: Brightness adjustments clearly show a better-looking image.

6

Correcting Contrast

. . . .

In This Chapter

▷ Finding out how contrast affects your images

▷ Making contrast adjustments automatically

▷ Correcting image contrast with the Brightness/Contrast command

▷ Using the Adjust Color Curves tool

▷ Working with the Shadows/Highlights tool

▷ Undoing edits

. . . .

*I*n Chapter 5, we talk about making Levels adjustments for tonal and brightness corrections. The most important aspects of these corrections are setting a white point, a black point, and a Gamma adjustment for the midtones. These edits only get you halfway, however, in terms of creating an image with overall pleasing brightness. You next need to consider editing image contrast.

Conceivably, you could have an image with a pure white point, a rich black, and a good overall brightness appearance that's still much too contrasty or flat.

This chapter picks up where Chapter 5 leaves off: After you make adjustments for brightness in the Levels dialog box, you're ready to take a look at some solutions for getting a proper contrast balance.

Correcting Image Contrast

What do we mean by *image contrast?* After you set the white and black points to obtain a full tonal range in the image, the resulting image contrast can actually vary all over the place. It all depends on the original tones and lighting of the subject matter and your personal tastes for the way you want the image to appear.

For a better understanding of what we mean by changing image contrast, check out the photo shown in Figure 6-1. This still-life image has a full range of tones from white to black and a full set of midtones — something we achieve just by using the Levels dialog box. We include a 15-step grayscale in the figure to help show what we mean by changing midtone contrast. The contrast is just right in the photo shown in Figure 6-1.

Figure 6-1: The proper image brightness and contrast make this photo look tasty!

Figure 6-2 shows the same photo after we edited it to reduce the image contrast. Notice the loss of contrast in the center area of the grayscale. You can see less visible difference in tone from one step to the next.

We edited the file in Figure 6-3 to increase the image contrast. We greatly increased the contrast of the midtones. You can see a much greater difference in tone from one midtone step to the next.

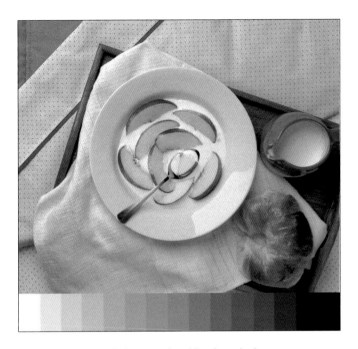

Figure 6-2: You can darken your breakfast by reducing contrast.

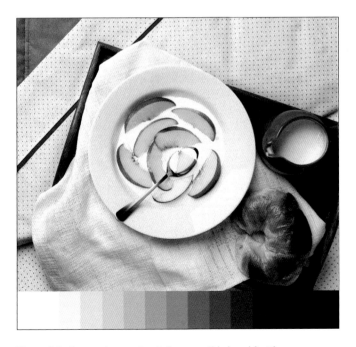

Figure 6-3: Increasing contrast sharpens this breakfast image.

In both of the modified files, all the tones are still there. The contrast adjustments just rearranged the tone distribution. Both files still have pure white and black tones with no tonal losses. A look at the histograms in the Levels dialog box confirms the fact that each of the images has a black point, a white point, and tone separation, as you can see in Figure 6-4. On the left, you see the histogram for the original file (Figure 6-1), in the middle is the file with a lower image contrast (Figure 6-2), and on the right you see the histogram for the high-contrast photo (Figure 6-3). If you start with a low- or high-contrast image and need to change image contrast, you can't use Levels exclusively to make an image contrast correction.

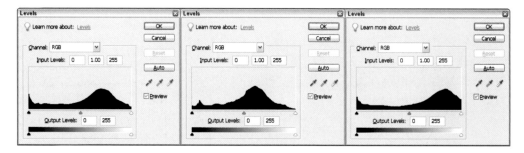

Figure 6-4: See the difference in the histogram for a normal image (left), a low-contrast image (middle), and a high-contrast image (right).

You can use one of two methods to adjust image contrast. Elements has a quick-and-dirty method for adjusting contrast called the Brightness/Contrast menu command. The other method involves making edits with the Levels dialog box and the Adjust Color Curves command.

You need to make your black- and white-point adjustments first when you're editing for contrast. Use one of the methods we cover in the following section to adjust the white point and the black point. After a quality Levels edit, changing the image contrast really means modifying the tonal contrast of the midtones.

Fixing Contrast Problems with the Auto Contrast Command

The Auto Contrast command (Enhance➪Auto Contrast) sets the black- and white-point limit for you. Unfortunately, Elements doesn't offer any controls that enable you to change the Auto Contrast attributes. The command simply examines your file data and sets the black and white points based on the assumption that one-tenth of one percent of your image pixels (one in a thousand) should be pure white and the same proportion should be pure black.

It should really be called Auto Black and White Points because that's what actually happens when you use the command. It doesn't have a clue about the original overall image contrast of your file. It can, however, be a very useful edit for some files.

The Auto Contrast command does nothing on a file that already has some full white and black tones if the black and white pixels comprise more than one in a thousand of the total image pixels. Elements doesn't allow you to custom set the black-and-white clipping percentages like its big brother, Photoshop CS2, does. The default setting is a kind of best average, and you can't change it. The following example shows how it works.

To follow along in these steps, use the `missouri.jpg` file you can download from the Chapter 6 folder on the Wiley companion Web site.

To edit an image with the Auto Contrast command, follow these steps:

1. **Open an image that appears flat and doesn't have true black or white pixels.**

   For this example, we use the photo shown in Figure 6-5. You can download this image from the Chapter 6 folder on the companion Web site if you don't have a photo with similar brightness and contrast problems. Because this photo has no white or black pixels, using Auto Contrast will set the black and white points by using the default settings.

Figure 6-5: This battleship is looking a little flat.

2. **Press Ctrl+L (⌘+L for Macs) or select Layers⇨New Adjustment Layer⇨Levels to open the Levels dialog box and take a look at the histogram, shown in Figure 6-6.**

   After checking the histogram, click Cancel to close the dialog box.

3. **Select Enhance⇨Auto Contrast to run the Auto Contrast command.**

4. **Reopen the Levels dialog box and check the histogram again.**

   After using the Auto Contrast command, the histogram appears as shown in Figure 6-7. You can see the change in the remapping of the tone curve in this histogram, compared to Figure 6-6, as a result of the Auto Contrast adjustment. After the Auto Contrast edit, you can see confirmation that the black and white points have indeed been reset.

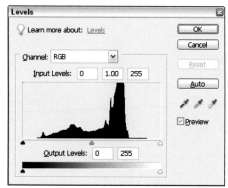

Figure 6-6: The Levels dialog box for the battleship image shows you where the data fall on the histogram.

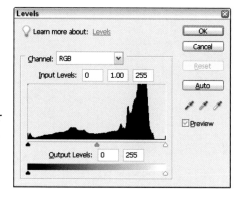

Figure 6-7: The battleship's histogram after using Auto Contrast.

The Auto Contrast command got pretty close to the best setting in Figure 6-7. Black and white points *were* reset. But should you routinely use Auto Contrast for image editing? It depends. A custom setting of black and white points in Levels allows you to decide exactly where you want the black and white points to be for best possible results. Also, you can change image brightness by adjusting the Gamma slider in the Levels dialog box. Therefore, in many cases, the Auto Contrast feature can't give you the results you can get by using custom adjustments.

On the other hand, if you have 200 photos of a kid's birthday party to edit, you may find Auto Contrast a real time-saver. Doing 200 custom adjustments may just be impractical. As a matter of practice, you may want to manually correct images for brightness and contrast when time permits.

In the example in this section, a Levels adjustment took care of the brightness and the contrast, and it did a pretty good job. You won't always be that lucky, though. After adjusting the brightness in Levels, you may need to use other methods to either boost or lower contrast. Everything depends on your image data and the results you want. In this chapter, we stick to making adjustments on a single layer. You have more options for contrast control when you use additional layers, as we explain in Chapter 7.

Working with the Brightness/Contrast Command

Under the Enhance⇨Adjust Lighting menu, you can find a tool called Brightness/Contrast. You might be wondering why we didn't use that tool for our contrast example in the preceding section. We have a very good reason: The Brightness/Contrast command is a completely bogus tool that should have been deleted from both Photoshop Elements and Adobe Photoshop long ago.

Never use this tool! We, the authors, have been serious Elements/Photoshop users for many years, and we never, ever use this tool. Just forget it exists altogether, please! We have a much better way to perform high-quality edits for brightness and contrast. In order to use the tools for these edits properly, we have to introduce the use of adjustment layers, which we explain in Chapter 7.

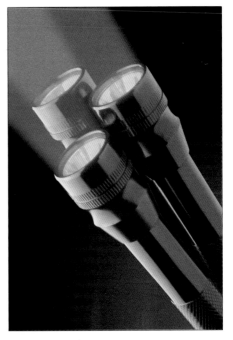

You may have heard from others that you should never use the Brightness/Contrast command, but perhaps you don't know why — or maybe you haven't seen any comparative images showing the differences between using the command and using other correction methods. In this chapter, we show you exactly why you want to avoid the Elements Brightness/Contrast command if you want quality results when you change overall image contrast.

In Figure 6-8, you see an image you might want to edit for image contrast. Download the `lights.jpg` file from the Wiley companion Web site in the Chapter 6 folder.

Figure 6-8: The image of these flashlights needs an overall contrast adjustment.

An image of this nature can work well with different amounts of contrast, depending on personal taste. This section compares reducing contrast by using the Elements Brightness/Contrast tool to doing the same adjustment with a contrast reduction layer. You can find the steps for creating and using contrast reduction layers in Chapter 7, but don't worry too much about that now. In this section, we're just illustrating why the Brightness/Contrast tool doesn't measure up to other methods of contrast correction.

The results of the two methods appear in Figure 6-9. On the left side of the figure, you can see just about the best contrast adjustment we could get by using the Brightness/Contrast dialog box. The right side of the figure shows a contrast adjustment we made by using a contrast reduction curve and an adjustment layer (which we explain how to do in Chapter 7).

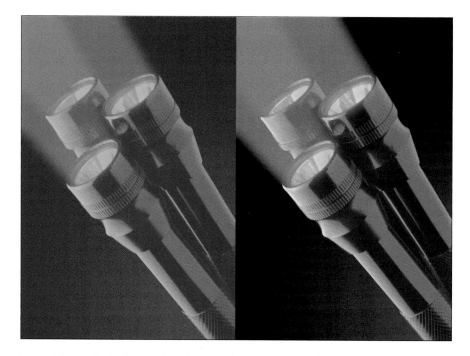

Figure 6-9: The flashlights got the Brightness/Contrast treatment (left) and a contrast adjustment layer (right).

Notice how flat and awful the image on the left in Figure 6-9 looks. The tool really only resets the black and white points toward gray. When you open the Levels dialog box and look at the histogram for the image on the left side of Figure 6-9, you can easily see what happened to the data. (See Figure 6-10.) The file was wrecked in a single edit! You end up with a grayed-out, veiled file.

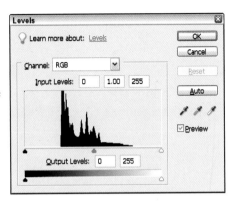

Figure 6-10: A histogram showing the results of the Brightness/Contrast tool on the flashlights image.

Now, compare Figure 6-10 to Figure 6-11, which is the histogram for the image corrected with a contrast reduction curve. Image contrast is nicely reduced, but you still maintain a full tonal range. The histogram shows you've maintained some true full black and white tones.

Next, compare results from the Brightness/Contrast tool when you use it to increase contrast, compared to the results from using a contrast increase adjustment layer. Figure 6-12 shows the results of trying to produce a moderate contrast gain by using the Brightness/Contrast tool on the left and a contrast increase curve on the right.

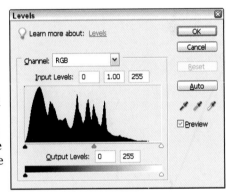

Figure 6-11: You get a nice tone curve in the flashlights image histogram by using a contrast reduction curve.

Observe the bright highlights on the left side of the flashlights in Figure 6-12. The Brightness/Contrast adjustment tool completely clipped the white highlight values, leaving behind blank posterized white areas. (*Posterized* refers to areas that are supposed to be subtle gradations of color but have instead morphed into patchy areas of abrupt color transition.) The bright illuminated tops of the flashlights have areas clipped to paper white. Much of the shadow detail has turned to posterized black values.

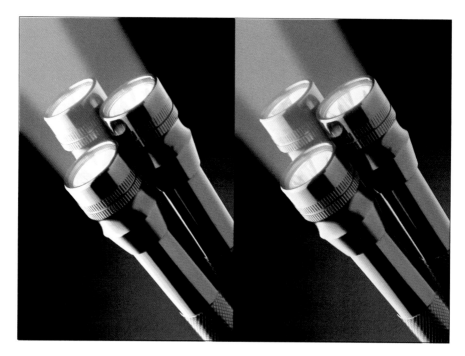

Figure 6-12: The flashlights get a contrast boost with the Brightness/Contrast tool (left) and a contrast increase curve (right).

The contrast increase layer resulted in a smooth transition of highlight tonal values without abrupt posterization to white. Notice also the way the layer retained shadow detail in the dark areas of the flashlights. The resulting histograms from the two files shows why you get such a difference in final quality. In Figure 6-13, the histogram on the left is from the original unedited file (Figure 6-8). The middle histogram is from the Brightness/Contrast adjusted file (Figure 6-12, on the left). Using Brightness/Contrast simply sets the black and white points closer to the center of the histogram, exactly as if you'd pushed the black and white sliders too far into the histogram. You end up with severely clipped black and white points. On the right, you can see the histogram from the file edited by using a contrast increase curve (Figure 6-12, on the right). A contrast increase curve changes the contrast of only the midtones and leaves the black and white point settings unaltered. The histogram shows no tone clipping.

You might look at Figure 6-13 and wonder why we say the middle histogram has tone clipping. Take a careful look at the center histogram in Figure 6-13 — you can find spikes at either end of the histogram. These spikes represent the data shoved up against a wall: It can't go any farther. If the data could go farther, it would travel outward and eventually dwindle out. Because they can't reach beyond the edge of the histogram, the data are smashed together, and the tones that could have extended beyond the histogram are cut off — or *clipped*.

Compare the center histogram with the one on the far right. You don't find spikes at the histogram edges. The data just stop before they reach the edge, so the histogram on the right doesn't show clipped tones.

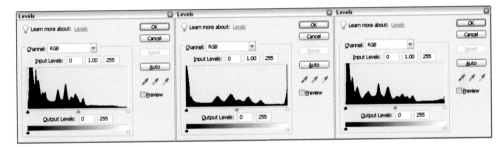

Figure 6-13: Histograms from the unedited flashlights image (left), the Brightness/Contrast adjusted file (middle), and the file after using a contrast increase layer (right).

Modifying Contrast with Adjust Color Curves

Without getting into how to make complex edits for contrast by using adjustment layers (we go into adjustment layers in Chapter 7), you have a couple of other ways you can modify image contrast in Elements without using the dreaded Brightness/Contrast command.

Elements 5 has introduced a new feature called Adjust Color Curves. This feature is a dumbed-down version of the Curves command found in Adobe Photoshop. Photographers and professional image editors routinely use Curves in Photoshop to adjust images for brightness, contrast, and color correction. (See Chapter 16 for more on Photoshop Curves.) In an effort to provide Elements users with a tool to perform similar edits, Adobe introduced the Adjust Color Curves tool in Elements 5.

Photoshop Elements 4 for the Mac doesn't have the Adjust Color Curves feature. Adjust Color Curves is a new feature in Elements 5 initially introduced on Windows only. Until Elements 5 for the Mac appears, you won't be able to use this feature. If you're a Mac user, don't be disappointed. To be honest, we don't find this tool a great addition for correcting brightness, contrast, or making color corrections. You can access all the other methods we talk about in this book on the Mac by using Photoshop Elements 4.

The Adjust Color Curves command, in its present form, doesn't really work as well as it could because of some built-in limitations, but you can use an option in the tool called Midtone Contrast to perform minor contrast adjustments without wrecking your file.

You may not intuitively think that you should use the Adjust Color Curves tool for correcting brightness and contrast because you access it from the Adjust Color submenu. When you open the Adjust Color Curves dialog box, however, you soon find out that you have options for adjusting brightness, contrast, midtone contrast, and shadows. All of these options are targeted at making brightness and contrast corrections, as well as color adjustments. (For more information on correcting color, see Part III.)

To open the Adjust Color Curves dialog box, select Enhance➪Adjust Color➪ Adjust Color Curves. The Adjust Color Curves dialog box opens, as shown in Figure 6-14.

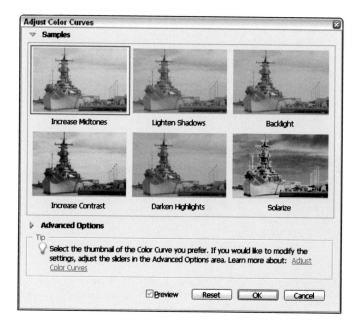

Figure 6-14: The Adjust Color Curves dialog box offers some good tools for correcting brightness problems.

As you can see in Figure 6-14, the Adjust Color Curves dialog box provides you some thumbnail previews for midtone, contrast, and shadow adjustments. Using this pane in the Adjust Color Curves dialog box is similar to using the Color Variations dialog box we talk about in Chapter 10: Click an image preview, and that particular adjustment is applied to your image. You have but one shot at making a correction here. In other words, if you click Increase Contrast once, you can't click again to add more contrast. These options are single fixed edits, and you have no control over the attributes for the adjustment.

Below the image previews, you can see a right-pointing arrow to the left of the words *Advanced Options.* Click the arrow, and the Adjust Color Curves dialog box expands to provide additional choices, as shown in Figure 6-15.

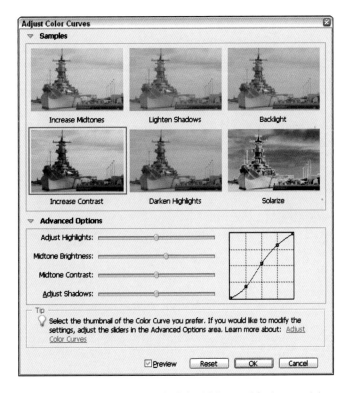

Figure 6-15: Click the arrow to the left of Advanced Options, and the dialog box expands to provide more options.

You can best adjust highlights, shadows, and midtone brightness in the Shadows/Highlights dialog box, which we talk about in the following section. Forget about the Shadows/Highlights dialog box for now and take a look at the Midtone Contrast slider in the Adjust Color Curves dialog box. If you move the slider, the points on the graph that appears on the right side of the

Advanced Options section move just to show you a visual of the tone curve. You might be able to make some slight contrast corrections by moving the slider, but be careful to not move it too far in either direction: You can create some problems by over-editing in the Adjust Color Curves dialog box.

Our impression of Adjust Color Curves is that the points represented by the five squares on the tone curve were placed too close together to be an effective tool. You can't grab any of the tone points or plot additional points on the curve. You're stuck with moving those three points in the center of the graph by using the sliders. (And if you adjust the Increase Contrast slider, only the third middle-tone point moves.) You can't move the white and black points, shown at the lower-left and upper-right corners, at all.

Because these tone points are fixed at the default locations, and Elements doesn't give you any options for plotting additional points or exercising more control than the sliders provide you, you run the risk of flattening the midtones if you move the sliders too far. The tool isn't completely useless — you can make a few useful adjustments by using Adjust Color Curves.

Using the Shadows/Highlights Tool to Adjust Contrast

The Shadows/Highlights tool is a very useful feature for tone editing in Elements. This tool has the best contrast adjustment available in Elements, outside of using adjustment layers. (See Chapter 7 for details on using adjustment layers.) Shadows/Highlights also supports 16-bit file editing. (For more on 16-bit file editing, see Chapter 12.)

The Shadows/Highlights tools that adjust contrast do so without changing the image color saturation. (The Adjust Color Curves tool can't change contrast without affecting color saturation.) You can usually use the contrast adjustment in Shadows/Highlights more easily because any preset image saturation will be maintained. The contrast change isn't as smooth across the tonal range as the results you get when you use contrast adjustment layers (see Chapter 7), but the Shadows/Highlights tool is still very useful.

To use the Shadows/Highlights tool for contrast control, select Enhance⇔ Adjust Lighting⇔Shadows/Highlights. The Shadows/Highlights dialog box opens. First, you want to bring the Lighten Shadows slider all the way to the left. This slider move turns off the default shadow lighting. Next, for contrast control, work with the Midtone Contrast slider as shown in Figure 6-16. Moving the slider left decreases contrast, whereas moving it right increases contrast. Click OK when you're finished making adjustments.

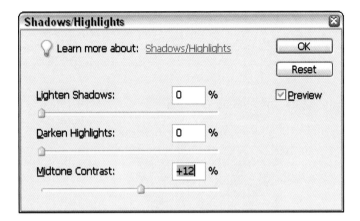

Figure 6-16: With the Shadows/Highlights dialog box, you can really control your contrast adjustments.

The Shadows/Highlights tool is a very useful editing feature in Elements. With this tool, you can make tonal adjustments that you can't with any of the other tone-editing tools. This tool works much differently than either Levels or Adjust Color Curves.

The Shadows/Highlights tool works by zeroing in on just the highlight or shadow tones when editing. It automatically creates masks of just the light or dark portions of your file. The tool is designed to lighten shadow tones or darken bright highlight tones, or it can do both at once.

A *mask* is a kind of digital overlay window on the image. The tool then works on just what it can see through the mask. This feature makes the tool different than Levels or Adjust Color Curves. Any time you make a tone change in Levels or Adjust Color Curves, such as lightening the file, you lose tone information everywhere in the picture as a result. There's no free lunch in digital editing.

With some kinds of files, the Shadows/Highlights tool is the only solution to fix problem tones. To understand when the Shadows/Highlights tool is the best tool for the job, take a look at an image with poor contrast and edit the file by using just Levels and a contrast adjustment curve.

To follow the steps precisely, you can download the file `photographer.tif` from the Chapter 6 folder on the Wiley companion Web site.

In Figure 6-17, we have a photo that needs a contrast boost. Follow these steps to make an adjustment by using Levels and a contrast adjustment layer:

1. **Open an image that needs a contrast adjustment in Elements in Full Edit mode (Standard Edit mode on the Mac).**

   The photo in Figure 6-17 is a snapshot of a photographer working on a foggy day. The flat lighting resulted in a dreary-looking image. The foggy sky is the light source, and it's much lighter than the rest of the image.

Figure 6-17: This photographer needs a boost in contrast.

2. **Open the Levels dialog box by pressing Ctrl+L (⌘+L for Macs).**

   As with all tone edits, you should make a Levels adjustment first. At the very least, take a look at the histogram and see how the data fall on the tone curve. The tone curve for our image shows an absence of white in the image.

3. **Move the white slider to the left, to the bottom of the histogram hill.**

   By moving the slider, you get a full tonal range, but the main subject is too dark. You can see some subtle tonal separation in the foggy sky.

4. **To make a second Levels edit, move the Gamma slider a little to the left to lighten up the main subject.**

   The picture lightens up, but it looks flat and lacks contrast, as you can see in the image on the left of Figure 6-18.

Figure 6-18: The original photographer image (left) gets adjusted with Levels (right).

5. **Adjust contrast.**

   Next, try adding a contrast increase layer to bump up the contrast. (We cover this edit in detail in Chapter 7.) You can see the results of using the contrast increase layer on the right of Figure 6-18.

The result you can achieve by following the steps in the preceding list has more contrast, but notice that the sky is lacking tonal separation and looks almost blank, as shown in the image on the right of Figure 6-18. This is what we meant by no free lunch when tone editing. To get more contrast in the midtones, you have to lose contrast and tonal separation in the highlights. With many files, this loss doesn't matter, but in this file, it destroys the mood of the image.

As an alternative to using just the Levels and a contrast increase curve, this time, edit the same file by using the Shadows/Highlights tool and compare edits. You can't forget Levels entirely because all your tone edits always begin with a Levels adjustment.

To use the Shadows/Highlights tool for making a contrast boost, follow these steps:

1. **If you haven't done so already, make the edits in the Levels dialog box described in the preceding step list.**

2. **Select Enhance⇨Adjust Lighting⇨Shadows/Highlights to open the Shadows/Highlights dialog box.**

    When the dialog box opens, the shadow slider is set to 25% by default. This image needs a little more correction than that, so move the slider to 35%. This setting opens the dark tones nicely, without changing the lighter image tones.

3. **While you have the dialog box open, move the Highlights slider right to a 5% setting. This slider adjustment adds some nice tonal separation to the bright sky. Only the brightest tones in the image are darkened.**

    The image is much improved. The main subject has lightened nicely, and the background sky has maintained its original tonal separation. Click OK in the Shadow/Highlights dialog box when finished.

4. **Open the Levels dialog box by pressing Ctrl+L (⌘+L for Macs).**

    After your Shadows/Highlights edit, the image is still a little dark overall, so you need to make a final pass through the Levels dialog box settings to lighten the image a bit and tweak the black and white points one final time.

5. **Move the Gamma slider slightly to the left to add a little more brightness to the image and then move the black- and white-point sliders a little farther into the histogram to add more brilliance to the image.**

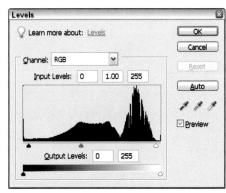

The results of the Levels adjustments are shown in Figure 6-19.

Figure 6-19: Our final Levels adjustments to the photographer image.

Look at Figure 6-20, which shows the edit made with the Levels and contrast adjustment layer on the left and the file edited by using the Shadows/Highlights tool on the right.

You can also use the tool subtly to add small amounts of shadow detail enhancement. It's not just for fixing big errors. In Figure 6-21, you can see the original photo on the left; when editing the right image, we used a 15% Shadow slider move to open up the dark background and show more details, such as the rose leaves. The edit didn't change the foreground flowers at all.

Figure 6-20: The photographer on the left was edited using a contrast increase curve; on the right, he got worked over by the Shadows/Highlights tool.

Figure 6-21: A Shadow-slider edit to the image on the right brings in some background without affecting the foreground flowers.

Take care when you use the Shadows/Highlights tool: Because of the masks that the tool uses, extreme edits can cause *haloing,* an effect you can see in Figure 6-22, and other generally strange-looking results.

Figure 6-22: Haloing doesn't make the photographer in this image look heavenly.

The Auto mask in the Shadows/Highlights tool has a very soft edge and will cause halo effects near darker edges. In Figure 6-23, we set the Shadow slider to 100%. This extreme move causes a large loss of midtone tonal separation. If you use the Shadows/Highlights tool carefully, you can greatly improve problem files, but pushing the sliders to extremes can produce unsatisfactory results.

For files that need major repairs to brightness and contrast problems, you're probably better off using another method. You can find these other methods in Part III, where we cover correcting a variety of snapshot files.

Figure 6-23: The photographer looks a little strange without his midtone tonal separation.

Traveling Back in Time with the Undo Command

If you don't like the edits you make to some of your images, never fear: You can select the Undo command (Ctrl+Z for PCs, ⌘+Z for Macs; or Edit➪Undo) to undo edits you make while using the Levels dialog box and other tools that don't provide you with options for reediting the last applied settings. Elements also permits you to travel back in time (well, sort of) in your edits. For example, if you apply a Levels edit or perform other editing tasks and want to undo a series of steps, you can select the Undo command repeatedly, undoing several edits.

You can control the number of undos you can perform in the General Preferences dialog box. Press Ctrl+K (⌘+K for Macs), or select Edit➪ Preferences (Windows) or Photoshop Elements➪Preferences (Mac), to open the General Preferences dialog box. As shown in Figure 6-24, the default number of History states is 50. You have an undo available for each History state. For just about any editing session, 50 states is sufficient. You can increase the number, but doing so gobbles up some valuable memory.

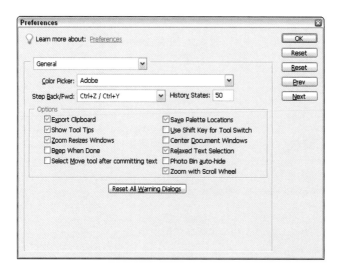

Figure 6-24: You can change the number of undos available in the History States text box.

You can also perform undos via the History palette, which records the number of states you set in the General Preferences. Again, by default, that number is 50. Select Window⇨ Undo History, and the Undo History palette (shown in Figure 6-25) opens.

Click any state listed in the Undo History palette, and you travel back to that edit. All states after the selected state are undone.

Figure 6-25: The Undo History palette records your edits.

When you perform tonal and color corrections, you may need to experiment periodically and travel through a series of steps to view a result. If you don't like the result, you can choose to Undo back to the last step that you want to keep as part of your edits.

Sometimes, you may find completely starting over more practical than undoing edits. If this is the case, select Edit⇨Revert. Your file then reverts back to the last saved image. However, you still have access to the states recorded in the History palette up to the number identified in the General Preferences. If, for some reason, you use Revert and then want to go back to an edit prior to reverting to the last saved version, just click the state you want that appears prior to the Revert state.

Using Adjustment Layers

*I*n this chapter, we extend our discussion on brightness and contrast editing, which we begin in Chapters 5 and 6, to include working with adjustment layers. In this chapter, you can find out how to create adjustment layers and why adjustment layers can often be the best choice for making tonal corrections on problem files. Hopefully, this chapter can help you not only appreciate the flexibility you have working with adjustment layers, but also begin to routinely use these layers.

An *adjustment layer* is a special layer created from several different editing options, and you can view and manipulate this layer in the Layers palette. You can reopen the layer you create to show the last settings you applied in various editing dialog boxes, and you can reedit those settings. This kind of flexibility provides you with opportunities to tweak and refine edits you make for settings, such as brightness and contrast adjustments.

In addition, in the Chapter 7 folder on the companion Web site for this book, we provide two Curves adjustment layers we created in Photoshop that you can apply to your images in Elements. These layers significantly enhance the types of contrast corrections you can do in Elements.

Adding Adjustment Layers to Your Editing Arsenal

You may, at first, find using adjustment layers a little confusing, but there's nothing to be afraid of. An adjustment layer works exactly the same as an image adjustment, but the advantage is that an adjustment layer gives you the ability to revisit the adjustment at any time and change the settings. For example, if you apply a Levels correction and click OK, the only edit you can make is to immediately undo the edit. After that, you're stuck with the correction. If you later want to tweak the tone points, you can't go back to the same Levels settings you last applied. However, if you use a Levels adjustment layer, you can make several edits after you make a Levels correction, and then you can go back to the same Levels adjustment and rework the sliders.

All of the editing options in the Levels dialog box are available to you as adjustment layers. All of the options in the adjustment layers work the same as they do in the dialog box, but as reeditable Layer options instead of just image-editing commands.

Creating Adjustment Layers

You create adjustment layers in Elements by using a menu command. When you create an adjustment layer, the dialog box for the type of adjustment layer you're working with opens, and you can apply settings options. When you click OK in the dialog box, a new adjustment layer is added in the Layers palette.

You can see the options available to you when creating adjustment layers in Figure 7-1. Choose Layer⇨New Adjustment Layer and make a choice from the submenu that appears. Both Levels and Brightness/Contrast, which we talk about in Chapter 6, are available as adjustment layers in this submenu.

To create an adjustment layer and return to the adjustment layer for revising edits, follow these steps:

1. **Open a file that you want to edit by using Levels in Full Edit mode (Standard Edit mode in Elements 4 on the Mac).**

   Choose any file you want to edit, using any one of the number of methods we cover in Chapters 5 and 6 for using the Levels tool. The file you use for these steps isn't as important as understanding the process of creating a Levels adjustment layer.

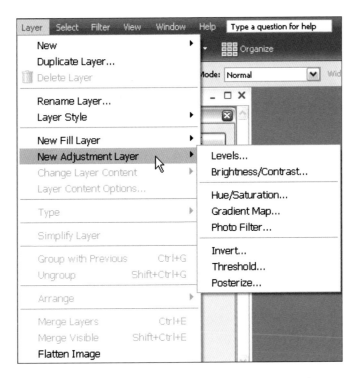

Figure 7-1: Select an option from the New Adjustment Layer submenu to create a new adjustment layer.

2. **Select Layer⇨New Adjustment Layer⇨Levels (or press Ctrl+L on PCs, ⌘+L on Macs) to open the New Layer dialog box.**

   In the dialog box, you can type a descriptive name for your layer or leave the default name, as shown in Figure 7-2. In our example, we use the default name, Layer 1, for the layer. Click OK.

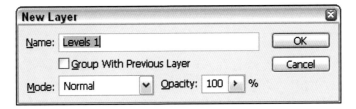

Figure 7-2: In the New Layer dialog box, type a name (or leave the default name) and click OK.

3. **Make adjustments to the black, white, and Gamma sliders as needed for the image you're editing. Click OK when you're done.**

   The Levels adjustment is applied to your image.

4. **Reopen the Layers dialog box by pressing Ctrl+L (⌘+L for Macs).**

   When you open the Layers dialog box, you see the last edits you made. For example, if you moved the Gamma slider to 1.5, you see the Gamma slider at 1.5 when you reopen the Layers dialog box. Click Cancel in the Levels dialog.

5. **Double-click the Levels adjustment layer in the Layers palette to reopen the Levels dialog box.**

   As shown in Figure 7-3, you see a thumbnail graph of the Levels dialog box in the Layers palette. Double-click the left thumbnail, shown in Figure 7-3, to reopen the Levels dialog box.

6. **Make any changes you want in the Levels dialog box and click OK.**

   The new edits are applied to the image.

   Figure 7-3: The Layers palette allows you to see all the layers you're working with.

The layers are *stackable,* meaning you can add several layers to any file. You can create multiple adjustment layers and even multiple adjustment layers of the same type.

As a matter of practice, you should always try to make tone adjustments by using adjustment layers. You never know when you may need to return to a particular edit, especially for color corrections. Make brightness adjustments first, then go about correcting color. If you need to return to a brightness correction, adjustment layers afford you that opportunity.

For information on using adjustment layers for color correction, see Chapter 8.

Working with Adjustment Layers

Photoshop Elements is truly a great program that offers many options for making quick fixes for fast results. A lot of these options just don't appear in more sophisticated programs, such as Adobe Photoshop. However, for all the great features Elements offers, it also has some limitations. Among the most limiting absences in Elements is the lack of a tool for adjusting individual tone points. You can accomplish just so much in the Levels dialog box by making adjustments to the white point, the black point, and the Gamma.

What Elements needs is a tool to make more precise tonal adjustments, but it simply doesn't exist. As a workaround, you can borrow a number of custom settings, using tools in Adobe Photoshop, and introduce the custom settings into an Elements workspace. You don't need to purchase Adobe Photoshop to use such custom settings because we've uploaded the files you need to the Chapter 7 folder on the companion Web site. Keep these files stored on your computer, and you can make the same tone adjustments described in the remainder of this chapter.

Changing the opacity of layers

You can control the strength or degree of any layer by changing its opacity. If you create a Levels adjustment layer, for example, the Opacity setting is 100% by default, but you can control the strength of the layer edits by reducing or increasing opacity.

For example, if you import a Curves layer from Photoshop, you can't edit the Curves layer itself, but you *can* control how much of the Curves adjustment you use by changing the Opacity setting of the Curves layer. The maximum Opacity setting you can use is 100%. The minimum is 0%, which results in no change on layers below the adjustment layer.

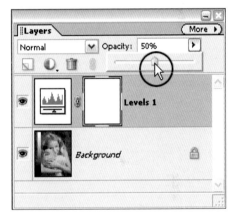

To adjust opacity, click the arrow to the right of the Opacity option in the Layers palette. A slider appears, as shown in Figure 7-4. Drag the slider back and forth to change opacity. Your results are dynamically shown on the image in the Image window.

Figure 7-4: Drag the Opacity slider to modify the strength of an adjustment layer.

Moving adjustment layers between files

You can drag adjustment layers from one image to another image. Adjustment layers are resolution-independent, which means the file size of the image doesn't matter as far as the adjustment layer is concerned. For example, you can drag an adjustment layer from a 32K file to a 10MB file. You don't need to worry about image resolution when using adjustment layers. The files we've provided in the Chapter 7 folder on the companion Web site are small, but they work with any file you edit in Elements.

To use the Curves adjustment layers from the companion Web site, you need to open the files in Full Edit mode (Standard Edit mode on Macintosh in Elements 4).

Open the file you want to add the Curves adjustment layer to and position both the file and the adjustment layer in view in the Image window. Select one of the Curves adjustment layers to make it active and observe the Layers palette. You should see the adjustment layer in the Layers palette. Click the adjustment layer and drag it to the top of the image you're editing, as shown in Figure 7-5. We set the Curves layer opacity at 50% as our default setting. To add more of the curve effect, move the Opacity slider toward 100%. To decrease the effect, move the Opacity slider toward 0%.

When you click an image in the image window, the image becomes the active document. The Layers palette shows you all the layers in the active document. In Figure 7-5, the `contrastIncreaseCurve.tif` file is the active document, and as such, the Layers palette shows you the adjustment layer in that file. When you drag the adjustment layer to another file, a copy of the adjustment layer is added to the target file, and that file then becomes the active document. Dragging an adjustment layer between files doesn't delete the layer from the original file.

Click the adjustment layer and drag it on top of the image you are editing.

Figure 7-5: Drag an adjustment layer from the Layers palette to the image you're editing.

Choosing a layer blending mode

Another option you have when using adjustment layers is choosing a blending mode. By default, the Normal mode is set as the blending mode. Click Normal or the arrow to the right of Normal in the Layers palette to see a long list of blending mode options, shown in Figure 7-6. When you select one of the options, the layer in which you change the mode uses the selected mode attributes to blend with the lower layers in the layer stack.

For a good many of the tone edits we make by using adjustment layers, we choose the Luminosity blend mode. This blend mode restricts the blending of the adjustments to just the brightness and contrast, without changing color saturation.

Figure 7-6: The blending mode options in the Layers palette.

Correcting Image Contrast with a Curves Adjustment Layer

To get full control of the file tone qualities of your image, you need a means of modifying image contrast with a high-quality editing tool, such as Curves. *Curves* is a classic tool from Photoshop that allows you to have full control of the tone qualities of a file. You can use Curves to modify any tonal area of a file, along with changing contrast, and Curves can do everything that the Levels tool can do, as well.

Unfortunately, Elements 5 doesn't have a real version of Curves as an adjustment layer, and the new Adjust Color Curves tool introduced in Elements 5 is a poor effort at duplicating the Curves dialog box in Photoshop. (See Chapter 6 for more information on using the Adjust Color Curves feature.)

However, we have a solution to the problem: You can load a Curves adjustment layer created in Photoshop into any 8-bit file in Elements! You can't edit the curve itself, but you *can* choose the amount of the Curves adjustment you want to use by changing the Opacity setting of the Curves layer.

By using just a pair of Levels and Curves adjustment layers, you can have full control of your image brightness and contrast, with far better quality than you can get by using the standard Elements editing tools. By using a Levels adjustment layer along with a Curves adjustment layer, you can enjoy full control of image brightness, black and white points, and overall contrast with just two layers. Not all files need a contrast change after a correct edit in Levels, but it's a wonderful option to have available.

Increasing image contrast

Because you can't create a Curves adjustment layer in Photoshop Elements, we provide two essential files that can greatly help you edit images to increase and decrease image contrast. Check out the Wiley companion Web site and download the folder contrastCurves from the Chapter 7 folder to follow the steps in the following sections. You need the files contrastDecreaseCurve.tif and contrastIncreaseCurve.tif.

Follow these steps to use a Curves adjustment layer to increase image contrast:

1. **Download the contrast Curves files from the Chapter 7 folder of the companion Web site, if you haven't done so already.**

    The contrastDecreaseCurve.tif file and the contrastIncrease Curve.tif file both appear in the same folder. Open these files in Elements.

2. **Store the files in the Photo Bin.**

    Click the Minimize button in the top-right corner of each file (the Dash icon in the title bar). Minimizing the windows hides them from view, but you can easily make the files visible by clicking the image icon in the Photo Bin.

3. **Open the Photo Bin.**

    The Photo Bin displays an image thumbnail preview for each open file. To expand the Photo Bin, click the Photo Bin button, shown in Figure 7-7. In Figure 7-7, you see the two contrast Curves files loaded in the Photo Bin.

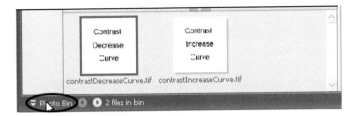

Figure 7-7: Click the Photo Bin button to expand the Photo Bin.

To maximize a document, click the image thumbnail in the Photo Bin. The file opens in the Image window and becomes the active document.

4. Open a file to edit.

To follow the steps precisely, you can download the file `islandView.jpg` from the Chapter 7 folder on the Wiley companion Web site.

Figure 7-8 is a photo taken in Hawaii that shows a distant view of a pretty island seascape. It's a nice photo, but a light haze subdued the image contrast. The bright sky caused the camera meter to underexpose the image a little. A little editing can take this photo to picture-postcard quality.

Figure 7-8: The light haze in this photo makes the landscape look muted.

5. Choose Layer⇨New Adjustment Layer⇨Levels and click OK.

The Levels dialog box opens. As usual, you should start by first using Levels to examine the file and make basic adjustments (which we describe in Chapter 5).

6. Use the Levels preview option to set the white and black points.

This file had many little bright spots. Set the white-point slider carefully by pressing the Alt/Option key and dragging the white slider until you can see just a few pure white spots. Move the black-point slider a bit into the histogram by pressing the Alt/Option key and dragging the black slider until you can see a hint of pure black in the bottom foreground. Don't clip the black and white points any farther than that, or you run the risk of posterizing important image tones. You can see the settings we used in our example in Figure 7-9. The file is improved, but it needs more contrast for best overall quality.

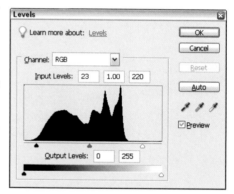

For more information on using the Alt/Option key while moving Levels sliders, see Chapter 5.

Figure 7-9: These Levels adjustments correct image brightness.

7. To add an image contrast curve, click the Contrast Increase Curve file in the Photo Bin and drag the Layer icon in the Layers palette onto the Island file image window.

The layer becomes active, and the image contrast increases. At the default Opacity setting of 50% for this adjustment layer, the file is much improved. At this point, you have two adjustment layers. You added one adjustment layer with the Levels edit, and you added the other adjustment layer by dragging the Increase layer from the Contrast Increase Curve file.

To see even more contrast, move the Opacity slider in the Layers palette to 100%. You can see the Layers palette in Figure 7-10. The result of adding the two adjustment layers brings the file to life with much improved brightness and contrast.

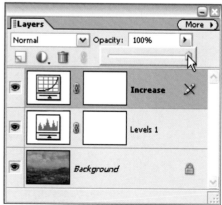

Figure 7-10: Move the Opacity slider for the Contrast Increase Curve to 100%.

Now that you've set contrast to your liking, the image may seem a little too dark for your taste. If you think a little lighter would be better, making this change isn't a problem when you use adjustment layers.

8. **Click the Levels layer in the Layers palette to make the Levels layer the active one again, and then double-click the Layers icon in the Layers palette.**

   The Levels dialog box opens again, showing the last settings you made to Levels.

9. **Move the Gamma slider to the left to lighten the image, and then move the black-point slider a few more Levels to the right to enhance the blacks a bit more. Click OK in the Levels dialog box after making your edits.**

   In our example, we moved the Gamma slider to 1.16 and the black-point slider to 25. This final adjustment in Levels produces the image shown in Figure 7-11.

Switching back and forth between adjustment layers to get the image tones right where you want them isn't unusual. In fact, it's the main benefit of using adjustment layers.

Figure 7-11: The island comes to life after some clever editing.

Reducing image contrast

Figure 7-12 shows a surf shot that's pretty but high in contrast and a little underexposed. The high contrast is a result of the subject matter and the lighting. The foreground rocks were nearly black in color, and the bright foamy white surf is in full sunlight. The camera just wasn't able to hold the full tonal range.

Figure 7-12: This high-contrast surf shot needs some contrast reduction.

With this file, you need to edit first to correct the underexposure, and then edit to reduce the overall contrast. To follow these steps precisely, you can download the file surfRaw.tif from the Chapter 7 folder on the Wiley companion Web site.

To edit a high-contrast image by using adjustment layers, follow these steps:

1. **Open a high-contrast photo in Full Edit mode (Standard Edit mode on the Mac).**

2. **Select Layers⇨New Adjustment Layer⇨Levels to create a Levels adjustment layer.**

   The Levels dialog box opens.

3. **Adjust the black point.**

   Because our example file was a little underexposed, the histogram extends
   full left to the full black portion of the dialog box. A standard black point
   preview (holding the Alt/Option key down and clicking the black slider)
   shows that a tiny move to the right (just one tone level) gives you some full
   black tones, as shown in Figure 7-13. Because you want to recover some
   of those shadow tones, be very careful to not over-edit the black point.

4. **Press Alt/Option and drag the white-point slider until you see the first
   appearance of pure white pixels, as shown in Figure 7-14.**

   In our example, the white point needs the most adjusting because of the
   underexposure of the file. You need to make a much larger move of the
   white point slider to create a few pure white highlight tones on the
   bright surf.

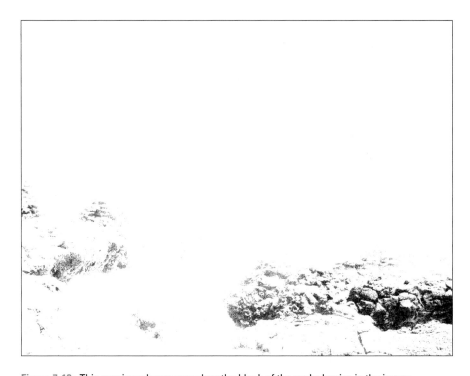

Figure 7-13: This preview shows you when the black of the rocks begins in the image.

Figure 7-14: You can see when the white begins in the surf of the image with this preview.

5. Adjust the Gamma slider.

After setting the black and white points, the image may still seem a little too dark. A small move of the Gamma slider to the left lightens the file somewhat. The settings we use for black, white, and Gamma in our example appear in Figure 7-15.

The bright surf in our example is lacking in tonal separation and the darkest rocks are lacking in shadow detail because of excessive image contrast, as shown in Figure 7-16.

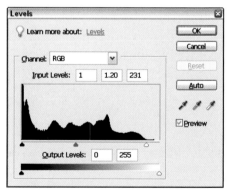

Figure 7-15: Levels adjustments for white point, black point, and Gamma can help you get the image you want.

Figure 7-16: The Levels adjustments lighten the image of the surf and really bring out its details.

6. **Open the Contrast Decrease Curve file in the Image window.**

If you opened the contrast Curves files that you downloaded from the Chapter 7 folder on the Wiley companion Web site, your Contrast Decrease Curve file should be in the Photo Bin. Click the Photo Bin icon to open the Photo Bin and click the Contrast Decrease Curve file to maximize it and make it the active document. In the Layers palette, you can see the Curves adjustment layer.

7. **Drag the Curves adjustment layer in the Contrast Decrease Curve file to the Image window on the file you're editing (in our example, the surfRaw.tif file).**

You end up with essentially the same view in the Layers palette as shown in Figure 7-10. At the default Opacity setting of 50%, the photo already has an improved contrast reduction.

8. **Increase opacity to further reduce contrast.**

   A little more contrast reduction might give you the visual look you're after. In our example, we push the Opacity slider in the Layers palette to the right and bring the Opacity up to 76%, which reduces the contrast more.

   After we finish adjusting the contrast reduction curve, the file still seems a little too dark to us. (Remember that these judgments are subjective. Using the Photoshop Elements tone controls allows you to have the image exactly the way *you* want it.)

9. **To lighten the image a little more, click the Levels adjustment layer and double-click the left icon to open the Levels dialog box again and make a Gamma slider adjustment.**

   Move the Gamma slider to lighten the image. We moved the slider left toward black a little to lighten up the file to suit our taste. (The actual Gamma setting we used was 1.36.) Click OK after making the edit. The final edited image appears in Figure 7-17.

Figure 7-17: The Hawaiian surf looks bright and beautiful after Levels and Curves adjustments.

Part III
Color Corrections

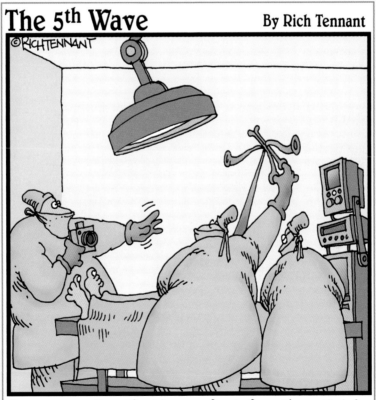

The 5th Wave   By Rich Tennant

"Ooo – wait! That's perfect for the clinic's home page. Just stretch it out a little further...little more...Now let me adjust the lighting so the flesh tones look just right."

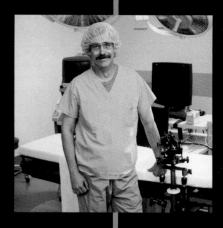

In this part . . .

*T*his part contains the meat of the book. These five chapters help you discover color correction and many different methods for solving a variety of different color problems.

We start by discussing how to identify colorcasts and color problems in Chapter 8, then we move on to Chapter 9, the first of the technique chapters, in which we talk about correcting skin tones. In Chapter 10, we introduce additional tools you can use for color correction. Chapter 11 helps you learn advanced color correction techniques. We finish off this section with Chapter 12, which talks about color correction as it specifically relates to camera raw images.

Identifying Color Problems

*T*he Holy Grail of digital image editing is the art of color correction. Probably no editing issue is more confusing to folks figuring out how to use image-editing software. The fact that a program such as Photoshop Elements has such an array of different tools to use doesn't help. Some of these tools are automatic, and others are fully manual. However, with all the automatic tools and methods that Photoshop Elements provides you to correct color in your pictures, you may find figuring out where to use them pretty tough.

To help simplify matters for you, this chapter gives you some basic steps to help you identify color problems. We cover how to fix many of these color problems in Chapters 9 through 12. In this chapter, we stick to viewing photos and identifying any problems.

In most cases, first getting the tonal quality of your file corrected makes color correction much easier. If you want to know more about adjusting tonal correction, look over Chapters 5 through 7.

Identifying a Colorcast

What do you do if, after you finish doing your best to correct the brightness and contrast on your photos, the color still just doesn't look quite right? Most of the time, an excess of a primary color (or two) in the file is causing the problem.

When your image has a primary-color problem, you typically see a *colorcast*, which means that all of the photo colors are tinted a particular color, and the photo just doesn't look right. Sometimes, you can very easily discover a colorcast if the photo in question contains any neutral grays and whites, or at least some colors very close to neutral gray. You may find photos that lack neutrals or contain only bright vivid colors more difficult to correct, and you can have problems identifying the particular colorcast in those photos.

To start with something simple, Figure 8-1 shows a color-correct version of a white marble statue close-up.

Figure 8-1: These ladies have all the right colors.

The photo looks normal because the tones are neutral. In Figure 8-2, you can see the same photo, this time with colorcasts from the six basic primary colors. (Refer to Chapter 1 for a review of the six basic primary colors.)

It's obvious that these files have colorcasts. You can see why known grays and near whites are the easiest to use to determine a colorcast if you observe each of the six photos in Figure 8-2. Because whites and grays are neutral, they take on the exact hue (color) of the colorcast.

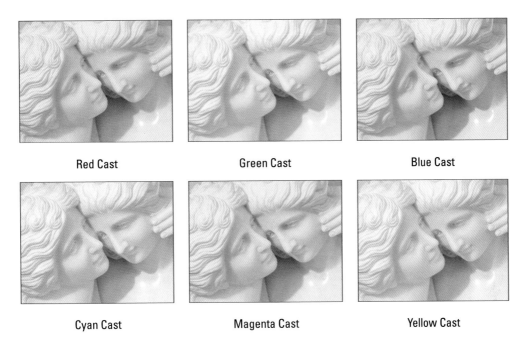

Red Cast   Green Cast   Blue Cast

Cyan Cast   Magenta Cast   Yellow Cast

Figure 8-2: Colorcasts from the six basic primary colors give the statue these different looks.

In Figure 8-2, you can see how Photoshop Elements defines the primary colors. A red or yellow colorcast doesn't necessarily jump out at you, and the green or cyan color itself might look a little different than your own idea of green or blue, for example. The colorcasts, as shown in Figure 8-2, represent their appearance in the way Photoshop Elements defines them. You may find getting familiar with the way Elements defines color very helpful as you develop your color-editing skills.

Discovering Memory Colors

Sometimes, an image doesn't contain any easy-to-identify neutral colors. With that type of image, you must make a guess at the colorcast based on what are known as memory colors. *Memory colors* are common hues that you know — you have a very real expectation of what they're supposed to look like.

Common memory colors are flesh tones, sky blues, plant greens, earth browns, wood browns, and similar objects you can easily identify from memory. The trick with colorcasts in memory colors is figuring out exactly what color the colorcast is. This colorcast identification is a little harder than with neutral colors, but with a little practice, you can do it fairly easily.

For example, in Figure 8-3, you see a snapshot with a strong green cast in the left image. The image really has no neutrals, but because of your color memory, you can easily tell something isn't right about the flesh tones. On the right, you see a corrected image with the color making the flesh tones look natural.

Figure 8-3: The kids on the left look a little green, but the flesh tones on the right look natural.

Figure 8-4 shows a photo with a different colorcast. Sky blues are a powerful memory color. The red cast in the image on the left gives the sky a purplish hue. You can easily tell something's wrong because we all know what a sky is supposed to look like, as shown in the image on the right. Clouds don't normally have a pinkish color, and the plants in the image on the left are lacking a vibrant green hue. Your color memory lets you know that the color isn't quite right, even if you can't figure out exactly what's wrong with the image.

Figure 8-4: Familiar objects, such as skies, clouds, and foliage, can help you identify colorcasts.

Getting Familiar with Color Saturation

As we explain in Chapter 1, *color saturation* refers to the vividness of color. Adjusting color saturation can be an important aspect of getting the color correct in your file. It's perfectly all right to increase the color saturation of a photo for extra drama or impact, such as you might want to do with a pretty sunset. Likewise, intentionally reducing saturation can be just fine if you want to give an image a certain mood. You can even reduce saturation completely to create a black-and-white image.

In this book, we concentrate on showing you how to view normal saturation in photos and edit your files for the most normal-looking color you can get. Controlling saturation can be just as important as removing a colorcast if a correct rendering of the image's memory colors is the goal. Compare the right photo in Figure 8-3, in which you see the corrected color, to Figure 8-5. In Figure 8-5, the color is oversaturated.

Figure 8-5: This photo of the kids has too much saturation.

The color balance in this file is exactly the same as the color balance of the image shown on the right in Figure 8-3, but Figure 8-5 has 40 percent more color saturation. The skin tones look unnatural — almost cartoon-like.

Therefore, some files can have two potential problems with color — a problem with a colorcast and also with color saturation.

Fortunately, Photoshop Elements allows you to easily correct color for both colorcasts and color saturation. When all is said and done, you make successful color corrections by finding and recognizing the assumed neutral tones in a photo or by using memory colors as a reference to identify a colorcast. You correct color in photos by removing colorcasts and adjusting color saturation when you need to.

As with any skill you master, you need some practice at color correction. The first step in correcting color after you make tonal adjustments is to identify the color problems. After you know where the problems lie, you can develop a roadmap for correcting them. In the following chapters, we talk about how to correct images that have both colorcasts and saturation problems. Before you jump into any of the other chapters in this part, look over many different photos and carefully study them to try to identify color problems. The more you practice viewing photos for the purpose of identifying color problems, the easier all your color correcting editing tasks will be.

Color Correcting Skin Tones

9

In This Chapter

▷ Making corrections with the Adjust Color for Skin Tone tool

▷ Adjusting color saturation with the Hue/Saturation command

▷ Using the Remove Colorcast tool

*W*hen we were getting ready to write this book, we did a little research to determine the most popular subject matter for color snapshots. Our conclusion was that, by far, the most popular subjects for professional snapshot photographers, as well as many serious amateurs, are children. All kids have skin, so correcting flesh tones is a good place to start with correcting color on your pictures.

As you can read about in Chapter 8, skin tones are memory colors you can easily identify in photos, and colorcasts and saturation problems on skin tones are some of the easiest problems to identify.

In this chapter, we look at methods for correcting skin tone problems in Photoshop Elements.

Correcting Skin Tones

Photoshop Elements includes an excellent tool for correcting flesh tones called the Adjust Color for Skin Tone tool. In fact, Elements users are one step ahead of Photoshop users when it comes to correcting flesh tones. The full version of Photoshop CS2 doesn't have the Elements Adjust Color for Skin Tone tool. (But we wish it did.) It's a great tool that works well on more than 90 percent of the files we've tried it on.

As we talk about in Chapter 8, the first step of correcting color is to view a photo and identify any potential problems. In Figure 9-1, you see an outdoor photo of a little boy in a garden. The auto white balance in the camera was fooled by all the surrounding yellow-green leaves, so the colorcast of the flesh tones is magenta-blue, the exact opposite of the leaf colors.

Figure 9-1: This boy's skin tones help you identify the photo's magenta-blue colorcast.

To color correct this file, use the auto color-correction option in Photoshop Elements that corrects skin tones, the Adjust Color for Skin Tone tool. The nice thing about the Adjust Color for Skin Tone tool is that you don't have to identify the colorcast to use it. It works on files needing color correction for skin tones, and it doesn't disturb photos that are properly color corrected.

If you want to work along with this example, you can download the `boy.jpg` file from the Chapter 9 folder of the companion Web site.

To use the Adjust Color for Skin Tone tool in Elements, follow these steps:

1. **Open a photo in which you see a colorcast on skin tones.**

2. **With the image open in Full Edit mode (Standard Edit mode on the Mac in Elements 4), choose Enhance⇨Adjust Color⇨Adjust Color for Skin Tone.**

   The Adjust Color for Skin Tone dialog box opens, as shown in Figure 9-2.

   After the dialog box opens, your cursor changes to a target circle with cross hairs when you place it inside the image window.

3. **Drag the Adjust Color for Skin Tone dialog box aside by clicking and dragging the dialog box's title bar until you can clearly see the image.**

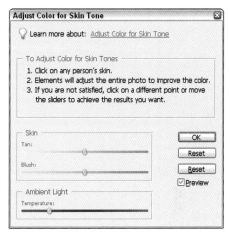

Figure 9-2: Use the Adjust Color for Skin Tone dialog box to help eliminate colorcasts on skin tones.

4. **Move the cursor inside the image window and click a flesh-tone area in the photo to sample a skin tone.**

   Elements color corrects the file based on the flesh-tone sample under the cursor. If you get the result you want from your first sample effort, you can just finish up by clicking OK in the Adjust Color for Skin Tone dialog box.

   For our first effort, we clicked to the right of the child's eye, as shown in Figure 9-3. Notice we moved the dialog box away from the photo so we could clearly see the photo in the Image window.

REMEMBER

   The result of our first effort seems a little cool for our preferences (too blue). The color of skin varies on the face, arms, and hands, so you want to try different sampling points on the subject's skin to see which sampled area gives the most pleasing result.

Use the Eyedropper to sample a color.

Figure 9-3: Move the cursor to a skin-tone area and click to sample the color.

5. **(Optional.) Click the dialog box's Reset button, move the cursor to a different place on the skin, and click again to resample another area of the skin tone.**

For our second attempt, we sampled the little boy's cheek. The result is too green, as shown in Figure 9-4. The little boy has rosy cheeks, which fooled the tool because it assumed that all the skin was as red as the cheeks.

You should usually avoid the cheeks on most faces — especially on photos of women, who often wear makeup. Try to pick an average area of skin color to sample.

6. **Repeat Step 5 as often as necessary to get a sample you like.**

Follow Step 5, clicking Reset and clicking again on another area of skin. Little kids have great skin with none of the battle scars many adults have, so we sampled his hand on our third attempt.

Figure 9-4: A sample from the boy's cheek resulted in a color shift to green.

This sample came close to perfect, but it needs just a little fine-tuning. In the Adjust Color for Skin Tone dialog box, we can perform fine-tuning adjustments by moving the sliders.

The result seems a tiny bit too blue for a little boy's flesh tone. We need to fine-tune the color result a little because we're picky about our flesh tones. However, if you like the result you get after clicking on a good patch of skin, you're finished!

7. **If you want to continue tweaking the result, use the sliders in the Skin and Ambient Light boxes to fine-tune the correction.**

Here's how you fine-tune the result after clicking the cursor on the skin. After you click a flesh tone, the color slider tabs become visible. The box called Skin has two sliders named Tan and Blush. The Tan slider is really a yellow-blue fine-tuning adjustment, and the Blush slider fine-tunes the cyan-red balance of the flesh tone. (See Figure 9-5.)

Less yellow   More yellow

Less red   More red

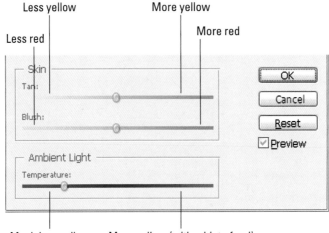

Much less yellow   More yellow (with a hint of red)

Figure 9-5: The Tan slider adjusts yellow-blue balance, and the Blush slider adjusts cyan-red balance.

The Ambient Light Temperature slider is actually just like the Tan slider, but it exaggerates the edit a great deal more. You can see the Ambient Light Temperature slider move slightly as you adjust the Tan slider. As a rule, if the Tan slider can't get the yellowness of the skin color where you want it, try sampling a new area of skin before resorting to using the Ambient Light Temperature slider.

The Tan and Blush sliders are designed for fine-tuning the color balance of the skin color. Large moves of the sliders make small changes in the color balance, so don't be afraid to move them around liberally when you're fine-tuning.

The little boy has very fair skin, and he's standing in open shade. We felt that the flesh tone color was a little too cyan-blue for our own personal preference, so we moved the Tan slider to the far right to add yellow and the Blush slider a little to the left to add a bit of red to the flesh tone, as shown in Figure 9-6.

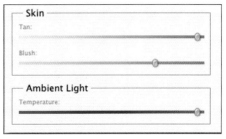

Figure 9-6: Move the Tan and Blush sliders to fine-tune your skin tone adjustments.

The final result makes the little boy's skin look the most pleasing to our eyes, as shown in Figure 9-7. Not all files are quite that easy. In some cases, you need to adjust the saturation of the skin color, too. As a rule, you can first color balance a flesh tone with low or normal color saturation before you adjust saturation.

Figure 9-7: The boy finally has a healthy skin tone after a final color correction.

You can best handle photos with excessive flesh-tone saturation by reducing color saturation before attempting to use the Adjust Color for Skin Tone tool, which brings us to the very important Hue/Saturation tool in Elements.

Using the Hue/Saturation Tool

The Hue/Saturation command is one of the most important color correction tools available to you in Elements. The command allows you to adjust the color saturation of your entire image, or you can limit your adjustment to include just the colors you want to change.

You can also modify the hue (color) of any primary color you want, while leaving the rest of the image colors unchanged. We revisit Hue/Saturation in some of the following sections to solve the most common color-correction problems. We do our best to show you just the features of the tool that you'll need, without boring you with esoteric techniques that no one ever really uses.

You can use the Hue/Saturation command as a standard editing tool or as an adjustment layer. To access the Hue/Saturation dialog box, select Enhance⇨Adjust Color⇨Adjust Hue Saturation or press Ctrl+U (⌘+U for Macs). To access Hue/Saturation as an adjustment layer, select Layer⇨New Adjustment Layer⇨Hue/Saturation, and then click OK in the New Layer dialog box that appears. Either menu command opens the Hue/Saturation dialog box, shown in Figure 9-8.

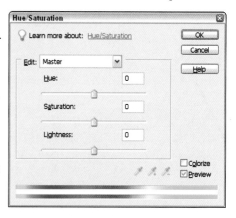

Figure 9-8: Adjust the color saturation of all or a little bit of your image by using the Hue/Saturation tool.

Understanding the Hue/Saturation dialog box

Figure 9-8 shows the Hue/Saturation dialog box as it appears when you first open it, either from a menu command or as an adjustment layer. In the center of the dialog box, you can see the Saturation slider. The Saturation slider changes the saturation of all image colors equally. You can ignore the Hue and Lightness sliders when the Edit menu is in the Master position.

Clicking the down arrow opens the Edit menu, where you can make color selections, as shown in Figure 9-9. Picking a primary color limits the Hue/Saturation edit to just the hue you select from the menu commands.

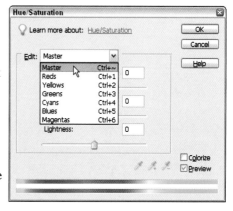

Figure 9-9: Click the down arrow to open the Edit menu.

When you select Reds from the Edit menu, the slider appears at the bottom of the Hue/Saturation dialog box under the red in the color spectrum, which you can see on the left side of Figure 9-10. On the right side of Figure 9-10, Blues is selected from the Edit menu, and the slider appears under the blue area in the color spectrum. The two rainbow color bars represent a color wheel laid out flat.

You use the eyedroppers to the left of the Preview check box to sample a color in your open file. The eyedroppers allow you to set the Hue/Saturation for a color that doesn't fall exactly in the center of the six primaries in the Edit menu. The eyedroppers are very handy if you want to work with a non-primary color, such as orange or yellow-green.

If you keep the Preview check box checked at all times, adjustments made in the Hue/Saturation dialog box are dynamically displayed in the Image window.

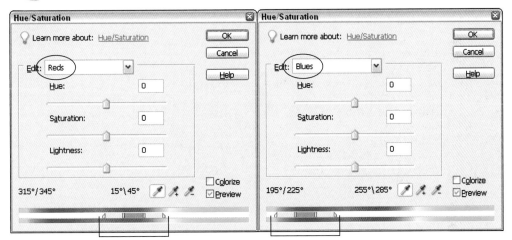

Figure 9-10: Select a color from the Edit menu (Reds on the left, Blues on the right), and the slider moves to the respective color on the color wheel.

Editing Hue/Saturation

An initial Levels adjustment can go a long way in correcting color. You also have the option to use the Adjust Color for Skin Tone tool to help bring skin tones into correct color balance. But what happens when these tools don't do the job and your image also has a color saturation problem? To discover when to use the Hue/Saturation tool, as compared to corrections made with Levels and Adjust Color for Skin Tone, take a look at a photo on which you need to use Hue/Saturation first to bring the image saturation under control.

To follow along with edits made in this section, download the swim.jpg file from the Chapter 9 folder on the companion Web site.

Take a look at Figure 9-11. This photo looks strange for a few reasons. It's a little underexposed, and the white balance of the camera was set to daylight. Light reflecting from the water created a cyan-blue cast to the photo. Even worse, the type of inexpensive digital camera used to take the photo tends to oversaturate the colors when the capture is underexposed. The photo looks cartoon-like, even before we do our standard first edit in Levels.

Figure 9-11: The two in this underexposed photo look a little cyan-blue.

After the standard Levels edit (which we talk about in Chapter 5), the over-saturation looks even worse. The flesh tones are clown-like, and the skin color variation between the tanned woman and the pale little boy looks unrealistic, as you can see in Figure 9-12.

The high color saturation also makes the Adjust Color for Skin Tone tool act erratically because the normally subtle differences of skin tones are so exaggerated because of the excessive image saturation.

But when you try to correct a saturated file such as this with the Adjust Color for Skin Tone tool, you run into more problems. We clicked the Hue/Saturation cursor on the girl's forehead because her forehead gave us a good average sample for her skin color. But the image ends up with a severe blue colorcast. Her reddish, oversaturated skin tone caused the tool to overcorrect the file toward blue, as you can see in Figure 9-13.

Figure 9-12: A standard Levels edit makes the color imbalance worse.

Figure 9-13: Sampling the young woman's skin gives the image a blue colorcast and reddish skin tones.

Minimum and maximum saturation

The Hue/Saturation slider is a powerful editing tool. The slider can completely remove all color saturation or increase saturation to 100 percent overall. If you completely desaturate a photo by moving the Saturation slider all the way to the left (0 percent), your color photo appears in black and white, completely devoid of color. All color saturation is removed because full desaturation converts all image colors to gray, as the following figure shows.

Pushing the Saturation slider all the way to the right brings the file color saturation to 100 percent overall (which you can see in the following figure). You may find this slider move fun if you want a bizarre result, but it's off the scale for normal editing purposes.

Next, we tried sampling the little boy's chest area because it seemed to have the purest color for the sample. The oversaturation of the file caused the skin tone to shift the file color balance far too yellow in most of the colors. The color of the girl's skin and the background water don't look like memory colors, as you can see in Figure 9-14.

The remedy for this problem is easy. We have to reduce color saturation *before* we attempt to balance the color. To desaturate a photo before you make color corrections, follow these steps:

1. **Open an oversaturated photo that features at least one person.**

   In our example, we use the `swim.jpg` file you can download from the Chapter 9 folder on the companion Web site.

Figure 9-14: Using the boy's skin tone as the sample leaves the photo with too much yellow.

2. **Select Enhance➪Adjust Color➪Adjust Hue/Saturation to open the Hue/Saturation dialog box.**

3. **Desaturate the photo.**

   When the Hue/Saturation dialog box opens, move the center Saturation slider to the left to decrease overall image saturation, until the image colors seem to have a more normal vividness. In this example, we move the Saturation slider to –35, and the result gives the file a lower, more normal color-saturation appearance, as shown in Figure 9-15. Of course, you still have to deal with the colorcast.

   Try to reduce color saturation until the image seems to appear a little on the pastel side. You can use the Adjust Color for Skin Tone tool much more easily on a file that's a little low on color saturation, and you can easily add back some color saturation by adjusting the Saturation slider in the Hue/Saturation dialog box after you remove the colorcast.

4. **Select Enhance➪Adjust Color➪Adjust Color for Skin Tone to open the Adjust Color for Skin Tone dialog box.**

5. **Click the cursor on an area of skin to remove any colorcast from the file and click OK.**

Figure 9-15: Moving the Saturation slider to –35 reduces the color saturation.

We clicked on the little boy's chest to remove the blue color-cast in our example. The skin tones now look much more realistic, as shown in Figure 9-16.

If you like the look of your edited image, you're done and can skip the rest of the steps.

If you still want to change the look of your image, you can now return to the Hue/Saturation command and further adjust the image color saturation.

As a rule, you need to make a final small adjustment if you had to desaturate the file before you color corrected it.

Now that you have pleasing flesh tones in the example image, maybe you think the pool water just doesn't look quite right. The water color seems too dull

Figure 9-16: Both the tanned woman and pale child look much more realistic.

(desaturated). This time, use the Hue/Saturation dialog box to adjust only the color saturation of the pool water. This is one of the best features of the Hue/Saturation command. It allows you to modify just certain hues (colors) in the image, without affecting the rest of the image colors. In the professional world, this kind of change is known as *local color correction*.

6. **Press Ctrl+U (⌘+U for Macs) to open the Hue/Saturation dialog box.**

7. **Open the Edit menu. From the menu, pick the primary color that you think is closest to the color you want to modify.**

In this example, we pick Cyans. *Note:* Don't worry about picking the exactly correct primary color. Step 8 takes care of that for you.

After you pick a primary color from the menu, the sliders at the bottom of the dialog box move to the selected color range in the color spectrum. (See Figure 9-17.)

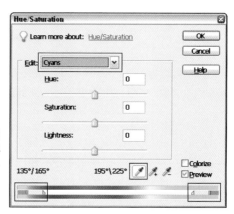

Figure 9-17: Select Cyans and click the left-most eyedropper tool to modify a color in that range.

The little eyedropper icon with the gray background is the color sampler, and the gray background means it's active and ready to use. This eyedropper tells the Hue/Saturation command the exact color you want to modify.

8. **Move the cursor to an average-colored area of the background you want to edit and click the mouse once to sample a color, as shown in Figure 9-18.**

Figure 9-18: Click an area of the water to sample a hue you want to saturate.

The color slider on the bottom of the Hue/Saturation dialog box moves slightly when you sample a color. The eyedropper sampler centers the color slider to the exact hue you pick with the cursor.

You can actually set the color menu to any color, even if that color isn't close to the hue (color) you want to modify. After you click the color sampling eyedropper on the image color you want, the color menu resets itself to the color you chose automatically.

9. Add saturation to the selected hue.

The saturation edit needed for the background water is subjective. We wanted the background to match the foreground people, so we moved the Saturation slider to the right, to +25 percent. Because we selected just Cyan hues for the edit, only the water changes, as shown in Figure 9-19, and the flesh tones stay the same.

Figure 9-19: The swimmers photo after saturating the Cyans +25 percent.

Correcting flesh tones involves using the Adjust Color for Flesh Tone tool, along with adjusting overall color saturation, to give the photo a natural appearance. When your photos have saturation problems, always make a saturation adjustment before adjusting for tone and color corrections.

Removing a Colorcast

The Adjust Color for Flesh Tone tool works by comparing a known reference color to the flesh color in the file you select with the tool cursor. Elements then automatically calculates the color change needed to remove the colorcast from the image.

In techie terms, the tool works by matching a *target color* (your file), to a *reference color* (a flesh tone stored in memory).

The Remove Color Cast tool works exactly the same way as the Adjust Color for Flesh Tone tool. The difference is the reference color. Remove Color Cast works by using neutral gray as the reference color. Elements then assumes that the file area you click with the Remove Color Cast cursor is supposed to be gray, and it changes the file color balance to make the reference area gray.

How do you know what's really a true neutral gray in the image? Well, you make a guess and see what happens. If you get an odd-looking result, you simply try again.

Of course, the tool is useful only in photo files that contain some neutral colors, but many photos have a neutral area to sample if you look for it hard enough.

The area you sample doesn't have to be a perfect middle gray. Light or dark grays can work well, too. To use the Remove Color Cast tool, follow these steps:

1. **Open a file containing a colorcast and a neutral gray.**

   To follow our example in these steps, download the file `greenCast.jpg` from the Chapter 9 folder of the Wiley companion Web site.

   In Figure 9-20, you see one of the authors photographed with a digital point-and-shoot camera. The color balance has a greenish cast. The photographer had her camera set on daylight balance, and the room was lit with fluorescent lighting, resulting in the green colorcast.

   Because the room has a lot of neutral colors, the Remove Color Cast tool will work well on this image.

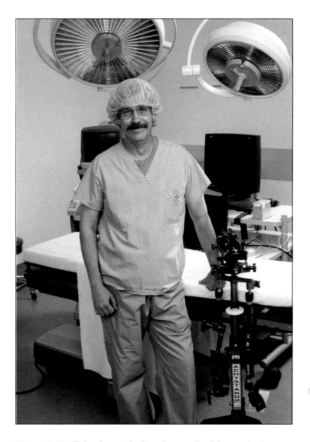

Figure 9-20: This photo of a handsome devil in scrubs has a green colorcast.

2. **Select Enhance⇨Adjust Color⇨Remove Color Cast to open the Remove Color Cast dialog box, shown in Figure 9-21.**

Figure 9-21: You can correct a colorcast by using the Remove Color Cast dialog box.

3. **Sample a gray color in the photo.**

   Because you can't be sure where the best neutral gray in the image is located, simply make a guess to determine the best place to click the cursor in the image. If you like the result you get with your first sample, you don't need to follow the rest of the steps. Just save your work — you're done!

   For our first try, we clicked the cursor inside the paint trim on the back wall. The result looks too blue. The paint stripe must have been a warm gray. Adjusting the paint stripe's warm gray to perfect gray by using the cursor made the overall color balance too cool, as shown in Figure 9-22.

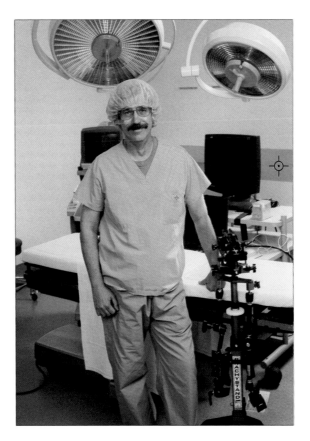

Figure 9-22: A click on the paint trim in the photo produces this too-blue appearance.

4. (Optional.) Make a second sample.

If you don't like the result of Step 3, just click the cursor somewhere else in the image. You don't need to reset the tool each time, as you did with the Adjust Color for Flesh Tone tool. Next, we click the cover cloth hanging off of the exam table. It appears to be a white cloth, so it should give us a neutral color.

This sample produces a much better result, but the photo still has a slight magenta colorcast, as shown on Figure 9-23. The white cloth must have picked up some reflected green light from the green floor.

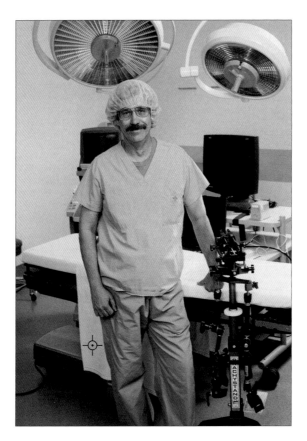

Figure 9-23: A sample from the exam table's white cloth makes the picture look slightly magenta.

5. Continue sampling until the image appears with a correct color balance.

You can continue clicking to sample neutral grays, blacks, and whites until you see the photo come into a good color balance. We clicked this time on the side of the exam table cover sheet. The sampled area seems to be just right, and the overall color balance looks normal, as shown in Figure 9-24.

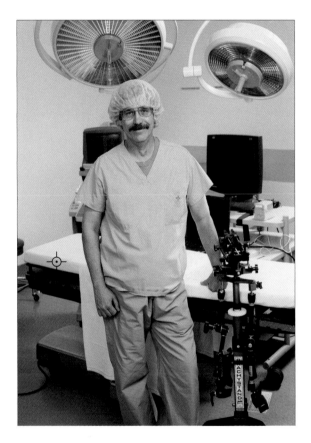

Figure 9-24: The sample from the side of the exam table brings the colors into balance.

Keep in mind that it takes far longer to read this procedure than it took us to make three sample clicks. If you don't like the results you get, just keep clicking around until you see a result that looks good.

10

Using Levels and Color Variations to Make Color Corrections

In This Chapter

▷ Adjusting color with Levels

▷ Using Color Variations

*T*wo useful tools for color correction in Photoshop Elements are Levels and Color Variations. We cover how to use Levels for tone corrections in Chapter 5, but Levels has much more to offer than just adjusting brightness and contrast: You can also use Levels to correct color.

In addition to Levels, Elements provides you a more visual approach to color correction with the Color Variations dialog box. These two tools, combined with the Hue/Saturation, Adjust Color for Skin Tone, and Remove Color Cast tools (which we discuss in Chapter 9), provide you with flexibility and numerous options for correcting color.

In this chapter, you discover how to use Levels for color correction and how to use the Color Variations dialog box for visual color corrections.

Using Levels for Color Correction

The Remove Color Cast command, which we discuss in Chapter 9, is actually a tool that's been around since the very first version of Photoshop. It's really not new: Elements just gave it a fancy new name. The tool in its original form is still with us in the Levels dialog box, as an eyedropper.

In the Levels dialog box, you can see three eyedropper icons. From left to right, they're the White, Gray, and Black eyedroppers. For now, just pay attention to the Gray eyedropper, shown in Figure 10-1.

The Gray eyedropper

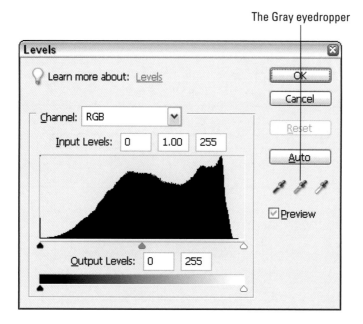

Figure 10-1: You can use the Gray eyedropper, in the center, to sample midtone grays.

This eyedropper works exactly like the sampler in the Remove Color Cast command we discuss in Chapter 9. There's no difference at all in its function, but there are real advantages to using the Gray eyedropper in Levels rather than the Remove Color Cast tool:

✓ You can use the Gray eyedropper right after doing your basic Levels tonal edit if the file has some gray values to reference.

✓ The Levels Gray eyedropper works on 16-bit files, whereas Remove Color Cast and many of the other color correction tools work only on 8-bit images.

✓ You can use Levels as an adjustment layer, which can have many advantages if you want to change your mind later, as we discuss in Chapter 7.

✓ It allows you to use the Gray eyedropper in combination with other color correction tools, if you wish, when used as an adjustment layer (for example, a Hue/Saturation adjustment layer and a Levels adjustment layer).

✓ You can actually reset the Gray eyedropper to a different color of your choice, if needed. We discuss this eyedropper adjustment in Chapter 11 when we talk more about advanced color-correction techniques.

Correcting color by using Levels

To use Levels for color correction, follow these steps:

1. **Open a file with a colorcast problem.**

   For this series of steps, we use the `gym.jpg` file that you can download from the Chapter 10 folder of the companion Web site. The picture was shot to show off a brand-new high school gymnasium. The camera white balance was set for fluorescent lighting; but the gym had Mercury Vapor lights, and the result was a severe cyan-green colorcast, as you can see in Figure 10-2. To make things even more difficult, a small amount of natural outside light was coming in from some doors behind the camera. Although the picture doesn't have any obvious gray areas to sample, click around inside the image by guesswork and see if you can bring the image into a more reasonable color balance.

Figure 10-2: The lighting in this gym gave the photo a cyan-green colorcast.

2. **Press Ctrl+L (⌘+L for Macs) or select Layer⇨New Adjustment Layer⇨ Levels to open the Levels dialog box.**

3. **Click the middle eyedropper (the Gray eyedropper) in the Levels dialog box to activate it.**

   When the cursor moves into the image area, the eyedropper appears with a gray fill.

4. Sample a gray area in the photo.

Take a guess, click an image sample, and see what happens. If you don't like the result, just click again somewhere else in the image. If you hit the right sample the first time, you're done! No need to follow the rest of the steps in this list.

As a first effort, we tried clicking on the neutral-looking folded gym seats. The resulting color balance was too cyan-blue, as shown in Figure 10-3. The folded seats must be a warm tan color.

Figure 10-3: This version of the gym photo has a cyan-blue colorcast.

5. (Optional.) Sample a second gray area in the photo.

If the first attempt doesn't bring the image into color balance, click in another area of the photo.

This time, we tried clicking on one of the doors on the rear wall. The result is much better, but the photo looks a little too yellow-green overall, as shown in Figure 10-4.

6. Continue sampling colors until the image appears balanced in color.

Last, we sampled the ceiling in the upper-right corner. This sample gave us the result we liked best.

Note: The gym ceiling is actually painted white, but it's lit mainly by reflected light from the floor, so the ceiling tends to take on the color of the floor. As you can see in the final result, shown in Figure 10-5, the ceiling is many different shades of white, from cool to warm.

Figure 10-4: In this edited image, the gym has a yellow-green colorcast.

This is a common situation in all color photography. Just because you know that an object in the photo was really white or gray doesn't guarantee you'll get a perfect color balance from sampling that object. Color reflection from the lighting environment can tint the neutrals, which leads to errors in color sampling. So, just keep on clicking until you find the right spot!

Figure 10-5: The third time's a charm, giving us a color-balanced image.

Image saturation should be normal or undersaturated for best results. A file with high color saturation makes the Remove Color Cast command, or the Gray eyedropper in Levels, much more difficult to use. Do your best to normalize the overall image color saturation with the Hue/Saturation command's Saturation slider, if needed, before you try to color balance the image. (See Chapter 9 for reducing saturation by using the Hue/Saturation tool.)

Analyzing the Levels adjustments

When you use Levels to correct color, you can review the tone distribution as you make adjustments. Levels provides you feedback not only for the result in the composite image, but also when you view each color channel. (You can access Red, Green, and Blue channel information in the Levels dialog box.) In this section, we take a look at what really happens to the tone distribution when you follow the steps in the preceding section.

After you click the Gray eyedropper in the image, the color balance changes, and you might notice that the histogram seems to change, too. Elements makes changes in all three color channels in order to bring your file into color balance. You can see what actually happens when you click the Gray eyedropper by viewing the individual Red, Green, and Blue channel histograms.

Clicking the Channel menu in the Levels dialog box reveals the separate channel options available. To view the individual color channels, select Red, Green, or Blue from the menu options. Alternatively, you can press Ctrl+1 (⌘+1 for Macs), Ctrl+2 (⌘+2 for Macs), and Ctrl+3 (⌘+3 for Macs) to view the Red, Green, and Blue channels, respectively. Ctrl+~ (⌘+~ for Macs) returns you to the composite RGB channel. Note that these keyboard shortcuts work only when the Levels dialog box is open.

The separate color channel histograms, shown in Figure 10-6, all look somewhat different from each other because you're looking at information from a full-color photograph. The proportions of the different colors vary. The histograms all match only if the entire image is comprised of nothing but pure gray tones.

Also, the Gamma sliders in all three channels have moved away from the center position. That channel move is the result of using the Gray eyedropper. Elements moves the individual color channel Gamma sliders to brighten or darken Red, Green, and Blue primary color components to change the overall color balance of the file.

You can also move the Gamma sliders manually in each channel to modify the image color balance, if you want. We tell you more about that in Chapter 11.

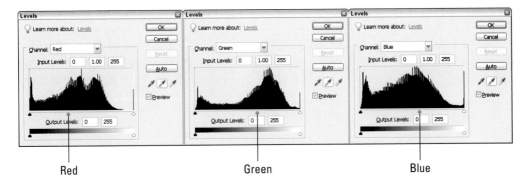

Red   Green   Blue

Figure 10-6: Histograms for the Red, Green, and Blue channels after Levels edits.

Working with Color Variations

Another very useful tool in Elements for color correction is a command called Color Variations. Color Variations is a visual color-correction tool that allows you to make color-balance judgments by using visual comparisons.

Color Variations is a throwback to the classic days of making color prints in a darkroom. To help determine the best color settings when making color prints from color negatives, the photographer printed a set of color variations. The color variations were based on the six basic primary colors and helped a great deal when the photographer was trying to determine what settings would help eliminate a colorcast. This proof set is called a *ring around*. The color variations followed the classic layout of the color wheel, hence the name ring around.

The Color Variations command in Elements follows the same general idea, but you might find the labeling a little confusing at first. To open the Color Variations dialog box, choose Enhance⇨Adjust Color⇨Color Variations. The Color Variations dialog box opens, as shown in Figure 10-7.

At the top of the dialog box, you can see the Before and After image windows. The Before window always shows you the original state of your image, and the After window shows the real-time results of any editing changes you make in Color Variations.

At the bottom-left of the dialog box, you can find the Select Area of Image to Adjust radio boxes and the Adjust Color Amount slider. Moving the Adjust Color Amount slider increases and decreases the overall amount of color you apply when you click a ring-around thumbnail in the Color Variations dialog box.

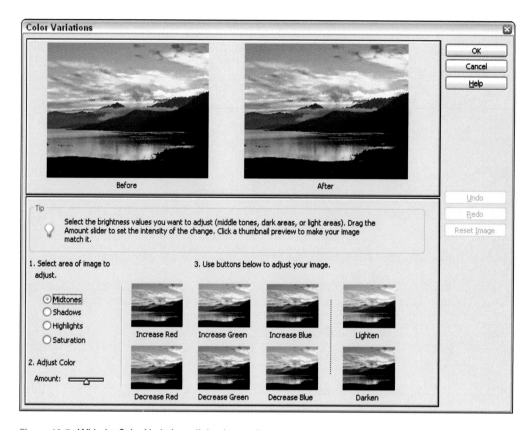

Figure 10-7: With the Color Variations dialog box, color corrections are at your fingertips.

Actually, leaving the Midtones radio button selected under Select Area of Image to Adjust radio boxes allows you to make changes to the color balance of the entire image, not just the midtones. We recommend always leaving the default midtone setting when you use Color Variations for color balancing your image. Using the Shadows or Highlights settings destroys your black- and white-point settings in Levels and tints the real whites and blacks. If you already set your white and black points in Levels (which we talk about in Chapter 5), you don't want to mess that up by using Color Variations. (Remember, always make your tonal adjustments first in Levels.)

In the center of the dialog box, under Use Buttons Below to Adjust Your Image, you can see the Color Variations options — the ring around. Below each thumbnail, you see a text description for what happens when you click that thumbnail. For example, click the top-left corner thumbnail, and you increase reds, as described in the text below the thumbnail. You can click any one of the six thumbnails repeatedly to add or remove primary colors.

Using the Color Variations command is fairly straightforward. By default, the tool is set to affect the midtones. You simply click the cursor over the ring-around color option you like in the dialog box, and the result appears in the After image preview.

The Amount slider is a little heavy-handed at the default setting. We suggest moving it a little to the left, as shown in Figure 10-8, in order to make the file changes less severe with each click on a color-option thumbnail.

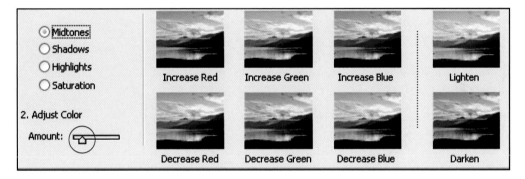

Figure 10-8: To apply more subtle corrections, move the Amount slider to the left.

We think the color labeling in the Color Variations dialog box is a bit confusing. We modified the text in the dialog box in Figure 10-9 to show you how it would look if the six primary colors were all actually identified in the dialog box.

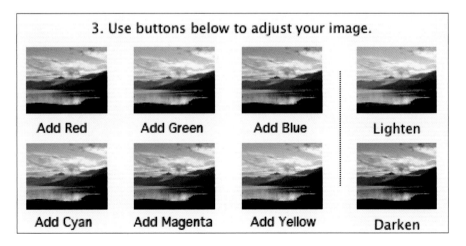

Figure 10-9: We relabeled the color options according to the six primary colors.

As you can see, the complementary colors (the opposites) are placed one above the other. To help understand the concept a little more, take a look at the color wheel we introduce in Chapter 1 (Figure 10-10). You can clearly see the color complements in the color wheel.

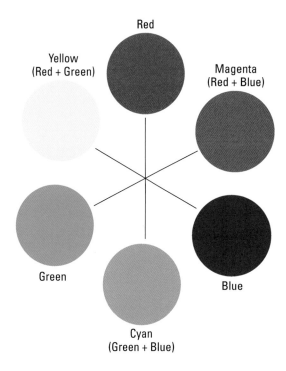

Figure 10-10: The color wheel clearly shows the complementary colors.

Correcting color with Color Variations

Color Variations is purely an eyeball editing tool. If you have reasonably good color vision, using Color Variations is easy and straightforward. To gain a little practice at using Color Variations, follow these steps:

1. **Open an image in Elements.**

   A photo that appears a little too cool or a little too warm would be best to use for these steps. For this example, we use the sunrise.jpg file, which you can download from the Chapter 10 folder on the companion Web site.

We start with the sunrise photo shown in Figure 10-11. The colors of a twilight scene are very subjective. We felt that the sunrise as captured by our digital camera looked a little on the cool side. We prefer a warmer morning look. But we're not exactly sure what particular color balance would look best, which makes this photo a good candidate for the visual judgments we can make in Color Variations.

Figure 10-11: This sunrise image looks a little too cool.

2. **Select Enhance⇨Adjust Color⇨Color Variations to open the Color Variations dialog box.**

   When the Color Variations dialog box opens, you can quickly view a number of color balance variations until you see what you like best.

3. **Reduce intensity by moving the Adjust Color Amount slider one place to the left and leaving the Midtones radio button selected.**

4. Add a warmer tone to the image by adding some yellow and a little red to the overall color balance.

To add some yellow, click the Decrease Blue option three times. (Remember, yellow is the opposite of blue. Decreasing blue adds yellow to the photo.)

Clicking three times on the Decrease Blue thumbnail produces the effect shown in Figure 10-12.

Figure 10-12: We clicked the Decrease Blue thumbnail to get this warmer sunrise image.

The added yellow seemed to put us on the right track, but adding a little red to the file will make it look just right for our taste. (Adding some red with the yellow in combination results in adding some "orange" to the file.)

We click the Increase Red option twice, and the After preview shows us the overall color balance we like best. You can see the final result in Figure 10-13.

Figure 10-13: The final edited sunrise image after adding more red.

Darkening and lightening images

On the far right of the Color Variations dialog box, you can see the Lighten and Darken options. Should you use them?

Using these options to make small final adjustments to your file after you get the color where you want it is okay. But keep in mind that your initial edit in Levels should have gotten your overall image brightness close to where it should be. (You did edit first in Levels, right? We cover Levels edits in Chapter 5.) As a matter of practice, you shouldn't have to use the Darken and Lighten options in the Color Variations dialog box, except for some last-minute subtle adjustments.

Saturating images with Color Variations

Color Variations enables you to make changes to an image's saturation. Remember, however, that although you can use the Color Variations tool to make final slight adjustments to an image, the Hue/Saturation command we discuss in Chapter 9 gives you far more control for changing image saturation.

For this example, we chose a file that needs correct color rendition rather than a subjective color balance for a pleasing mood.

To adjust image saturation with the Color Variations tool, follow these steps:

1. **Open an image in Elements in Full Edit mode (Standard Edit mode on the Mac in Elements 4).**

   To follow our example in these steps, download the file `classroom.jpg` from the Chapter 10 folder on the Wiley companion Web site.

   Figure 10-14 is a picture shot for a high school yearbook. The classroom had some kind of warm white fluorescent lighting, and the digital camera auto white balance did a poor job of guessing the correct white balance setting. The result is an image with a yellow-green colorcast.

Figure 10-14: This classroom photo has a strong yellow-green colorcast.

   The lighting isn't color consistent in this file, so Color Variations is a good choice to color balance the image.

2. **Open the Color Variations dialog box by selecting Enhance⇨Adjust Color⇨Color Variations.**

3. **To reduce the yellow in the file, add blue to the file (because blue is the opposite of yellow).**

   If you need to, quickly review the color wheel in Figure 10-10 to confirm the complementary color you need.

Figure 10-15 shows the image after we click the Increase Blue option twice to begin our corrections. The picture is improved, but it's still not quite right.

Figure 10-15: Clicking Increase Blue reduces the colorcast, but the classroom still needs a little work.

A colorcast is seldom composed of a single primary color, such as red or yellow. You usually need to adjust two primaries to get the file looking just right.

4. **Remove some green in the file by clicking the Remove Green option, and then click OK.**

Viewing the Color Variations thumbnails confirms that the file seems to have an excess of green after we remove the excess yellow from the colorcast in Step 3. A single click on the Remove Green option brings the file to a pleasing and more realistic color balance. You can see the final result in Figure 10-16.

You can also use Color Variations to color balance the flesh tones or grays in any file if you're comfortable enough using the command. Color Variations is also a good training tool when you're figuring out how to recognize colorcasts. Working with opposite color primaries to neutralize a colorcast is the basic skill you need to correct your color photos like a professional.

Figure 10-16: Removing green from the image gives the class a more realistic color balance.

Advanced Color-Correction Methods

*T*hroughout this book, we show you techniques that work well for most of the color problems you'll encounter with your digital photographs. However, you can't properly correct some color problems with the methods we describe in Chapters 8 through 10. So, for the more courageous Elements users, we want to introduce a few custom color-correction methods that the professionals commonly use.

In this chapter, we talk about some advanced color correction methods you should try when you can't seem to correct images with the techniques we describe in earlier chapters.

Cleaning Up the Whites

Figure 11-1 is a photo of a child's first theatrical appearance, shot by a proud parent. The stage lights provided the lighting, which resulted in a severe yellow-red colorcast. If you tried to fix this file with any of the methods we demonstrate in earlier chapters, you'd probably be heading back to the bookstore for a full refund.

Figure 11-1: This school production photo has a strong yellow colorcast.

We tried our best to correct this photo by using Levels and Color Variations methods that you can find in Chapter 10. We set the black and white points in the Levels dialog box and used the Color Variations tool to reduce the excess yellow and red from the file, but the results look very bad. The little white fence is pink, the flesh tones look strange, and the little girls' dresses are a sickly-looking yellow-green, as shown in Figure 11-2. We couldn't get one hue right without ruining another. What went wrong?

The camera white balance was far too warm, and the photo was underexposed, so the Blue and Green channels are far more underexposed than the Red channel. The file has an orange colorcast, but that colorcast is much more severe in the highlights. That's why the standard color correction methods don't work with this file.

In the professional world, we'd say that the three color channels aren't *linear*, or in other words, the color channels have different tonal ranges. We have to fix the channels independently in order to make the color look normal.

Figure 11-2: Our best Levels and Color Variations correction effort left the image still looking terrible.

For this file, you can actually fix the individual channel tonal ranges very easily. Just use the Auto Levels command to correct the color in this file. Open the Levels dialog box and click the Auto button. Alternatively, you can select Enhance⇨Auto Levels or press Shift+Ctrl+L (Shift+⌘+L for Macs). With a single click, the file looks better. Most of the colorcast is gone, as shown in Figure 11-3.

Figure 11-3: A single click on Auto Levels improves the little performers' image.

The white fence is white, the yellow dresses look normal, and the flesh tones look much improved. What actually happens when you use the Auto Levels command? To find out, check out the following section to examine all the color channels in Levels.

Examining color channels in Levels

To examine the same file we use as our example in this chapter, download the `kidsPlay.jpg` file from the Chapter 11 folder on the Wiley companion Web site. We use this file to examine the tone curve in individual channels, using the Levels dialog box. Your first stop is viewing the default RGB channel. Open the Levels dialog box (Ctrl+L for PCs, ⌘+L for Macs), and you see the histogram reporting the tone distribution in the composite RGB channel. The histogram looks fairly normal, as shown in Figure 11-4.

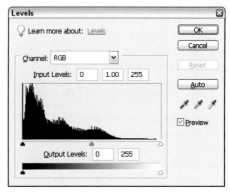

Figure 11-4: The Levels dialog box shows that the kidsPlay.jpg photo has a normal tone curve.

To examine the different color channels while you have the Levels dialog box open, select the channels from the Channel menu. An easier method is to use keyboard shortcuts. Press Ctrl+1 (⌘+1 for Macs) to see the Red channel, Ctrl+2 (⌘+2 for Macs) to see the Green channel, and Ctrl+3 (⌘+3 for Macs) to see the Blue channel. You can see the histograms for each of the individual channels in Figure 11-5.

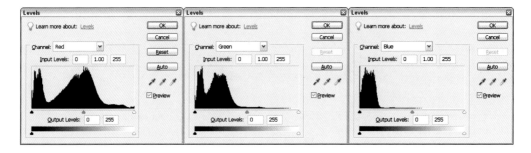

Figure 11-5: Histograms for the Red, Green, and Blue channels.

What do the histograms tell you? Looking at the Red channel histogram, you can see red in the highlights of the image. (The data on the right side of the histogram represents the highlight information.) In the Green channel, the histogram shows only a little data in the highlights. A tiny bit of data appear to the right of the midtone point in this channel. In the Blue channel histogram, you see no data to the right of the midtone point toward the highlight area. This histogram indicates that no blue exists in the highlights at all.

From looking at these histograms, you can tell that this image has a lot of orange in the highlights. (A lot of red mixed with a little green makes orange. Go back to the kindergarten lesson we give in Chapter 1 to figure out the results of mixing colors.)

In this photo, the right side of the histogram for each of the three channels is very different. Because the file should show some true white tones (such as in the picket fence), the histogram white points have to match up in order to bring the highlight values into an accurate neutral color balance. You can't fix the color balance across the entire tonal range until you set a white point by evening up the histogram white points. Because the standard edits for making Levels and Color Variations adjustments that we describe in Chapter 10 can't do the job, you need to use another method for setting the white point.

Using Auto Levels

To edit the file shown in Figure 11-1, you can use the Auto Levels option in Elements. When you use Levels to make tone adjustments in the composite channel, all channels are equally edited with the same tone adjustments. We suggest you use Auto Levels because this option applies a custom Levels edit that sets each individual color channel's white point to equalize the tonal range in each channel. Here's how to do it:

1. **Open the `kidsPlay.jpg` file in Full Edit mode (Standard Edit mode on the Mac in Elements 4).**

   You can download the file from the Chapter 11 folder of the Wiley companion Web site.

2. **Open the Levels dialog box (Ctrl+L on PCs, ⌘+L on Macs).**

3. **Click the Auto button in the Levels dialog box.**

You can also use the Enhance⇨Auto Levels menu command. Using this command makes the same edit, but it doesn't give you the option of examining what happened in each channel. For this series of steps, use the Levels dialog box and click Auto so you can then examine the individual channels to see how Elements moves the tone points.

After you make a Levels adjustment in the Levels dialog box, the new slider positions appear under the histograms for each channel. When you click OK in Levels, the tone curve is remapped according to your adjustments. However, if you reopen the Levels dialog box, the histogram shows the new tone point mapping, but the black, white, and Gamma sliders return to their default positions.

 4. **Select the Red channel from the Channel menu or press Ctrl+1 (⌘+1 for Macs).**

Continue examining each of the three individual color channels, choosing Green and then Blue from the Channel menu or pressing their shortcut keys (Ctrl+2 for PCs or ⌘+2 for Macs, Ctrl+3 for PCs or ⌘+3 for Macs, respectively). In Figure 11-6, you can see the three color channels after the Auto Levels adjustment in Step 3. The white-point slider moves to the left in the Green and Blue channels. Seeing the neutral highlights in the photo clean up nicely confirms that using Auto Levels was the correct editing move.

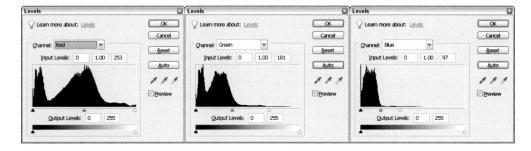

Figure 11-6: The three color channels after the Auto Levels adjustment.

 5. **Adjust the Gamma slider to the left, to the 1.18 position.**

Auto Levels evened out the color channels in Step 3, but you can still tweak the file a little for the very best result. With the Levels dialog box open, make some final adjustments to image brightness and readjust the white and black points. In this step, you move the Gamma slider to the left to lighten the image overall in the RGB composite channel.

 6. **Move the black-point slider right, to the 18 position.**

7. Adjust the white point by moving the slider left, to the 248 position.

This small move of the white-point slider adds a little extra sparkle to the highlights. You can see the final result, after all edits in the RGB composite channel, in Figure 11-7.

Figure 11-7: This final edited image shows the girls at their color-correct best.

Keep in mind that you can also use Hue/Saturation, Color Variations, or any of the other color correction tools after you make the Auto Levels edit to bring your file to perfection. We liked the look of this file with a little extra saturation to enhance the mood of the stage lighting, so we didn't bother making a Hue/Saturation adjustment.

Almost any file with heavy colorcasts in neutral highlight areas can benefit from a pass through Auto Levels.

Figure 11-8 gives another example of how Auto Levels can bring a photo into a good tonal range. The photo on the left, an unedited image shot with a digital camera, is an average snapshot with a heavy highlight colorcast. On the right, you see the image edited with a single pass in Auto Levels. The image's large areas of real white tones allow Auto Levels to do a good job.

Figure 11-8: A snapshot with a heavy highlight colorcast (on the left) and edited with Auto Levels (on the right).

Be very selective with your use of Auto Levels. Unlike the Auto Contrast command (which we talk about in Chapter 6), Auto Levels can cause large, unnatural, color shifts in files that lack real white values because Auto Levels tries to create some white pixels, even if the photo has no real white values. Carefully examine your photo for true whites before applying the Auto Levels command.

In Figure 11-9, an adjustment made with Auto Levels just didn't work. The file contains no neutral values at all. When you use the Auto Levels adjustment, the file is completely ruined because the image has no neutral highlights.

We had to edit this file by using custom edits with the Levels tool, the Adjust Color for Skin Tone command, and the Hue/Saturation tool, all of which we describe in earlier chapters. The final result is a pleasing overall color balance, as shown in Figure 11-10.

Figure 11-9: These young swimmers aren't showing any neutral highlights.

Figure 11-10: The swimmers' snapshot looks much better after making some edits.

Setting White and Black Points with the Levels Eyedroppers

You can't fix all files with severe highlight colorcasts by using Auto Levels. A file with clipped white- or black-tone areas can fool Auto Levels, making the Auto Levels feature not function as it should. Files with pure white and black areas don't work at all with Auto Levels.

With these types of images, you have to take control and reset all the color-channel white and black points manually. Figure 11-11 shows you an example of the type of image that needs manual white- and black-point adjustments. This photo was shot in a mixed-lighting environment. The background is much more yellow than the foreground. The ceiling light fixtures and the sign in the background are the brightest tones in the file.

Figure 11-11: This photo of cheerleaders in a school gym has a strong colorcast.

What happens when you use Auto Levels on this kind of image? Auto Levels sets the white point to those bright values in the sign and light fixtures. The result doesn't look very good, even though some real white tones exist in the main subject, as you can see after we apply Auto Levels in Figure 11-12.

You can find the solution to the problem in the Levels dialog box — the Black and White eyedroppers. These eyedroppers allow you to set a black or white point based on the area you select in the image. You have full control; Elements doesn't just make a guess for you. This control also allows you to ignore areas of the photo that aren't important to the main subject.

Figure 11-12: The cheerleaders still don't look color-balanced after an Auto Levels edit.

By default, the Black and White eyedroppers are set to full black and white. You want to neutralize the colorcasts without clipping the tones in the histogram. It can be difficult to guess exactly where the full white tones are in a file with a colorcast, so you need to reset the eyedroppers to very light gray and very dark gray rather than pure white and black. After you correct the colorcasts, you can fine-tune the white and black points just like any other file. It sounds complicated, but it's really easy. After you correct colorcasts by using the eyedroppers a few times, it becomes second nature. Just follow these steps:

1. **Open the `cheers.jpg` file, which you can download from the Chapter 11 folder on the Wiley companion Web site.**

2. **Open the Levels dialog box (Ctrl+L for PCs, ⌘+L for Macs).**

3. **Double-click the White eyedropper in the Levels dialog box to open the Color Picker, as shown in Figure 11-13.**

   The White eyedropper is the third eyedropper to the right, below the Auto button. Because this dialog box is the Color Picker for the White eyedropper, the words "Select target highlight color" appear at the top of the dialog box, as shown in Figure 11-13.

   At the top left of the large color box, you can see a small half-circle. This half-circle shows you the color selected for the White eyedropper. The eyedropper is positioned at the full-white default position. The far left side of the color box is all gray tones, with white on top and black on the bottom.

The color selected
for the Eyedropper

Before and after
color samples

RGB values

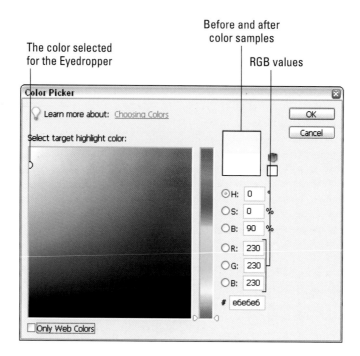

Figure 11-13: In the Color Picker, set all RGB color values to 230 to change white to light gray.

4. **Set the White eyedropper color to a light gray by typing** 230 **in each of the R, G, and B text boxes, and then click OK to close the Color Picker.**

   You can find the RGB value display on the right of the dialog box. (The R, G, and B values for white are always each 255.) To reset the White eyedropper to light gray, simply type values in the RGB text boxes. To set the eyedropper color to a light gray, you use 230 for all three RGB values, as you can see in Figure 11-13. (Alternatively, you can click and drag the circle in the color spectrum, but getting a precise value by dragging the circle is a little bit of a chore.)

   A change occurs in the before-and-after sample box at the top-right of the color box. At the top of this box, you can see your new color selection. (The bottom half of the box represents the default color before you made a color change.)

   After you click OK, the White eyedropper is now set to light gray.

5. **Much like you did for the White eyedropper, double-click the Black eyedropper in the Levels dialog box.**

   The same Color Picker opens again, except this time, the text over the Color Picker box says "Select target shadow color," and the target circle is on the bottom-left, set to full black (the RGB values are shown at 0, 0, 0).

6. **Type** 25 **in all three RGB value text boxes. Click OK in the Color Picker, and both eyedroppers are set and ready to go.**

After you've done this a few times, custom setting the eyedroppers takes about five seconds.

7. **Set the white point in the photo.**

The cheerleader uniforms have what seems to be pure white trim on the top. You can use that as your target area for the White eyedropper. (The cheerleaders' white socks and shoes would make good targets, also.)

Click the White eyedropper cursor in the Levels dialog box. Move the cursor to the photo and click the brightest white area you can find on the uniform. In Figure 11-14, we clicked on the uniform of the girl on the far right. (When you move the eyedropper to the photo, you can click anywhere in the photo to reset white to the area you click.) The eyedropper sets the value to a neutral light gray, and the highlights clean up nicely.

Figure 11-14: Click the White eyedropper in a bright area of the photo, the uniform of one of the girls.

8. **Set the black point in the photo by clicking the Black eyedropper tool in the Levels dialog box and then clicking the tall, black speaker, as shown in Figure 11-15.**

Set the black point to a known neutral black area to ensure all the color channels reasonably match each other for the main subject of the photo. The tall, black speaker cabinet in the background is a good choice because you know it's probably a neutral tone and it's in the same lighting as the cheerleaders.

Figure 11-15: Click the Black eyedropper in the darkest area of the photo, the speaker cabinet.

Note: If you notice any hue change in the highlights after you set the black point, click the White eyedropper on your highlight target again. If you guessed correctly for your white and black targets, the image color balance looks much improved.

9. **Manually set the white point by moving the white-point slider.**

   With the Levels dialog box still open, complete the edit by setting full white and black points.

   Note: Because you set the White and Black eyedroppers to light and dark gray to avoid tone clipping, you have to make a final, manual adjustment, using the white- and black-point sliders in Levels. This adjustment ensures the best possible tone quality in the file.

   Press Alt/Option to see a preview in Levels. Move the Levels white-point slider until you just begin to see a few white pixels in the white areas of the cheerleader's uniforms. The image should appear similar to Figure 11-16.

10. **Manually set the black point by pressing the Alt/Option key and moving the black-point slider until you see the first appearance of black in the main subject.**

    Move the black-point slider until you begin to see a few black pixels in the black areas just behind the cheerleaders. Ignore the shadow clipping on the ceiling because that area isn't important to the main subject. Your screen should appear similar to Figure 11-17.

Figure 11-16: Move the white-point slider until you see the first appearance of the girls' white uniforms.

11. **Make a Gamma adjustment by moving the Gamma slider to the left.**

    After Step 10, the file looks much improved, but wait: There's more to be done! The image looks a little too dark, so moving the Gamma slider to the left lightens it up nicely.

Figure 11-17: Move the black-point slider until you see the first appearance of black in the main subject area in the photo.

With the image lightened, you can see that the cheerleaders seem to be standing on neutral-colored mats.

12. **Click the Gray eyedropper in the Levels dialog box and click the foreground area on the mat (see Figure 11-18) to get a small improvement in the color balance for the main subject.**

Those mats must have been a true gray tone: The color balance is improved after the adjustment.

Figure 11-18: Click the gym mat with the Gray eyedropper to improve the color balance.

13. **Complete the Levels edit by clicking OK to save the changes and close the dialog box.**

Figure 11-19: A dialog box asks if you want to save the new target colors as defaults.

After you click OK, a dialog box appears (as shown in Figure 11-19) asking if you want to save the new target colors as defaults.

14. **Click No.**

Clicking Yes leaves your custom settings in place for any photos you open with Elements in the future.

If you click Yes by mistake, don't panic. Just open the White and Black eyedropper Color Pickers and reset them to full black (0, 0, 0) and pure white (255, 255, 255). Be sure to click Yes when the prompt appears again.

The last problem with this file is the strong, yellow saturation in the background. The gym must have had some sodium vapor lights back there. An adjustment with Hue/Saturation can help solve the problem.

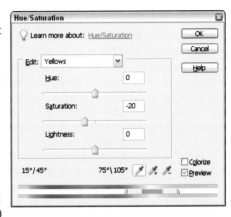

15. **Select Enhance⇨Adjust Color⇨ Adjust Hue/Saturation or press Ctrl+U (⌘+U for Macs) to open the Hue/Saturation dialog box.**

16. **Select Yellow from the Edit menu and drag the Saturation slider to the left.**

Moving the Saturation slider left to –20 percent (see Figure 11-20) brings the yellow saturation under control without affecting the main subject too much.

Figure 11-20: Edits in the Hue/Saturation dialog box help bring down the overly saturated yellow in the photo.

The final edited image appears in Figure 11-21.

Figure 11-21: After all that editing, these cheerleaders' color balance is in top form.

At first, you may find these edits take up a lot of time. With a little practice, however, making these kinds of edits can become second nature. The real key to working fast is carefully analyzing your file to determine what tools and steps you need to make corrections. After you know where you want to go with your corrections, making those corrections is a breeze.

Fine-Tuning with the Hue/ Saturation Command

In an ideal digital world, setting a perfect gray balance in your digital file would give you perfect reproduction of all the color captured in your photo. In the real world, you can seldom achieve perfect color-reproduction accuracy in digital imaging, but fortunately, you don't really need absolute perfection to get pleasing results. You don't usually have the opportunity to compare your final color output to the original scene captured, so you don't often notice small errors in hue reproduction.

Digital cameras have inherent hue-reproduction errors. Creating a camera profile that will work in all shooting conditions is almost impossible. Additionally, different brands and types of digital cameras each have their own unique color signatures, just as different color films had in the analog film photography days.

If you've worked hard to edit and color correct your file, but a memory color still doesn't look quite right, this is the section for you.

Figure 11-22 shows a snapshot from a theme park. We followed all the rules and tried to balance the file with methods we describe earlier in the book, but we wound up with a strange-looking sky.

Figure 11-22: This photo of a theme park castle looks less than royal.

The sky color has an excess of magenta (not enough green), and it just looks strange. All the other memory colors look just fine. If you try using Color Variations to produce a normal-looking sky, the rest of the image winds up with a greenish colorcast. We clicked twice on Increase Green in the Color Variations dialog box, and the photo ends up looking like Figure 11-23.

The solution to the problem lies in correcting only the blue-cyan portions of the photo because the other hues seem to look just fine. To perform this kind of edit, you need to use the Hue/Saturation command.

To follow these steps, download the `castle.jpg` file from the Chapter 11 folder of the Wiley companion Web site. To use Hue/Saturation to fix the problem shown in Figure 11-22, just follow these steps:

Figure 11-23: The photo as it appears after clicking twice on Increase Green in Color Variations.

1. **Open the `castle.jpg` file in Full Edit mode (Standard Edit on the Mac in Elements 4).**

2. **Open the Hue/Saturation dialog box by selecting Enhance⇨Adjust Color⇨Adjust Hue/Saturation or pressing Ctrl+U (⌘+U on Macs).**

3. **Adjust the blue hue to correct the sky color by selecting Blues from the Edit menu.**

4. **Click the left eyedropper to open the Color Picker and then click in the sky area to set the exact blue color in the Hue/Saturation command.**

Moving the Hue slider adds the adjoining primary color to the hue you select in the Edit menu in Step 3. The color gradient at the bottom of the dialog box shows you the degree of change your edits make, as does your image preview. Extreme moves of the Hue slider can change the target color you select into a completely different hue, making the Hue/Saturation command function just like the Replace Color command. (Hue/Saturation and Replace Color are really the same tool, but with differing controls.)

For color correction, you need to make only modest adjustments in Hue/Saturation.

To adjust the sky hue, first look at the color gradient at the bottom of the Hue/Saturation dialog box. The gradient color to the left (in the lower-left corner of the dialog box) looks more like the real color of a sky. The right side shows a more cyan hue that adds more green to the sky color.

5. **Move the Hue slider to the left until the sky looks right.**

That's all there is to it. All other blue hues in the photo similar to the sky receive the same color edit.

The blue spires on the castle also change color, as you can see in Figure 11-24.

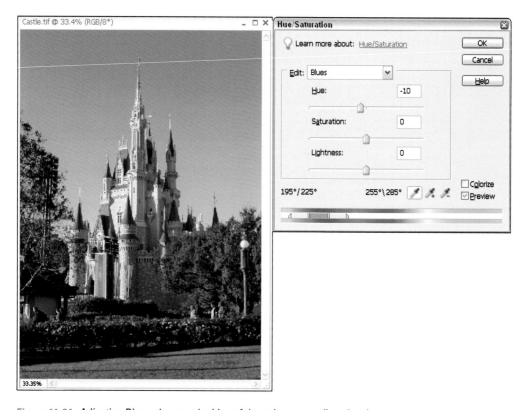

Figure 11-24: Adjusting Blues changes the blue of the spires, as well as the sky.

6. Adjust lightness and saturation by moving the Saturation slider to +58 and the Lightness slider to –67.

The sky now looks correct, and you didn't change the color balance in the rest of the image. You can also change the brightness and saturation of your target color at the same time, if you want. In the first edit, you color correct the sky. You can darken the sky and add a little more saturation to the sky's blue by adjusting the Saturation and Lightness sliders.

You can think of the Lightness slider as the Add White or Black slider. Keep in mind that any change you make to the targeted image color with the Lightness slider results in a loss of saturation (black and white have no saturation). Add saturation with the Saturation slider after you change the Lightness setting if you want to maintain the original amount of saturation in the target color. In our example, you make a large move of the Lighten slider toward darken, to +58, so you need a large move of the Saturation slider (–67) to add saturation to the resulting darkened sky. You can see the final edited image in Figure 11-25.

Figure 11-25: The photo after making all edits in Hue/Saturation.

Always do your best to bring a file into the best overall color balance before you resort to the Hue/Saturation command for local color-correction control, but feel free to use Hue/Saturation to fix a problem color in a file when all the other memory colors look normal.

Correcting Overexposed Saturated Files

Chapter 5 covers working with overexposed files. In this chapter, we want to talk about working with overexposed saturated images — we constantly hear about these kinds of problem images from amateur photographers.

Light-metering systems in point-and-shoot digital cameras vary a great deal from brand to brand. Some are pretty accurate, whereas others seem to have a tendency toward always shooting a little light or dark, depending on the camera.

You can usually edit underexposed photos far more easily because the important highlight detail is preserved; the viewer tends to see shadow detail, which you often lose in overexposed images, as less important than rich highlight detail.

Overexposed files can suffer from severe clipping in important highlight regions of the image; colorful subject matter combined with overexposure can create severe loss of tonal separation in the brightest saturated colors.

The best remedy for this problem is understanding your camera's default tendencies and modifying the camera setup properties to prevent the problem from happening. If you find that your camera tends to generally over- or underexpose your digital files, use the available metering system overrides to try to solve the problem.

If your pictures constantly come out overexposed, set your metering option to expose less, in general, for your photos. Most cameras have an option for setting exposure in plus (+) or minus (–) values, usually in $f\frac{1}{2}$ or full f-stop increments. Try setting the camera to a $f\frac{1}{2}$ f-stop (– $f\frac{1}{2}$) option and leave it there by default for general picture taking. Remember, the default setting isn't really correct if your photos always look too light and have blown-out highlights.

Inversely, if your photos come out too dark most of the time, you need to override the camera metering system to add a little exposure for most situations. Setting the override option to + $f\frac{1}{2}$ or 1 f-stop should solve the problem.

Remember, the correct setting is the one that works best for you and the kind of photos you like to shoot.

When your metering system fails or you're working with lighting conditions that leave you with an overexposed photo, you need to adjust the tonal balance. Figure 11-26 shows you a typical example of an overexposed, highly color-saturated image. The dark background fooled the camera metering system, and the foreground blossom was overexposed as a result.

If you like shooting pictures of flowers, you'll run into this kind of a problem a lot. Shooting flowers in full sunshine isn't really the best idea if you like doing close-ups — soft light works much better. But sometimes you don't have a choice and end up with an overexposed image. To correct an overexposed image, follow these steps:

Figure 11-26: This daffodil is overexposed and highly saturated.

1. **Open the photo `daffodil.jpg`, which you can download from the Chapter 11 folder on the Wiley companion Web site, and examine the histogram in Levels.**

   After opening the photo in Full Edit mode (Standard Edit on the Mac in Elements 4), press Ctrl+L (⌘+L for Macs). The histogram shown in the Levels dialog box in Figure 11-27 confirms some highlight clipping and lack of a full, rich black in the shadows.

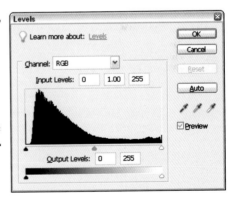

Figure 11-27: The Levels histogram shows a lack of full black, as displayed by the absence of tones on the left side of the histogram.

2. **Press Ctrl+3 (⌘+3 on a Mac) to open the Blue channel.**

   The daffodil blossom is mostly a very saturated yellow, so the blossom has almost no blue color. A quick check of the Blue channel in Levels (Figure 11-28) shows that there's no highlight clipping, so some unclipped tonal information is still in the photo.

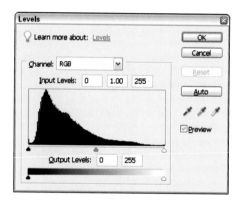

Figure 11-28: An examination of the Blue channel shows no highlight clipping and some shadow data in the histogram.

Wouldn't it be nice if you could transfer the Blue channel information to the clipped Red and Green channels? Well, you do have a way! You simply have to desaturate the file first before you begin any further editing.

A fully saturated color is one that's composed of just one or two color channels. The flower is yellow. Red and green make yellow on your monitor, so the blossom is almost all red and green. When we desaturate the file, Hue/Saturation has to add some blue to the yellow flower. Desaturation really just adds the complementary color. So, when you desaturate the file, Hue/Saturation takes information from the Blue channel and adds it to the Red and Green channels. You recover some of the lost tonal separation in the saturated yellow blossom.

3. **To desaturate the photo, open the Hue/Saturation dialog box (Ctrl+U for PCs, ⌘+U for Macs). Leave the Edit menu at the default selection of Master.**

4. **Move the Saturation slider to reduce file saturation by –40 percent.**

   The file looks very pastel at this point, but that's normal for this kind of file recovery. Don't worry; you can increase saturation if you need to later, after you finish your edit.

   After the desaturation edit, the histogram shows a nice recovery of highlight information. You can't see much highlight clipping in Figure 11-29.

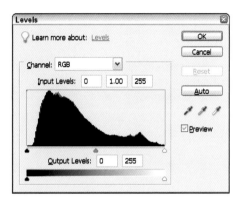

Figure 11-29: After the desaturation edit, the Levels histogram shows a nice recovery of the highlight information on the right.

5. **To adjust the Gamma, open Levels (Ctrl+L for PCs, ⌘+L for Macs), leave the black- and white-point settings as they are, and make a big Gamma slider move to the right, to 0.50, to darken the file.**

You need to enhance the highlight tonal separation as much as possible. You're just looking for a nice increase in tonal separation in the blossom, so don't worry about the overall darkness of the rest of the file. You can see the result of this edit in Figure 11-30.

The color saturation of the blossom increases a great deal after the Gamma adjustment. The Gamma adjustment, which you make to darken the image, increases contrast in the highlights. Increasing contrast

Figure 11-30: Making an extreme edit in the Gamma adjustment in Levels increases the tonal separation.

always results in increased saturation, unless you do the edit in Luminosity mode with a Levels adjustment layer, as we describe in Chapter 7. In this example, the saturation increase works in your favor.

6. **Click OK in Levels and select Enhance⇨Adjust Lighting⇨Shadows/Highlights. Move the Shadows slider to 50 percent. Leave the default settings for Highlights and Contrast at 0 (zero).**

   You need to make a Shadows/Highlights adjustment to recover shadow detail. Moving the Shadows slider opens the shadows up, but the picture's still a little on the dark side.

7. **Make some Levels adjustments for white point, black point, colorcast, and Gamma by following these steps:**

   a. **Click the Black eyedropper in Levels, leave it at the full black default setting, and click the dark shadow near the center of the image.**

   You can make the darkest portions of the background in this photo a full black tone because those dark areas are in deep shadow.

   b. **Pick the brightest petal you can find. Click the White eyedropper (leaving it at its default setting) and click the petal.**

   The small white flowers in the background are a good target for the White eyedropper.

   c. **Click around with the Gray eyedropper in Levels until you find just the right spot for a pleasing color correction to the slight cyan cast.**

   You can see all three sample areas in Figure 11-31.

   d. **Lighten the file slightly by moving the Gamma slider to the right, to 1.13, and click OK.**

Black eyedropper

Gray eyedropper

White eyedropper

Figure 11-31: Choose different areas of the daffodil image for the white, black, and Gamma adjustments.

8. **To pump up the saturation a little, open the Hue/Saturation dialog box (Ctrl+U on a PC, ⌘+U on a Mac) and move the Saturation slider to +10 percent, taking care to not overdo it and lose the tonal separation you worked so hard to recover.**

   You can see the result of the final edit in Figure 11-32.

Figure 11-32: The final edited image of the daffodil.

Correcting Color by Using Levels

Adobe created Photoshop Elements to provide a simplified and low-cost solution for digital image editing. Most of the color editing tools in Photoshop Elements give the user reasonable control of image color balance and tone characteristics, but they're limited by design. The full-featured Curves command in Photoshop is the best tone- and color-editing tool available, by far. Unfortunately, the Color Curves command in Elements is junk by comparison.

If Adobe added too many editing features to Elements, it could reduce demand for Elements' big brother, Photoshop. As a result, Elements doesn't contain the best controls available in Photoshop for precise manual color correction of your files, with one important exception: the Levels command.

The full-featured Levels command in Elements allows most of the color-balancing control available in Photoshop, but it's a little less handy to use than Curves. If you plan on moving up to the full version of Photoshop, figuring out how to use Levels as your main color-correction tool makes the learning curve much faster in Photoshop. Plus, you can use the Levels command in Elements as an adjustment layer. Add a Hue/Saturation adjustment layer, and almost all your editing needs will be met. (We talk about the advantages of adjustment layers in Chapter 7.)

Understanding the effects of adjusting color in Levels

The Levels dialog box allows you to select the individual Red, Green, and Blue color channels from the Channel menu at the top of the Levels dialog box. Each of the individual color channels contains its own Gamma slider. Moving the Gamma slider in a color channel dialog box changes the brightness of only the individual color channel selected and therefore changes the color balance of the entire file. This feature allows you to remove an unwanted colorcast from a file.

In principle, correcting a colorcast is simple. Either remove the color in excess or add its opposite (complementary) color. To understand the effects of moving the Gamma slider in individual color channels, take a look at Figure 11-33. This figure shows the results of selecting the three color channels and moving the Gamma slider left and right.

Here's what's going on when you make Gamma adjustments in individual color channels in Levels:

- **Red channel — Gamma left:** Select Red from the Channel menu in Levels and move the Gamma slider to the left. Only the Red channel brightens with a shift toward red.

- **Red channel — Gamma right:** Moving the Red channel's Gamma slider to the right darkens the Red channel, resulting in a shift toward cyan.

- **Green channel — Gamma left:** Moving the Gamma slider left in the Green channel shifts the image toward green.

- **Green channel — Gamma right:** Moving the Gamma slider right in the Green channel shifts the image toward magenta.

- **Blue channel — Gamma left:** Moving the Gamma slider left in the Blue channel shifts the image toward blue.

- **Blue channel — Gamma right:** Moving the Gamma slider right in the Blue channel shifts the image toward yellow.

Try to develop an understanding of how your image changes when you make Gamma slider moves in the individual color channels. After you know the effects of making these adjustments, you can effectively use Levels for color correction.

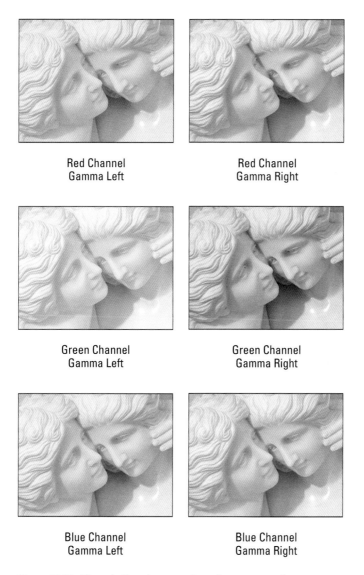

Red Channel
Gamma Left

Red Channel
Gamma Right

Green Channel
Gamma Left

Green Channel
Gamma Right

Blue Channel
Gamma Left

Blue Channel
Gamma Right

Figure 11-33: These ladies show you the colors you get when you move each channel's Gamma Slider left and right.

Color correcting a file with Levels

Adjusting color balance with Levels isn't really difficult, as long as you understand how to recognize a colorcast. After you try color correcting a file with Levels a few times, you'll find that reading about it takes far longer than just doing it.

If you've carefully calibrated your monitor for color according to the instructions in Chapter 3, you can eyeball the most pleasing color balance by using the color channel sliders in Levels. After you complete the basic Levels edits for the black and white point and the Gamma adjustment for overall image brightness (we talk about these edits in Chapter 10), you can then work to correct the colorcast. To correct the colorcast by using Levels, follow these steps:

1. **Open the file `interior.jpg` from the Chapter 11 folder on the Wiley companion Web site in Full Edit mode (Standard Edit in Elements 4 on the Mac).**

   The photo shown in Figure 11-34 is an interior photo shot for a design company. The white balance could use some improvement. The bright interior paint was a slightly warm white, but when viewed in Elements, the result looks obviously off color.

Figure 11-34: This photo of an auditorium has a red-yellow colorcast.

   The colorcast is red-yellow, although we aren't exactly sure of the hue proportions of the colorcast.

2. **To correct the colorcast, adjust the Red channel first by selecting Red from the Channel menu in Levels and then moving the Red channel Gamma slider to the right.**

   Move the Red channel's Gamma slider to the right, to 0.81, to remove most of the red cast from the image. (Moving the slider right removes red by adding cyan — red's opposite color.)

3. **To further correct the colorcast, adjust the Blue channel by selecting the Blue channel from the Channel menu in Levels.**

Moving the Blue channel's Gamma slider to the left, to 1.24, adds blue to the image, which neutralizes the yellow cast because blue is the opposite of yellow.

Now that you've removed the yellow component of the colorcast, you can see that the image still seems to have a little too much red, as shown in Figure 11-35.

Figure 11-35: The auditorium still looks a little too red after Red- and Blue-channel Gamma adjustments.

It's not unusual to have to work back and forth in the color channels to get the color balance just right. Because almost all colorcasts are a mix of two primary colors, you have to readjust as you go to get the color just right.

4. **Return to the Red channel by selecting Red from the Channel menu. Move the Red channel's Gamma slider a little more to the right, to 0.69, to further reduce the red cast in the image.**

The color balance of the image seems to be about as close as you can get to normal. The saturated blue color of the walls prevents an absolutely clean color balance because of blue light reflecting onto the more neutral surfaces, but the file looks pretty good to our eyes.

5. **Brighten the image by selecting the composite RGB channel from the Channel menu and moving the Gamma slider to the left, to 1.30.**

The heavy color editing dulled the original brightness of the image, so brightening the overall image improves its appearance.

In Figure 11-36, you can see the results of correcting a colorcast by using just the Levels dialog box.

Figure 11-36: The auditorium image is color corrected after edits in the Levels dialog box.

12

Camera Raw Color Correction

In This Chapter

▶ Getting a handle on camera raw features

▶ Putting the camera raw converter to work

▶ Processing camera raw files

▶ Returning to camera raw defaults

Camera raw is the file format used to capture and save all data that the camera's sensor can capture. This data is then processed by a special tool in Photoshop Elements called the *raw converter*. What's neat about camera raw is that you can process an image (which means you essentially make some settings adjustments and open the file in Photoshop Elements), and then you can go back and process the same raw image, using different settings.

Working with camera raw is sort of like having an opportunity to process film the traditional way, using chemicals and development time and, if you don't like the results, reverting the film to its state before it was processed and processing it again using a different development time.

Unfortunately, not all cameras support saving in camera raw format. Many of the consumer-grade point-and-shoot cameras give you only JPEG files saved to your media card. If your camera doesn't let you save in camera raw format, you can skip this chapter. But before you do, realize that camera raw gives you the best image to edit in Photoshop Elements. Why? Because it captures more data and provides you with many more editing options.

Understanding Camera Raw

We use the terms *raw* and *camera raw* interchangeably in this chapter. The term *raw* isn't an acronym that stands for anything: It's just a name for a file format. The file name extension can vary among the camera manufacturers, which often leads to a little confusion. File names ending with extensions such as `.crw`, `.mrw`, or `.nef` signify a raw format. The different camera manufacturers create these names, but the files all have common attributes. All the files are 16-bit images, and you need to convert the raw images in a raw converter.

Photoshop Elements provides you a raw converter when you install the program; therefore, you don't need special software to open a raw image.

Using the Raw Converter

If you're familiar with the basic image-editing controls in Levels that we cover in earlier chapters in this book, you'll find that the controls available in the raw converter are very similar. The only difference is the names given to the controls.

When you open a camera raw file in Elements (you can use any mode that you use to open files), the camera raw converter window, shown in Figure 12-1, opens first.

Some of the important tools in this window include the following:

- **Exposure:** This control works just like the white-point slider in Levels. The placement of the control determines the white point in your file. The same rules that you use when determining the best white-point placement in Levels apply when you set the Exposure slider. (See Part II for white-point adjustments with Levels.)

- **Shadows:** This control has the same function as the black-point slider in Levels. Its placement determines the black point in your file. You should exercise the same care with the Shadows slider as you do with the black-point slider when adjusting for best tonal range and shadow detail.

- **Brightness:** This control is really the Gamma control in the raw converter, and it works exactly like the Gamma slider in Levels. You use it to control overall image brightness.

- **Contrast:** This control changes the shape of the virtual tone curve in the raw converter.

White Balance eyedropper

Figure 12-1: A camera raw file is first opened in the Elements raw converter.

The Contrast slider works very much like the Curves adjustment layers we discuss in Chapter 7 and provide in the Chapter 7 folder on the Wiley Web site. A Contrast setting with a negative value reduces midtone contrast, very much like the Reduce Contrast adjustment layer. Setting the Contrast slider to a plus value increases midtone contrast and functions like the Increase Contrast adjustment layer.

✔ **Saturation:** This slider works exactly like the Master Saturation slider in the Hue/Saturation dialog box in Elements. Plus (+) values increase saturation, and minus (–) values decrease saturation.

As with the Hue/Saturation Master saturation control, a –100 value removes all color and produces a black-and-white image.

✔ **White Balance:** At the top-left corner of the raw converter, you can find the White Balance tool. This eyedropper works the same as the Gray eyedropper in Levels. The tool sets any area sampled in the raw preview to neutral gray. Similar to the Levels Gray eyedropper, you have to sample an area that's close to a real neutral value for the tool to work properly.

✔ **White-balance controls:** These controls have a number of options for color balancing your file. At the top, you have the White Balance presets. The White Balance menu offers a number of preset choices for your file's white point. (The White Balance menu is actually the overall color-balance control.)

- **Auto mode:** Elements averages all the colors of the file together and guesses at the correct color balance of the file. As a rule, the guess is never the optimum setting, but you can give it a try and see what happens, if you want.

- **Custom mode:** This mode is loaded by default when you use the White eyedropper, and it allows you to manually set the white balance with the Temperature and Tint sliders.

- **As Shot setting:** This setting preloads your digital camera's white-point setting.

Which preset should you use? That's easy. If the file color balance doesn't look quite right, try the different presets to see if one of them brings your file into a close color balance. Use the one that works best for the file.

If the file contains any identifiable neutral targets, use the White Balance eyedropper to set the color balance for you. If all else fails, you can use the white-point sliders (labeled Temperature and Tint) to bring the file close to where you want it.

Keep in mind that you don't have to get the file exactly correct before opening it in Elements. After the file is open, you can use the full range of color-balancing and tone-control tools in Elements to get the photo just right for your taste.

✔ **White-balance sliders:** You have two sliders for fine-tuning the white balance:

- **Temperature slider:** Changes the yellow-blue balance of your file.

- **Tint slider:** Changes the green-magenta balance of your file.

These sliders can seem a little clunky, compared to the RGB controls in Elements. If you need to manually adjust your white balance, we find that the best approach is to just get it close with the raw converter white-balance sliders and finish the color balance edit in Elements, using the easier RGB controls.

✔ **Depth:** One of the great advantages of working with camera raw files is working on 16-bit images. You have much more data to work with, and edits you make in the raw converter and the Levels dialog box are more forgiving. Adjustments you make to 16-bit files aren't as prone to destroying data as edits made on 8-bit files. As a matter of practice, keep the Depth menu (located in the bottom-left corner) on 16-bit when opening files from the raw converter.

✔ **Save:** When you look at the Save command, you may think that this control saves your adjustments and maybe opens the file in Elements. Not so. Clicking Save opens a dialog box in which you can save the raw image in Adobe DNG format. Because so many camera manufacturers create their own version of camera raw, Adobe developed the DNG (Digital Negative) format to try to create a standard. If you want to save a file in DNG format, click this Save button.

✔ **Open:** After making all your settings adjustments, click Open. The file opens in Elements in Full Edit mode.

To better understand the relationship between the adjustment sliders and the Levels tools, take a look at Figure 12-2.

In Figure 12-2, you can see the White eyedropper in the raw converter, on the right, connected to the midtone eyedropper in the Levels dialog box, on the left. The black-point slider in Levels matches the Shadows slider in the raw converter, the midtone slider in Levels matches the Brightness adjustment in the raw converter, and the white-point slider matches the Exposure slider in the raw converter.

The histogram in Levels differs from the one in the raw converter. The Levels histogram is a black histogram that describes the tonal range of your images. In the raw converter, you see a multicolored histogram.

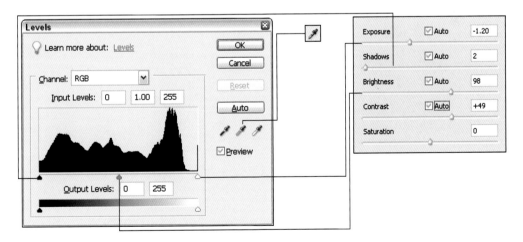

Figure 12-2: How camera raw tools match up with the raw converter tools.

In the Levels dialog box, you can select any one of the three RGB channels and view the data represented in each of those channels. Also, you can view the composite RGB channel in Levels. In the camera raw converter histogram, you can see a breakdown of data in the RGB channels represented by different colors in the histogram. The colors in the histogram represent the following data:

- **White:** White in the histogram shows pixels contained in all three RGB channels. This view is similar to the Levels histogram when you select RGB in the channels menu.

- **Red:** The red informs you of pixels that appear only in the Red channel, just as selecting Red in the Levels dialog box's Channels menu does.

- **Green:** Green represents pixels only in the Green channel.

- **Blue:** Blue represents pixels in the Blue channel.

- **Cyan:** Cyan shows you a combination of data in two channels. The Cyan color indicates an absence of pixels in the Red channel. So, Cyan shows a combination of pixels in the Green and Blue channels.

- **Magenta:** Magenta indicates an absence of pixels in the Green channel. Magenta shows a combination of pixels in the Red and Blue channels.

- **Yellow:** Yellow indicates an absence of pixels in the Blue channel, so Yellow shows you a combination of pixels in the Red and Green channels.

Some higher-end cameras, such as DSLR (Digital Single Lens Reflex) cameras, offer you a view of your picture in the LCD screen and an option to view the histogram for each picture in the same LCD screen. This feature is very helpful if you understand histograms and how they relate to tonal ranges.

Just like in the Levels dialog box, if you see the data slammed up against one side of the histogram with little data on the opposite side, you know your exposure is clipping data. After a quick preview on your camera's LCD screen, you can make some decisions about reshooting a file that you know will present some problems when you edit it in Elements. Perhaps changing the camera position relative to the lighting, using a different exposure value, adding flash, and so on might help get the exposure right.

We want to point out another set of adjustments in the raw converter dialog box. Click the Detail tab in the raw converter, and you find three adjustment sliders, as shown in Figure 12-3.

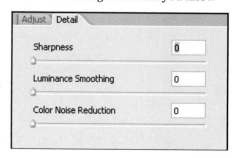

Figure 12-3: Clicking the Detail tab opens another pane that has more adjustment sliders.

The three options you have include Sharpness, Luminance Smoothing, and Color Noise Reduction. You use these sliders to adjust the amount of sharpness and reduce noise (artifacts) in your file. In Figure 12-3, we've pushed the sliders all the way to the left, so the raw converter makes no adjustments for these options.

You have some better options in Elements for sharpening and reducing color noise. As a default, keep these settings at a minimum and perform the adjustments after you open a file in Full Edit mode. This book is devoted entirely to tone, brightness, and color correction. We don't have the room to go into areas such as sharpening files and reducing color noise. For a good reference on making these adjustments, see *Photoshop Elements 5 For Dummies* by Barbara Obermeier and Ted Padova (Wiley Publishing).

Making Adjustments in Camera Raw

With all the settings adjustments you can make in the raw converter, you may find it difficult to know exactly where to start. You should make a good number of your corrections in Elements, using tools we describe in Chapters 5 through 11. You want to use camera raw only to get your tonal balance into a range where you have all the data you need to further edit a file effectively by using tools such as Levels, Hue/Saturation, Shadow/Highlight, and so on.

To follow the steps in this section exactly, download the `rawImage.CR2` file in the Chapter 11 folder on the Wiley companion Web site.

Follow these steps to edit a file in the raw converter:

1. **From Full Edit mode, select File⇨Open and open a raw file.**

   Figure 12-4 is a typical snapshot file taken with available light on a shaded porch. When you open the image in the raw converter, the auto settings make the picture look somewhat flat and dark.

2. **Deselect the Auto check boxes in the raw converter.**

   By default, all the Auto adjustment buttons are enabled when the raw converter opens. We usually turn them all off and make our edits from scratch, which gives us more control over the final edited image.

   If you shoot both camera raw and JPEG with your digital camera and you want a raw file to match your JPEG file, just turn off all the Auto options and open the JPEG file.

   The image brightness looks fairly close to normal, as shown in Figure 12-5. This tells us the camera exposure was close to correct.

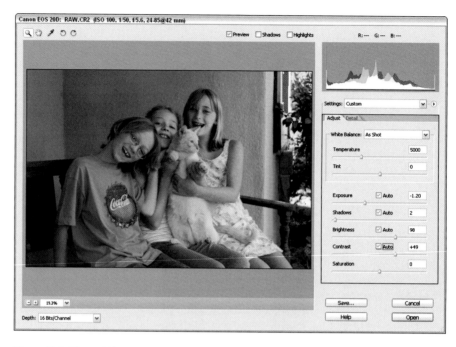

Figure 12-4: These kids and their kitty are displayed in the raw converter.

Figure 12-5: With auto correction turned off, the happy gang looks brighter.

The clipping preview is on, and the image preview shows some highlight clipping in the upper right of the image, where direct sunlight is falling on the wall of the house. If you plan to crop off that part of the image later, just ignore the clipping warning to the right and set your white point in relation to the main subject.

3. **Adjust the white point by moving the Exposure slider to the right to increase exposure.**

Moving the Exposure slider to the right has the same editing result as moving the white-point slider to the left in Levels. Move it too far, and you clip important highlight detail in important image areas of your photo. In our example, we went a little too far, and you can see the red clipping warning in the bright portions of the girl's dress, as shown in Figure 12-6.

Red clipping warning

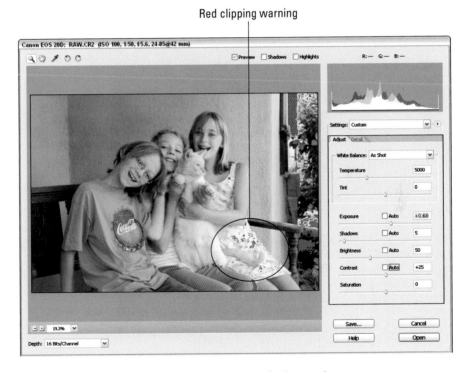

Figure 12-6: The red specks on the girl's dress are a clipping warning.

4. Fine-tune the white-point adjustment.

Usually, the first move you make for adjusting the white point (as you did by moving the Exposure slider in Step 3) gets you into a general range for setting the correct white point. If your first move isn't just right, move the slider farther or back it off, depending on the view you see in the image window. In this example, we moved the slider a little too much. We back off the Exposure slider a little until the clipping warning disappears on the dress, as shown in Figure 12-7.

Figure 12-7: Adjust the Exposure to eliminate the red clipping in the photo.

5. Adjust the black point by moving the Shadow slider to 2.

With the Shadow slider at 2, the shadow clipping warning disappears from the subject.

At the default 5 position on the Shadow slider, you can see some of the blue shadow clipping warning in the preview. To maintain as much shadow detail in the kids as you can get, back off the shadow slider to 2 or until the shadow clipping warning almost disappears from the main subject. We can't quite eliminate all the clipping, but we can get close, as you can see in Figure 12-8.

Figure 12-8: Adjust the Shadows, Brightness, and Contrast sliders.

6. Adjust brightness by moving the Brightness slider right to 60.

The Brightness slider is similar to the Gamma control in Levels. The image seems a little too dark, so you can lighten it up by moving the slider to the right, to 60. The Brightness slider works backward from the Gamma slider in Levels. Move the slider to the right to brighten rather than left, as you do with the Gamma slider in Levels. (See Figure 12-8.)

7. Adjust the contrast by moving the Contrast slider slightly to the right.

After you adjust the image brightness in Step 6, add a little more contrast to the image. A small move of the Contrast slider to the right makes the image contrast look just right, as shown in Figure 12-8.

Note: The Contrast slider in the Elements raw converter is a great tool. It works by modifying a virtual tone curve, and it gives excellent results. If you work with raw files in Elements, try to make your best contrast adjustment in the raw converter.

8. Adjust for color balance by moving the Temperature slider to the right.

The tonal editing is complete, so make a critical evaluation of the image color balance. In this photo, the image has a slightly cool cast overall (blue), so a small move of the Temperature slider to the right adds a little yellow to the image (Figure 12-9). The added warmth gives the photo the right mood, as shown in Figure 12-10.

Figure 12-9: Adjust the Temperature slider to remove a colorcast.

9. **Leave the Saturation slider in the default position.**

Never change image saturation in the raw converter because using the Hue/Saturation command in Elements gives you far better control over the final results.

10. **Click Open in the raw converter, and the file opens in Elements in Full Edit mode.**

You can see the results of the edits in Figure 12-10.

Figure 12-10: These four camera-raw characters look ready to be edited in Elements.

To see how the raw file compares to a JPEG file opened in Elements, compare Figure 12-10 with Figure 12-11. In Figure 12-11, we opened the same photo saved as a JPEG file. The JPEG file appears flat and out of color balance compared to the raw image.

Figure 12-11: The three kids and their cat as a JPEG, opened in Elements.

Working with Camera Raw Defaults

When you open an image in the camera raw converter and make settings adjustments to your file, the raw converter remembers the last settings you made. Therefore, if you want to open the raw file again in the raw converter, the last settings you used are shown in the converter window.

At times, you may want to start from scratch and apply new edits. The nice thing about using camera raw is that you can go back to the raw image in the raw converter and process your file a thousand times with different settings.

To start over again and change back to the default settings of a raw image, click the right-pointing arrow to the right of the Settings menu in the raw converter and select Camera Raw Defaults from the menu that appears. (See Figure 12-12.) Making this menu selection returns your file to the same view as when you first opened the file in the raw converter.

Figure 12-12: Select Reset Camera Raw Defaults to return to the default view of the raw image.

Part IV
Finishing Work

In this part . . .

This part is all about printing. In Chapter 13, we talk about printing pictures from several different color printers and show you all the controls you need to address when printing from these printers. Chapter 14 shows you how to use soft proofing to see how your printed pictures will look before you even print them.

13

Printing

After you correct your files' brightness, contrast, and color problems, you're ready to print your photos. You might output your prints to your own desktop printer or at a photo service center. For this chapter, we cover the aspects you need to know to print your files to desktop printers.

Just as you carefully prepare photos for corrections, you need to exercise care when it comes to printing. You have to select the right paper, understand how your printer works, and choose the right color profile.

In this chapter, you can discover how to optimize photos for printing, and you can get some guidelines for printing on a few of the more popular printers.

Preparing Files for Printing

You have many options for printing photographs. You can use your own desktop color printer or a mini photo lab, or you can even go to a service center that can print your photos with a variety of printing devices.

For your own desktop printing, you can choose to print files directly from either editing mode or the Elements Organizer. In this chapter, we stick to printing from the Full Edit mode (Standard Edit mode on a Mac).

Printing and image resolution

One of the most important aspects of printing your photos after you have them properly corrected for brightness and color is image resolution. You have three different resolutions to take into account: the resolutions of your camera (or scanner), your photos, and your printer. Remember that image resolution and printer resolution aren't the same, and they don't need to match up to each other when you print image files (at least not in a one-to-one relationship).

Here's what you need to keep in mind about the different types of resolution:

- **Camera/scanner resolution:** If you scan pictures, you need to look at the scanner resolution. Scanners often have two different resolutions. One resolution is the true resolution of your scanner and the other is the interpolated resolution. For example, say your scanner has a resolution of 1200/2400. The first figure (and always the lowest value) is the true resolution of your scanner. The second value is *interpolated resolution,* which means that the scanner upsizes the scanned image to create more pixels than the scanner can capture. For premium quality work, stick with the true resolution of your scanner.

  Digital cameras come in a variety of different resolutions. Most often, the price of a camera rises with the amount of resolution the camera can capture. Today, even the lowest-priced cameras start out at about 4 to 5 megapixels and go up from there. A 10-or-more-megapixel camera usually costs much more than a 4- to 5-megapixel camera. The camera resolution really determines how large a picture you can print. For 4-x-5-inch photo prints, any of the least-expensive cameras will work. But if you want to get prints of 16 x 20 inches or larger, look for a camera with a resolution of 6 or more megapixels.

- **Image resolution:** Image files are measured in pixels, so we often refer to a file's resolution as being measured in pixels per inch (ppi). What's the optimum ppi your printer needs to produce a quality print? That resolution might be 300 ppi or lower. Image resolution almost never needs to match device resolution. In other words, your Elements image doesn't need the same resolution as your printer is capable of producing.

  When you scan an image on a flatbed or slide scanner, the scanning software offers options to choose image resolution and size. You pretty much know, for example, you'll scan an 8-x-10-inch image at 300 ppi when you start your scan —at least that's what resolution you should use. With a digital camera, it's a little more confusing. A camera captures images at a particular size according to the number of pixels it can capture, but the resolution is always 72 ppi.

For example, you might have a camera that captures an image at 2000 x 1000 pixels. Another camera might capture an image at 3000 x 2000 pixels. Both images are 72 ppi, but when you resize the images in Elements, the image captured at 3000 x 2000 pixels produces a larger print than the other image at the same output resolution.

When you're using your own desktop printer, you may want to make many different test prints. If the optimum resolution of your printer is 300 ppi, you might be able to obtain satisfactory prints at resolutions as low as 200 ppi. Lowering the resolution enables you to print larger prints. Try to run some tests to find the resolution that produces the quality prints you're looking for, and you can determine how far you can go when you need to print larger prints.

✏ **Printer resolution:** Printer resolutions are perhaps the most confusing in the mix of the device resolutions. You hear printer resolutions such as 1440 x 720 from manufacturers, for example. This reference to the printer's resolution is a horizontal plotting value of 1440 pixels by a vertical resolution of 720 pixels. Printer drivers often let you change output resolutions at the time you print your files. Therefore, on a 1440 x 720 printer, you might be able to print 1404 x 1440 or 720 x 360. People often use the lower value for printing drafts and text documents.

Regardless of the resolutions your printer supports, realize that your file resolution doesn't need to match your device resolution. Just about any printer you use can print your photos at resolutions higher than your image resolution.

In this chapter, we use dpi (dots per inch) rather than ppi (pixels per inch) for the description of printers. Although the terms do represent slightly different measurements, they're most often used interchangeably.

Because you have three different resolutions to work with, the question you should consider is, "What resolutions should I use for my images to produce high-quality prints?" The one thing you can always control is the resolution of the file that your camera produces. You have little control over your camera's capture resolution, and you can't exceed the maximum resolution produced by the camera. (You may have an adjustment on your printer to choose from two or more different resolutions.) However, the real control you have is with your photo files — but only to a certain extent.

Changing image resolution

The last step you perform when printing files is setting the resolution of the image to the target resolution recommended by your printer manufacturer. You can find this value in the user manual for your printer. If you can't find any documentation on what resolution to size your images, you can use 300 ppi as a default with just about any desktop printer.

When you open the Print dialog box in Elements, you find options for scaling images to fit your paper. Although Elements provides you with scaling options, you always get the best results when you size your prints at a one-to-one ratio between image size and output size. For example, if you want to print a 5-x-7-inch image at 300 ppi, size the image to those dimensions and that resolution before you open the Print dialog box. If you try to print an 8-x-10-inch file at 600 ppi and later scale the image by using the Elements Print dialog box, you're sending more data to the printer than you need. Your image prints more slowly because the computer has to process more data. In addition, excessive resolution can actually degrade photos on most desktop printers.

To size images for output, follow these steps:

1. **Open an image in Elements that you want to print.**

2. **Select Image⇨Resize⇨Image Size (or press Alt+Ctrl+I for PCs, Option+⌘+I for Macs).**

   The Image Size dialog box, shown in Figure 13-1, opens.

3. **Deselect the check box for Resample Image.**

4. **Type a new width or height in the Width or Height text boxes.**

   As you type a value in the Width or Height text box with the Resample Image check box deselected, the image resolution shown in the Resolution text box changes in proportion to the setting you add to either Width or Height. As you type a higher number in either text box, the Resolution text box is proportionally lowered. When you type a smaller value in Width or Height, the Resolution goes up. If the Resample Image check box is selected, the resolution doesn't change.

   When you set either the Width or Height in the Image Size dialog box, the opposite value is proportionately sized automatically. For example, if you start with an 8-x-10-inch size and type **4** for the Width, the Height drops automatically to 5. Likewise, if you type **5** for the Height, the Width automatically drops to 4. Elements links these settings by default to prevent distortion of your image.

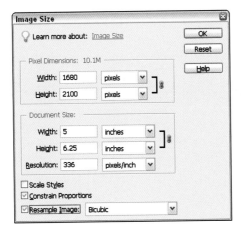

Figure 13-1: In the Image Size dialog box, you can size images for output.

5. **While still in the Image Size dialog box, select the Resample Image setting again and observe the value in the Resolution text box.**

   Is the value sufficient to get a quality print? If you drop far below the recommended resolution, you're trying to print a file larger than your printer can handle while still outputting a quality photo. You'd need to take another picture or scan another scan at higher resolution. For cameras, this might mean moving in closer to your subject. For scanners, you might need to boost the scan resolution.

   If the Resolution setting is larger than the recommended output resolution, you're in good luck. Just make sure the Resample Image check box is selected and type the output resolution you want in the Resolution text box. As you enter a value in the Resolution text box with the Resample Image check box selected, the Width and Height values stay fixed at the size you specify in Step 4.

6. **Click OK.**

   If you downsized your image in these steps, you'll see the photo in the Image window in Elements get a bit smaller. The file is downsampled to the resolution and size you set in the Image Size dialog box. You can recheck your settings by opening the dialog box again. Just press Alt+ Ctrl+I (Option+⌘+I for Macs), and the Image Size dialog box opens, showing your settings as the new default.

Cropping images

As we mention in the preceding section, if you set either the Width or Height in the Image Size dialog box, the opposite value is proportionately sized automatically. Elements links these settings by default to prevent distortion.

When you size photos for output, most often, one dimension isn't sized properly for the output size. For example, if you have an 8-x-10-inch image and you want to print a 4-x-6-inch photo, you can open the Image Size dialog box and set the Height for 6 inches. But doing so results in the Width automatically dropping to 4.8 inches. In order to get the size reduced to the exact dimensions you want, you need to crop the image. In this example, you would need to cut off the excess .8 inches from the width.

Follow these steps to crop a photo:

1. **Open the Image Size dialog box (Alt+Ctrl+I for PCs, Option+⌘+I for Macs) and type a value for the Width or Height. Leave the Resample Image check box deselected.**

   Make sure you type a value in either the Width or Height that results in an image size in the corresponding value that's larger than the size you actually want for that value. For example, if you want a 4-x-6-inch print, be certain Width is larger than 4 or the Height is larger than 6. You need to make one of the settings the exact size and the other larger than needed.

2. **Click OK, and the image is resized while preserving the image resolution.**

3. **Click the Crop tool.**

4. **In the Options bar at the top of the Elements window, type a value in the text box for the dimension that needs cropping.**

   For example, if you sized an image to a 6-inch height and need to crop off some width, type **4** in the Width text box in the Options bar, as shown in Figure 13-2.

5. **Drag the Crop tool across the full dimension of the setting you added to the Image Size dialog box in Step 1.**

   In this example, we draw the Crop tool to extend from the top to the bottom of the image to capture the full height. The width shows some area outside the crop dimensions because that's the data we're cutting off, as you can see in Figure 13-2. Note that the target crop region is represented by a dashed line in Figure 13-2.

Click the Crop tool button

Figure 13-2: Use the Crop tool to resize your image, cutting off a portion of the height or width.

6. **Press the Enter/Return key to crop the image.**

When you move the cursor inside the rectangle that you draw with the Crop tool in Step 5, the cursor changes to an arrowhead. You can click and drag the arrowhead cursor in the rectangle to decide what you want to crop off. When you're happy with the cropped image the rectangle surrounds, press the Enter/Return key.

7. **Open the Image Size dialog box again (Alt+Ctrl+I for PCs, Option+⌘+I for Macs) and take a look at the value in the Resolution text box.**

   Make sure you have sufficient resolution for your output and select the Resample Image check box.

8. **Type a resolution value that matches your optimized output resolution. (Use 300 ppi if you don't know the requirements of your printing device.) Click OK, and your file is ready to print.**

You may wonder about the settings for Width, Height, and Resolution in the Options bar. Yes, these options do exist, and you may think that you can bypass visiting the Image Size dialog box by just typing values in the Options bar when you use the Crop tool. In some cases, using the Options bar dimensions works fine. In other cases, you can inadvertently upsize your file. For example, if you start with an image of 4 x 5 inches and you want to crop to 5 x 7 inches at 300 ppi, the image resolution at the 5-x-7-inch size might drop below 300 ppi. The Options bar doesn't tell you that. The image will be cropped and upsized to 300 ppi without you knowing it. Using the steps in this section is a surefire way to be certain that you're not upsizing your images.

Converting Color

Printing your pictures and getting the color right requires knowing how to manage color at print time. You can choose to let Elements convert color from your workspace (sRGB or Adobe RGB) to your output profile, or you can convert to a color output profile yourself and then print the file.

You might convert color to an output profile when you're printing a proof print on your desktop inkjet printer for a file that you want to submit to a service center. If you have the appropriate color profile, you might want to print a test print (if you also have paper samples of material your commercial vendor uses) or preview a print on your calibrated monitor before sending it off to the service center.

We cover the actual steps for converting color to output profiles back in Chapter 4. After you convert color and save the file with the printer profile embedded, you go about printing the file much differently than printing files without converted color.

Printing to Epson Inkjet Printers

Print settings vary according to manufacturers, and we can't hope to cover all printers in this chapter. We discuss Epson printers as an introduction to printing to desktop color printers, but we also show some print options for HP and Canon low-end inkjets in sections later in this chapter.

 If you own a different brand of printer or use a service that uses other printers, just keep the process we outline in this chapter for printing your files in mind. Regardless of what type of printer you own, you need to know when to use a color profile and how color is either managed or not managed. You may have different check box selections and menu commands, but the general process is the same for any printer you use to print your photos.

Over the last few years, at least half of the many service-provider troubleshooting tech calls clients have made involved problems with accurate color output from Epson and some other inkjet printers. We're not talking about subtle changes between monitor and printer, but huge monstrous, color changes on output prints. As it turns out, almost all the strange output results originated from just one minor error the users made when setting up a file to print, involving either the when or how of managing color in the Print dialog box.

The settings we discuss in this chapter can help you get accurate results without stress or frustration. Just remember to use the settings exactly as described. When you use the proper settings, you can achieve superior results with either desktop or professional printers.

To help clarify and simplify the rules for the various types of profile usage, here's a quick summary:

- **Automatic profile selection:** This option is designed for novice users who want a simple means of printing without having to decide what profile to use. Use sRGB or Adobe RGB (1998), choose Printer Color Management from the Profile menu, and use the color controls in the printer driver dialog boxes. We detail this option in the following section.

- **Photoshop Elements Color Conversion:** You use this method when you want to make the profile selection yourself, but you want to choose from a list of generic profile types created for printing to a particular kind of paper. You might have profiles you download from vendor sites created for a line of papers, such as Kodak's Glossy Photo Stock papers. You have an advantage when you use this method or the following one because you can convert the color by using the target profile and then soft proof the image onscreen. (We cover soft proofing in Chapter 14.) Select the profile for your specific paper in the Print dialog box and choose Relative Colormetric for the Rendering Intent. Use the Relative

Colormetric setting as a default for all your photo images. Turn off all color management. We detail this method in the section "Selecting a printer profile manually," later in this chapter.

✔ **Converted color:** Use this method when you convert color by using a utility, such as the Dry Creek Photo Profile Converter or an AppleScript. Select Same as Source and use No Color Management in the printer driver. We detail this option in Chapter 4.

Using automatic profile selection

When you install your printer driver, the installation utility also installs a number of color profiles. You can choose those profiles in Photoshop Elements' Print dialog box and control all the printing by using the profile provided by your printer manufacturer.

You have a choice for how these profiles are used. You can select the profile in the Print dialog box, or you can choose an automatic method, in which the manufacturer created a no-nonsense process of automatic profile selection by using your printer driver. The color profile is automatically selected when you choose the paper source.

We want to explain the automatic method to you and let you know that it exists, but we don't recommend you use it for your printing. Among other things, you really can't tell by looking in the Print Preview dialog box what profile you're using to print your file. In addition, you don't have a way to convert your working-space color to the device profile for accurate soft proofing. (We cover soft proofing in Chapter 14.) But you should understand what goes on when the selection is made to be aware of some potential consequences.

The color engines in Photoshop Elements, ICM (Image Color Management in Windows), Colorsync (on the Mac), and the Epson Print Driver work in a similar manner, although they all show subtle differences when used to convert a file. For our setup instructions, we use the Epson Color Engine and work with an unconverted file, letting the printer driver automatically select the color profile. Our unconverted file is a photo still in its native color space, such as sRGB or Adobe RGB (1998). Assuming your file is open in Elements and you've already sized your file for the target dimensions and resolution for output, the following sections show you how to print from the native color space.

Printing in Windows

Here's how to print from Windows:

1. **Choose File⇨Page Setup. In the Page Setup dialog box that appears, select the orientation of your print (either Portrait or Landscape), as shown in Figure 13-3.**

Figure 13-3: Click the orientation matching your photo in the Page Setup dialog box.

2. **Click the Printer button in the Page Setup dialog box to open a second Page Setup dialog box.**

3. **From the Name menu, select your printer, as shown in Figure 13-4.**

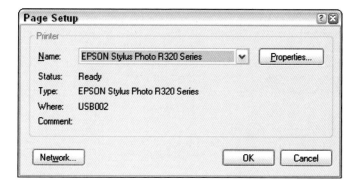

Figure 13-4: Choose your printer from the Name menu.

4. **Click OK in the second Page Setup dialog box to return to the first dialog box. Click OK in the first dialog box to close it, too.**

5. **Select File⇨Print to open the Print Preview dialog box.**

   By default, the Color Management options are hidden in the Print dialog box. To display choices for managing color and selecting printer profiles, select the Show More Options check box in the Print dialog box.

6. **From the Printer Profile menu at the bottom of the dialog box, select Printer Color Management, as shown in Figure 13-5.**

   This choice uses your current workspace color and will convert the color from your workspace to the printer output file when you open the print driver dialog box.

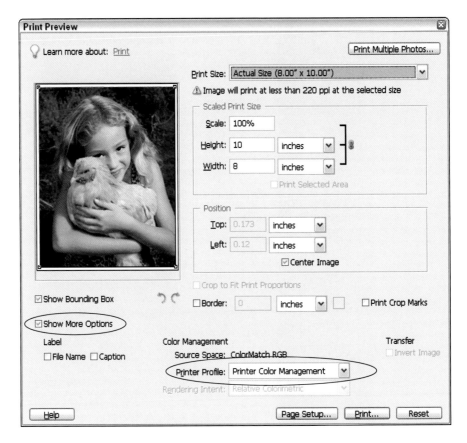

Figure 13-5: Select Show More Options and select Printer Color Management from the Printer Profile menu.

7. **Click the Print Preview button in the Print dialog box.**

   The file doesn't print yet. Instead, the Page Setup dialog box that appeared second in Step 2 opens again.

8. **Verify that your target printer is still selected and click Properties to open the print driver dialog box.**

9. **Set print attributes.**

   Each printer displays a different dialog box after you click Properties in the Page Setup dialog box. Figure 13-6 shows you the Epson Stylus Photo R320 Series Properties dialog box. Although many Epson printers use an identical dialog box, some Epson printers, especially the high-end devices, display different dialog boxes. Furthermore, printers from other manufacturers may appear with completely different settings in the print driver dialog box.

   For our Epson example, select Premium Glossy Photo Paper (or whatever kind of paper you're using) from the Type menu and click the Best Photo radio button, as shown in Figure 13-6.

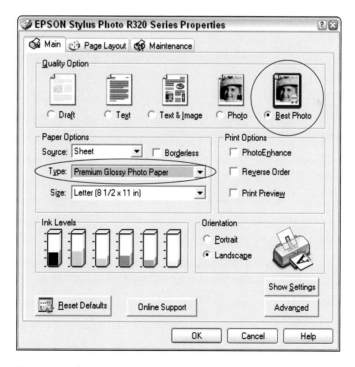

Figure 13-6: Select the paper type and Best Photo when you're printing photos.

10. To color manage your output, start by clicking the Advanced button.

Color managing your file is critical in your print-production workflow. For the Epson printer, click the Advanced button, which opens a warning dialog box. Simply click Continue to open the Advanced Settings dialog box, as you see in Figure 13-7.

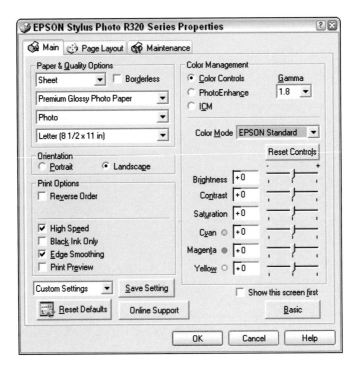

Figure 13-7: Click Advanced, and then click Continue to access the advanced settings in the Epson print driver.

11. Make the following choices in this dialog box:

- **Select a paper type under Paper & Quality Options.** The second menu in the Paper & Quality Options section of the dialog box determines what profile the printer will use for its automatic selection. Choose the same paper here that you did back in Step 9.

- **Turn color management on by clicking the Color Controls radio button.** This setting tells the print driver to automatically select a printer profile for the paper type you select.

- **From the Color Mode drop-down menu, choose Epson Standard.** Be certain to not use Epson Vivid. This choice produces inferior results on photos.

If you frequently use the same settings to print files, you can save your settings by clicking the Save Setting button.

12. Click OK, then click OK again in the print dialog box, and your file is sent to your printer.

The color is converted automatically from your source workspace of sRGB or Adobe RGB (1998) to the profile that the printer driver automatically selects for you.

Printing on a Macintosh

On the Macintosh, the Epson printer driver offers you some different settings, although the process is quite similar to that of printing from Windows (which we detail in the preceding section). Again, we're going to show you the automatic method for color conversion and let the print driver handle the conversion.

The Elements dialog box settings are the same for the Mac as you use in Windows. You make a choice for paper orientation and choose Printer Color Management in the Elements Print dialog box, just like Windows users. After you click the Print button in the Elements Print Preview dialog box, things begin to change. Follow these steps after you identify orientation and printer profile:

1. Click Print to open a second Print dialog box, shown in Figure 13-8. From the menu below Presets, select Print Settings.

The choices that the menu, shown in Figure 13-8, gives you are specific to your printer type. If you use a printer other than Epson, or even certain models of Epson, your menu choices will look different than the choices in Figure 13-8.

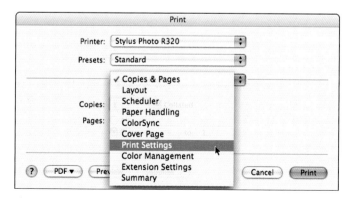

Figure 13-8: Select Print Settings from the menu.

2. **In the Print dialog box (with Print Settings selected), select the paper type from the Media Type menu.**

3. **Under Mode, click the Advanced radio button and select Best Photo from the Print Quality menu. (See Figure 13-9.)**

   You may have some other options for Quality if you're using a different brand printer. If so, choose the best quality from the list you see in the menu.

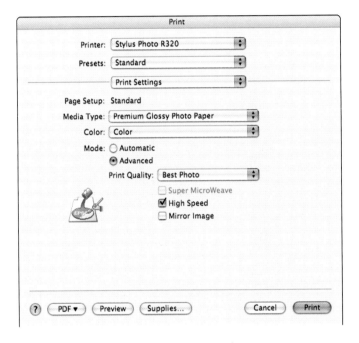

Figure 13-9: In the Print dialog box, you can choose settings for the best print quality.

4. **To select the color management method, select Color Management from the menu that shows Print Settings in Figure 13-9, as shown in Figure 13-10.**

5. **Select the Color Controls radio button and select Epson Standard from the Mode menu.**

   Selecting the Color Controls radio button tells the Print Driver to manage the color.

6. **Click Print, and the file prints with an automatic color conversion from your workspace color to the printer color profile.**

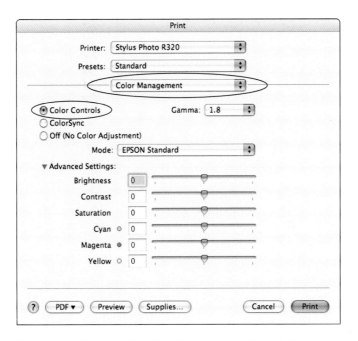

Figure 13-10: You can adjust the color of your print in the Color Management menu in the Print dialog box.

Selecting a printer profile manually

You can also manage color when printing files by selecting a printer profile manually from the available list of color profiles that were installed with your printer. The preceding sections use the printer to manage color (when you select Printer Color Management); this time, let Photoshop Elements manage the color. Again, the Windows options and Macintosh commands vary a little, so we discuss how to print by selecting a profile for each operating system.

Printing with a printer profile in Windows

The steps for setting up the page and selecting a printer are the same as those described in the section "Using automatic profile selection," earlier in this chapter. The steps change when you let Elements handle the color conversion, and you follow these steps in the Print dialog box:

1. **From the Printer Profile menu in the Print Preview dialog box, select the color profile designed for use with the paper on which you've chosen to print your image.** *Note:* Follow Steps 1–5 in the "Using automatic profile selection" section earlier in this chapter and start with this step after selecting your page size and printer name.

In this example, we use a heavyweight matte paper color profile, as shown in Figure 13-11. (Custom color profiles you acquire from a profiling service come with recommended color-rendering intents. For the paper in this example, Relative Colormetric is recommended and is selected in the Rendering Intent menu, as you see in Figure 13-11.)

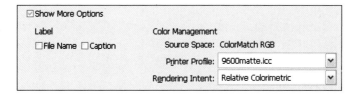

Figure 13-11: Choose a printer profile that matches the paper you use.

2. **Click Print, and the second Print dialog box opens. Click the Properties button (refer to Figure 3-4), and you arrive at the dialog box shown in Figure 13-7.**

3. **Select Best Photo from the Print Quality menu and then, from the Media Type menu, select the recommended paper choice.**

   Custom color profiles come with guidelines for selecting proper paper.

4. **Click the Advanced button and click Continue to arrive at the dialog box shown in Figure 13-7.**

   The paper choice selection is automatically carried over from the Properties dialog box (from Step 3).

5. **Click the ICM (Image Color Management) radio button and select the Off (No Color Adjustment) check box, as shown in Figure 13-12.**

   If you don't turn color management off, you end up double-profiling your print. For more on double profiling, see the sidebar "Problems with a magenta shift."

6. **Click OK and click OK again in the first Print dialog box to print your file.**

Figure 13-12: Choose the ICM radio button and turn off color adjustment to let Elements manage the color.

Problems with a magenta shift

If your photos have a strong shift toward magenta and the people in your photos look like they've been lying in the sun too long, you're *double profiling* your output. One of the most common problems with the Epson ink sets, either pigment or dye inks, is that a file converted for Epson output often has a strong magenta shift. It seems that an equal mix of all the inks produces a green-gray color. When converted, the magenta file bias tunes out this green balance of an equal ink mix, which is why a double-profiled file always has a strong magenta bias.

You can check to see if your file will print with a magenta shift before you actually print the file.

To see the magenta bias in a converted file, convert any small Elements file to an Epson output profile, such as Premium Glossy Photo Paper, by using the Dry Creek Photo Profile Converter (Windows) or an AppleScript (Mac), as we discuss in Chapter 14. Open the file in Elements and select File➪Save for Web. If a warning dialog box opens informing you that the image size exceeds the size that the Save for Web command was designed for, just click Yes to ignore the warning. Because Save for Web isn't profile aware, the magenta shift comes through nicely in the Save for Web dialog box.

Printing with a custom profile

Printing with a custom profile is very simple. Just remember that you must use the profile with the exact same settings you used to print the test target when the profile was created. For custom profiles, you *never* use color management throughout the output process.

Put another way, when you generate your test target for the profiling service from which you may order a custom profile for your printer, the service requires that you print the target without color conversions of any kind. The target has to reflect the actual colors generated by your printer, from a known sample file and using a known printing condition and media type, with no modifications whatsoever. The resulting profile tells the color engine exactly how to modify the output data to match the colors as closely as possible to your working space or a different, previously embedded color profile.

For all this to work properly, you can't allow the printer to modify the printing data in any way. Photoshop Elements has to do all the work.

If you've obtained a custom profile from a media supplier, you must use the specific media and intent settings they recommend for your printer, but you can follow all other instructions in this section.

So, if you have a custom profile ready to use, follow these steps to set it up:

1. **Use a profile converter, which we discuss in Chapter 4, to convert color.**

   In Windows, use a utility such as the Dry Creek Photo Profile Converter. On a Mac, use an AppleScript.

   If you create your own profiles for the same media, or you load profiles for each new media order from your paper supplier, add the creation date as part of the profile name. You can easily get confused if you have a number of profiles that you use for the same media and you haven't had time to delete the old profiles. Using the date in the file name helps you always select the right profile until you have time to delete old profiles.

2. **Open the converted file in Elements and then open the Print dialog box by selecting File⇨Print.**

3. **In the Print dialog box, select Same as Source for your Printer Profile, as shown in Figure 13-13.**

4. **Turn color adjustment off as you see in Figure 13-12.**

   Figure 13-13: Select Same as Source when printing files with converted color.

   Use the same settings for printing that we discuss in the earlier section, "Printing with a printer profile in Windows" to determine color. Be certain to turn Color Management off again, as well. (Refer to Figure 13-12.)

Printing to HP Inkjet Printers

Regardless of the printer you use, the process for printing follows the same logic. Unfortunately, each manufacturer uses different dialog boxes and different menu command names that can leave you completely confused if you try to apply one printer's steps for printing to a different printer.

The three methods for managing color (letting the printer driver determine color, letting Elements determine color by selecting a specific color profile, and printing files with converted color) apply to all printers, but the dialog boxes, buttons, and menu choices look different.

The critical steps you need to be concerned about when printing files is the profile selection, the paper selection, and when to turn color management off. If you own an HP printer, you probably know where to make your paper selection and your best photo selection. The most obscure setting is likely to be the color management choice. Rather than take you through each step for printing to an HP low-end desktop printer, the following sections take a look at how to manage color on your HP printer.

Printing to HP printers in Windows

Again, you have three choices when it comes to your printer's color:

- ✔ **Let your printer determine color.** Select Printer Color Management in the Print dialog box and click the Advanced tab in the printer driver dialog box that appears. Click Graphic and click Image Color Management. From the ICM Method menu, select ICM Handled by Printer, as shown in Figure 13-14.

- ✔ **Let Elements determine color.** Select a color profile in the Print dialog box and select ICM Disabled on the Advanced tab.

- ✔ **Print a file with converted color.** Select Same as Source in the Print dialog box and select ICM Disabled in the Advanced tab.

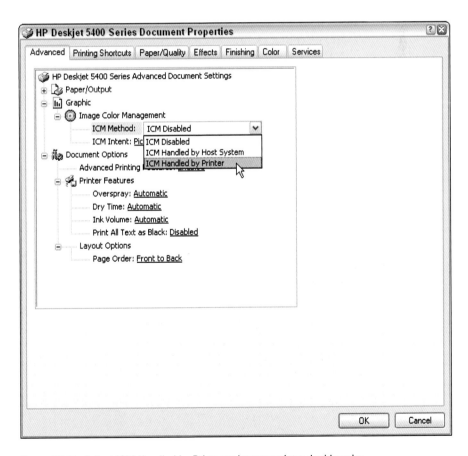

Figure 13-14: Select ICM Handled by Printer to let your printer decide color.

Printing to HP printers on a Macintosh

If there's a way to manage color on the Mac by using one of the HP Deskjet 5400 Series of printers, we haven't found it. HP and Windows go together like bread and butter, but using an HP printer with a Macintosh computer leaves a lot to be desired. Among the problems with using an HP printer on a Mac is that you can't turn color management off. Therefore, the only surefire method to print to an HP printer on a Mac is to let the printer manage the color. Don't attempt to use a specific color profile and don't try to convert color before printing.

When you open the Print dialog box, select Printer Color Management and click Print. In the HP printer driver dialog box, select the Paper Type/Quality from the menu below Presets and choose your paper type. Use only HP papers and make a selection for the HP paper type you use, as shown in Figure 13-15.

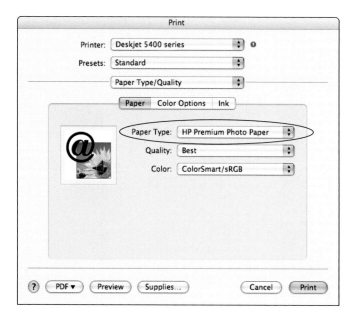

Figure 13-15: Select an HP paper in the Paper Type/Quality menu.

Because the printer driver determines the options in the Mac OS X Print dialog box, you don't have an option for color management like you do when you use a printer such as an Epson. With the HP printer driver, you don't get any color management options.

Printing to Canon Printers

When printing to a Canon printer, follow the same logic we talk about for Epson and HP printers earlier in this chapter and choose to either enable or disable color management. With Canon color printers, the area in the print driver dialog box is even more hidden than in Epson and HP desktop printers.

Printing to Canon printers in Windows

Control color management in one of these three ways:

- **Let your printer determine color.** Select Printer Color Management in the Print dialog box (click Properties in the Print dialog box) and select the Manual radio button under Color/Intensity in the Main tab, as shown in Figure 13-16.

  Click the Set button (in the Color Intensity area) to open the Manual Color Adjustment dialog box. Check the box for Enable ICM (Windows Image Color Management), as shown in Figure 13-17.

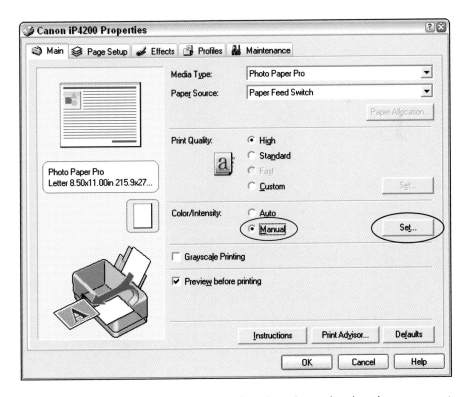

Figure 13-16: Click the Manual radio button for Color/Intensity to select the color management settings.

✔ **Let Elements determine color.** Follow the same steps as in the preceding bullet, but uncheck the Enable ICM (Windows Image Color Management) check box.

✔ **Print a file with converted color.** Select Same as Source in the Print dialog box and uncheck Enable ICM (Windows Image Color Management).

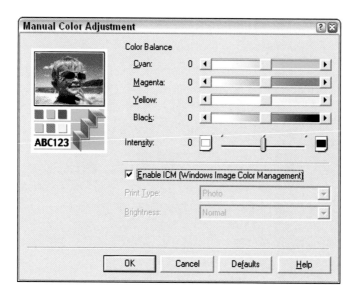

Figure 13-17: Check Enable ICM (Windows Image Color Management) to leave the color up to your printer.

Printing to Canon Printers on a Mac

You make the same choices on a Mac as you do in Windows for how you want to manage color on a Canon printer. If you want to let the printer manage the color, click Print in Elements and select Quality & Media from the menu below the Presets menu. The Quality & Media dialog box appears, as shown in Figure 13-18. Make a paper choice in the Media Type menu.

From the menu below the Presets menu, select Color Options, and then from the Color Correction menu choose BJ Standard when you want to let Elements determine color, None when you want to select a printer profile in the Elements Print dialog box, or Same as Source when printing a file with converted color. You can see the options in Figure 13-19.

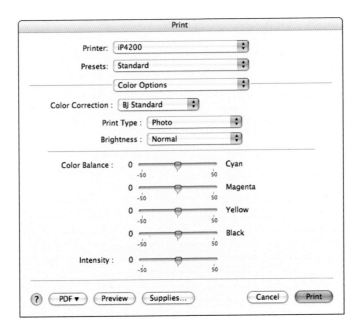

Figure 13-18: In the Quality & Media dialog box, you can choose your paper.

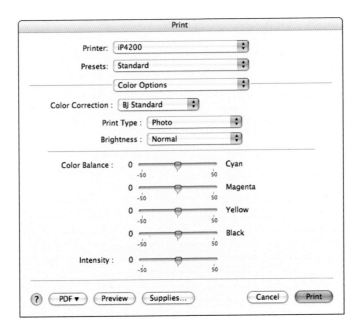

Figure 13-19: After selecting Color Options, you can determine the color yourself or have Elements do it for you.

Renaming Color Profiles

If you download a custom color profile or create one by using a color calibration system, you have to leave the profile name the same as the download or file you created. Changing the name of a color profile on your desktop nullifies the profile, and it doesn't appear in your list of profiles in the Print dialog box.

Mac users have an advantage because they have an easy way to rename a color profile that keeps the profile working properly and appearing in the Print dialog box. To rename a profile on the Mac, follow these steps:

1. **Open the folder in which you store your profiles and click the profile name once so the name becomes highlighted.**

2. **Type a new name for your profile.**

   You can find an AppleScript called Rename profile in your Scripts folder (`Macintosh HD/Library/ColorSync/ Scripts`).

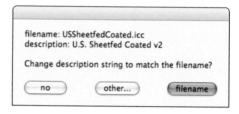

3. **Drag your renamed profile to the Rename profile script.**

   The dialog box shown in Figure 13-20 opens.

   Figure 13-20: To make your profile name change official, click Filename.

4. **Click the Filename button, and the dialog box closes.**

   Your profile now works properly with the new profile name.

If you don't run the AppleScript after renaming the file, the computer renders the file unusable.

Printing Contact Prints

A good way to proof files while conserving consumable materials is to print contact sheets. You can select a number of images in the Organizer and print the selected images on one or more sheets. When you print contact sheets, view your files in the Organizer, where you can easily select multiple files.

For contact sheet printing, don't bother to size your files in one of the editing modes. Contact sheet printing is the exception to the rule of sizing images for print. You can choose files of any size and let Elements size the files at print time. Sizing all the photos to small thumbnails and saving duplicate copies is much more time consuming than having Elements do the work for you.

To print a contact sheet, follow these steps:

1. **Open the Organizer by clicking the Organize button in the Shortcuts Bar in either editing mode.**

   Or you can open the Organizer when you first launch Elements and click the View and Organize Photos button in the Welcome screen.

   You should have already edited the files you select for printing for brightness and color corrections.

2. **Select the photos you want to print.**

   Hold down the Ctrl key (the ⌘ key on Macs) and click the photos you want to add to your selection.

3. **From the Organizer window, select File⇨Print.**

   The Print dialog box opens.

4. **Select Contact Sheet from the Select Type of Print menu. (See Figure 13-21.)**

   Below the menu, you can see an option for the layout.

5. **Type the number of columns you want in the Columns text box.**

   Elements automatically calculates the rows for you based on the number of columns you choose. As you increase the number of columns, you can print more images on a single sheet, but the images are smaller. If you're printing to check color, don't make the prints too small. About four columns is the most you can put on your contact sheet to see sizes large enough to examine color.

6. **Select the boxes to add Date, Caption, and Filename text labels to your contact sheet.**

   Selecting Filename makes filenames appear on the contact sheet, so you can more easily reference the files.

7. **Click the More Options button to access the More Options dialog box, shown in Figure 13-22.**

   You select the profile in this dialog box when printing contact sheets.

8. **From the Print Space menu, select the profile you want to use.**

   Follow the guidelines outlined throughout this chapter.

9. **Click OK in the More Options dialog box and then click Print in the Print dialog box.**

   Your printer driver dialog box opens, in which you can make choices for color management. Use the options for printing that relate to your printer profile choice. (We cover printer profile choices earlier in this chapter.)

Figure 13-21: You can choose how many images you want to include on your contact sheet under Select a Layout.

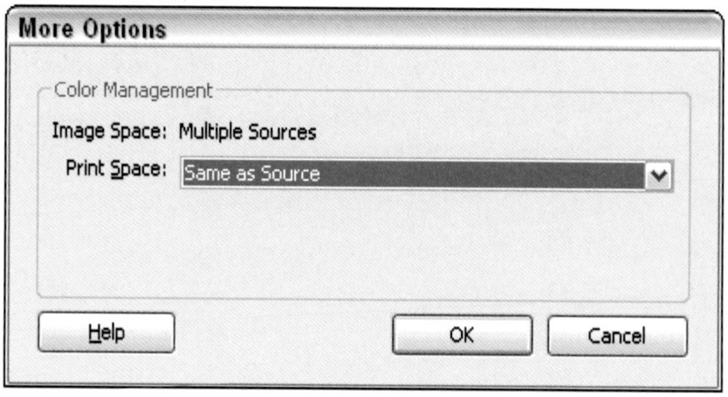

Figure 13-22: Select a color profile from the Print Space menu.

Choosing Paper and Inks

Photographers have always been concerned with the archival quality of prints when printing to inkjet printers. In the early days of the inkjet printers, you were lucky to get a lifespan of six months before your prints started to fade — a condition not acceptable to any photographer. As inkjet manufacturers improved their research and development, the inks have greatly improved, too.

Many inkjet printers support one of two kinds of inks:

- **Dye-based inks:** Dye inks were the first to appear for inkjet printers. The original inks had very poor archival qualities, but they printed more brilliant colors than the pigmented inks. Today, dye-based inks have much better archival qualities, and they still print more brilliant colors than the pigmented inks. But the gap is rapidly narrowing.

- **Pigmented inks:** Pigmented inks stay usable much longer than the dye-based inks (manufacturers claim pigmented inks have more than 100 years of life). When pigmented inks were first introduced, they tended to clog the heads on inkjet printers, and the colors weren't close to what the dye inks could offer in terms of saturation and brilliance. Newer pigmented inks flow easily through the heads on inkjet printers, and the color saturation has been greatly improved.

With the proliferation of so many different inkjet printers for consumers and pros, the printer manufacturers and paper suppliers developed an incredible array of different products. Most common are the photo-quality papers that appear similar to photo papers that photo finishing labs use. In addition to a variety of different coated stock photo-quality papers, you can find specialized material, such as Mylar, canvas, watercolor, LexJet, adhesive, matte, translucent, and so on. The list is long, and you have an abundance of choices.

Ideally, you should have a color profile for each paper you use. Papers have, among other things, different absorption responses that affect the color saturation. Be certain to make the paper selection that the paper or printer manufacturer recommends when you print to any paper. And be prepared to run many tests.

Soft Proofing Color

Soft proofing is a way of examining a file on your monitor before you print it. Creating soft proofs can save you materials and supplies. If your monitor is well calibrated and shows an accurate rendition of a printed piece, you can view files in the color space of your printer and, with a reasonable degree of accuracy, determine if your photos will print with the proper color.

In this chapter, we talk about soft proofing as a way to hopefully save you a bunch of money on paper and ink purchases for your desktop color printers.

Understanding Soft Proofing

What is soft proofing? *Soft proofing* means generating an exact monitor view of your printer output before you actually send it to the printer. If you go to the trouble of obtaining custom profiles for your printer or want to see the exact result of using your printer's driver profiles, soft proofing provides a preview of your printed output. (If you're unfamiliar with profiles, flip to Chapter 4, where we introduce how output profiles work and how to get custom or developer-created profiles.)

Note: Some of the newest Epson desktop printers don't allow you to access the profiles shipped by Epson, so you're out of luck unless you're trying to soft proof a custom profile.

Soft proofing is especially important if your file contains a lot of highly saturated color because hue errors are most common as you reach the limits of
your printer's color gamut. (For an explanation of color gamuts, see Chapter 1.)
Best of all, soft proofing saves money! You can catch printer output problems
before wasting expensive paper and ink. Of course, accurate soft proofing
depends on having a well-calibrated monitor. (We explain how to calibrate
your monitor in Chapter 3.)

Converting to an Output Profile

Soft proofing is one of the best features of a color-management workflow.
Unfortunately, Adobe didn't include this very important feature in Elements 5.
At the present time, you need Adobe Photoshop to get this feature as a menu
command.

To soft proof with Elements, you need to use a workaround. Elements has the
same accurate monitor compensation that Adobe Photoshop does. If you
open a file with an embedded printer output profile, the monitor compensation kicks in and shows you a very accurate soft proof view.

To make this work, you must convert the file to the printer output profile
outside of Elements and then open the file in Elements, which essentially provides you with the soft-proof file. You need to convert color to your printer
color, and with a well-calibrated monitor, what you see on-screen after converting to the printer color is what you'll get when you ultimately print the
file. The conversion process in Windows is different from that on a Mac, and
you can find steps for each operating system in the sections that follow.

The file you convert will be permanently altered. To keep your master file
intact, create a duplicate of your file. If you like the look of the soft proof, you
can save the duplicate as your printing file.

You may want to convert color not only for soft proofing a profile, but also to
get a file ready for printing to your home printer or at a printing service. If
you're soft proofing to check colors before sending your file or files to a printing service, by following the steps in one of the following sections, you then
have the color converted when you're ready to actually print. Chapter 13
covers printing in detail.

Converting color in Windows

In Windows, you can download a free utility from Dry Creek Photo that will
convert color from a workspace profile to a color profile. As an example,
assume you want to print some pictures at a discount store, such as Costco,

and you want to check how that store's profiles will impact your color and be certain you use the correct profile for the photo equipment that prints your pictures. You want to convert color from your color workspace (in this example, sRGB works best) to the profile for a photo printer and paper you want to use.

Before get starting with the conversion, download the utility by going to `www.drycreekphoto.com/tools/profile_converter` and clicking the link for `ProfileConverterSetup.zip`. After downloading the file to your hard drive, double-click the Setup file and follow the brief steps in the install wizard.

The Dry Creek Photo Web site (`www.drycreekphoto.com`) is one of the best sources of information available for color management and color profiling. In addition to offering custom color-profiling services, Dry Creek Photo hosts a number of different color profiles for many different commercial printers.

When you finish installing the Dry Creek Photo converter, follow these steps to prepare a file for soft proofing before sending it to a photo service, such as Costco:

1. **Make all the necessary edits you need to make in Elements and save your files in TIFF format.**

   You must use TIFF format to use the converter.

2. **Download color profiles from your photo service's Web site.**

   Almost all service centers post color profiles for their printing equipment. You can visit the Costco Web site at `www.costco.com`, click the Services link on the home page, and click Photo Center on the next page. You're prompted to set up an account, and then you come to a page on which profiles are listed. Costco makes the profiles available for stores in their geographic regions, and you usually find profiles for printing on their equipment and profiles best suited for different papers. This is something you need to pay attention to. If several profiles are available for downloading, be certain to use the right profile for the paper you want your pictures to be printed on.

   If you use a photo lab that wants you to convert color and embed profiles, you can visit that lab's Web site and download profiles, as well.

3. **Copy the profiles to your system color folder:** `C:\WINDOWS\system32\spool\drivers\color`.

   This is the folder in which all your color profiles are stored.

4. **Choose Start⇨Programs⇨Dry Creek Photo⇨Profile Converter⇨ICC Profile Converter.**

   The ICC Profile Converter dialog box opens, as you can see in Figure 14-1.

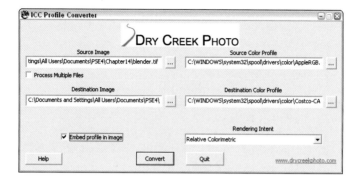

Figure 14-1: You can select the options for converting a color profile in the Dry Creek Photo ICC Profile Converter dialog box.

5. **Click the Source Image ellipsis (. . .) and select the source file.**

   The source file is the file you saved in TIFF format that you want to print.

6. **Click the Source Color Profile ellipsis and select the source color profile.**

   This is the color profile that's currently embedded in your source file.

7. **Click the Destination Image ellipsis and select the folder in which you want to save your file.**

8. **Click the Destination Color Profile ellipsis and select the color profile that your photo service's equipment uses.**

   You saved your color profiles to the Windows color folder, so be certain to look in this folder for the target printer color profiles.

9. **If you want to process multiple files, check the box for Process Multiple Files.**

10. **Be certain to check the box for Embed Profile in Image and then click the Convert button after you select all the options you want.**

    After you click Convert, the profile converter handles the profile conversion and saves your files to the target folder. See the section "Viewing the Soft Proof," later in this chapter, for details on proofing the color.

Although you need to convert your file to a TIFF to use the Dry Creek Photo utility, many consumer printing labs require you to send files in JPEG format. You can convert your file from one format to another and still keep the profile embedded in the image. We discuss working with profiles and file formats, including how to convert a file from one format to another, in Chapter 4.

Converting profiles by using operating system tools on a Macintosh

For Mac users, you don't have to look far when you want to convert color spaces in your photos. Mac OS X has a number of AppleScripts that few people know about. You can convert profiles for images just like Windows users who work with the Dry Creek Photo utility. On the Mac, follow these steps when you want to prepare files for a service, such as the Costco photo center:

1. **Make all the edits you need to make in Elements and save your files in the format that your service center needs.**

   In many cases, service centers use JPEG files. If you intend to print your pictures to your own desktop printer, use the TIFF format. Also, be certain to use sRGB or Adobe RGB (1998) as your workspace and save your files with the workspace embedded in the images (see Chapter 4 for how to save your photos while embedding a workspace profile).

2. **Open the AppleScripts ColorSync folder (which you can find by clicking through the following folders: `Macintosh HD/Library/ColorSync/Scripts`).**

   AppleScripts are mini programs installed with your operating system and custom scripts you can create with the AppleScript Editor (which is also installed with your operating system installation). On Mac OS X, a number of short scripts are installed that allow you to convert color spaces in files saved in the JPEG or TIFF format. To find the scripts used for converting color profiles, open `Macintosh HD/Library/ColorSync/Scripts`.

3. **Locate the script to convert the color in your photo(s).**

   Open the ColorSync folder and identify the scripts used for converting and embedding color output profiles. You have two choices, as shown in Figure 14-2. You can use either the Embed Chosen Profile or Match to Chosen Profiles script.

   If you have your files saved with the same color workspace profile, such as sRGB, and you want to convert the color to a specific output profile, use the Embed Chosen Profile script. If you want to identify a source profile (such as another profile that might have been saved with your file) and convert to an output profile, use the Match to Chosen Profiles script.

   If one script produces an error while it's attempting the conversion, use the other script.

4. **Drag a file (or files) to the script icon.**

   If you want to convert multiple files, select them from a folder in which you saved your files and drag the files on top of the script icon. You can process many files at the same time by dragging a selected group to the script icon. In this example, we use the Embed Chosen Profile script.

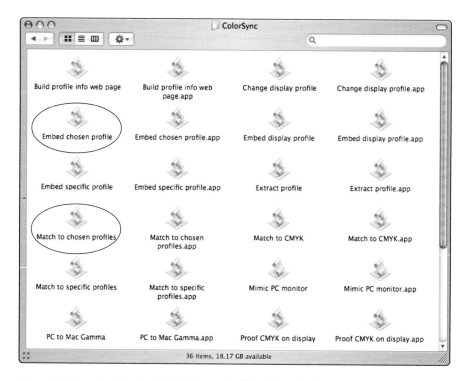

Figure 14-2: Locate either the Embed Chosen Profile or Match to Chosen Profiles icon.

5. Convert to an output profile.

The script makes it easy to identify the source and destination profile. If you use the Match to Chosen Profiles script, you need to identify a source profile when a dialog box prompts you. If you use the Embed Chosen Profile script, you're prompted to identify only your output profile.

Figure 14-3: You're first prompted to confirm your profile conversion.

Assuming you saved all your images that embed either the sRGB or Adobe RGB (1998) color profile, drag the files to the Embed Chosen Profile icon, and the dialog box in Figure 14-3 opens.

6. Click OK in the dialog box shown in Figure 14-3.

The Choose a File dialog box opens, as shown in Figure 14-4. The AppleScript automatically opens the folder in which your color profiles are stored.

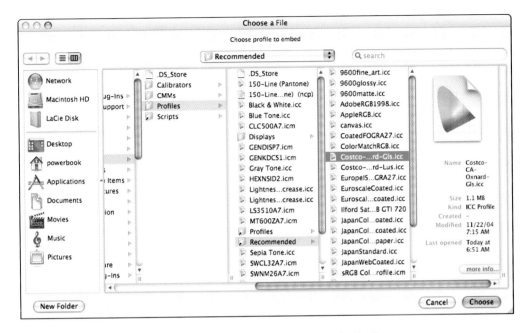

Figure 14-4: Select the output color profile that you want to use from the Profile menu.

7. **From the Profile menu, select the profile you want to use and click the Choose button.**

That's it! Your file is converted to your chosen output profile.

Viewing the Soft Proof

After you convert the color to an output color profile (which we talk about in the preceding sections), it's time to soft proof your image. Follow these steps to soft proof your image:

1. **In Elements, select Edit⇨Color Settings.**

The Color Settings dialog box, shown in Figure 14-5, opens.

2. **Click the radio button for Always Optimize Colors for Computer Screens and then click OK.**

3. **Open the file that you converted to an output color profile.**

What you see on-screen is what your printer will produce — simple as that, assuming you converted the file to the correct color profile.

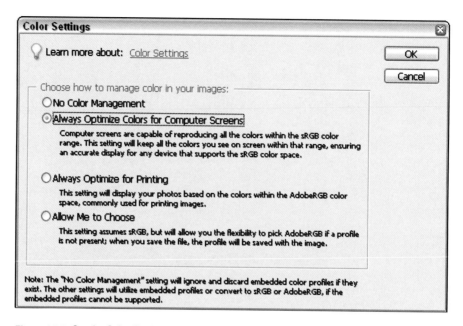

Figure 14-5: Set the Color Settings to Always Optimize Colors for Computer Screens.

4. Check the color profile in the image.

At the bottom of the image window, click the right-pointing arrow to open a menu, as shown in Figure 14-6. Select Document Profile from the menu options. The current color profile appears to the left of the right-pointing arrow. Verify that the file you're soft proofing contains the printer profile you intend to use for your printer and paper.

Be aware that soft proofing by using one of the profiles you received with your printer isn't always accurate because of manufacturing variations. Give the soft proof a try and see if the printer-provided profile is accurate. Sometimes, it is. In other cases, the color match isn't very close at all.

The profiles shipped with your printer are generic in nature. They're a kind of average for your printer, but they're not specific to your printer the way a custom-made profile is. A well-made custom profile gives you a soft-proof view that matches your print output very closely.

If you want to print the converted file that you just soft proofed, be sure to use the Same as Source setting and no color adjustment in the Elements Print dialog box, as we describe in Chapter 13.

Figure 14-6: Check your file's printer profile with the menu in the Image Window.

The lack of a soft proof feature in Elements 5 is the main reason we recommend using sRGB as your color workspace. The *color gamut* (or range of colors) in the sRGB space is much closer to most inkjet and photo paper gamuts than is Adobe RGB. For this reason, your monitor view will tend to be the most accurate without a soft-proof option.

Part V
The Part of Tens

In this part . . .

*T*he Parts of Tens section offers you some tips for how to get the best tone and color in your images, and it also gives you a look at getting more professional with your color-correction work.

In Chapter 15, we provide ten tips for better tone and color. In Chapter 16, we give you ten solid reasons why you might want to look at Adobe Photoshop for an upgrade. You can do a lot with Photoshop Elements, but if you intend to work professionally in photography, you might want to look at some of the reasons Photoshop can really help you out when it comes to tone and color corrections.

15

Ten Tips for Better Tone and Color

In This Chapter

▶ Using a calibrator and gray cards

▶ Shooting in proper lighting and using backgrounds

▶ Using Curves adjustment layers

▶ Working with high-bit images

▶ Editing important content

▶ Using filters

Correcting tonal balance and color in your pictures is always an easier job if you start off on the right foot. To make your tonal and color adjustments easier, you need to keep a few things in mind *before* you start shooting pictures. A little planning goes a long way in getting your pictures edited for the proper color balance.

Calibrating Your Monitor

We can't stress the importance of calibrating your monitor enough. You paid a fairly low price for Photoshop Elements — or you might have obtained a copy free with your digital camera. A very low-cost calibration device is an essential purchase if you intend to color correct any kind of photo. For the best deals, visit online resellers and pick up either the Pantone Huey or the ColorVision Spyder2express calibration device for as low as $69 U.S. Set up your computer monitor before you engage in any kind of color editing and run a lot of test prints to be sure that your output matches your monitor view. You can find details about how to calibrate your monitor in Chapter 3.

Using a Gray Card

Gray cards are sold at photo suppliers and used by professional photographers. These cards help you identify neutral grays when making tone and color adjustments. You can purchase a booklet of several gray cards, like the QPcard sold at www.calumetphoto.com, for a low cost. Keep the booklet of cards in your camera bag and use them when shooting your pictures. Follow these steps when shooting pictures, especially portraits:

1. **Set up your lighting for the photo shoot.**

2. **Have your subject hold a QPcard, as shown in Figure 15-1.**

3. **Shoot a second shot using the exact same lighting conditions of the subject without the QPcard.**

Figure 15-1: Shoot a photo with a subject holding a QPcard.

4. **When you open your photos in Elements, open both images. Use the Levels midtone sampler to sample middle gray in the photo with the QPcard while working on the photo without the card.**

   This method insures you of always having a neutral gray to sample when adjusting for brightness using Levels. In Chapter 10, you can find details about working with the Levels midtone sampler.

Or Using the GretagMacbeth ColorChecker

A more expensive solution for adding a prop to your photos for finding neutral grays is the GretagMacbeth ColorChecker. It costs more at about $69 U.S., but this card offers you not only neutral gray in a color swatch but a spectrum of colors that you can view to check the color on your monitor. You can find the card at online resellers such as `www.calumetphoto.com`. Like the method with the QPcard, shoot a scene with the GretagMacbeth ColorChecker and then shoot another scene without the color checker. You can use the middle gray swatch for sampling midtone grays as well as a number of other colors in the chart shown in Figure 15-2.

Figure 15-2: Shoot a photo with the GretagMacbeth ColorChecker.

Shooting Pictures in Proper Lighting

Shooting pictures in well-balanced lighting for normal exposures makes your editing job in Elements much easier. Try to avoid harsh background lighting whenever possible. When shooting portraits or people shots against harsh backgrounds, follow these steps:

1. **Move in close to your subject and take a light reading of the subject's hand, arm, or face.**

2. **Note the exposure reading and set the same reading to a manual exposure.**

3. **Move back and take your picture, ignoring all the background lighting.**

4. **When you edit your photo in Elements, adjust tone and color for the foreground subject.**

The background light might be overexposed, but your subject should be properly exposed, making the skin-tone corrections in Elements much easier. See Chapter 9 for the details about correcting skin tones.

Shooting Photos against a Background

Outdoor lighting can be a blessing or a curse. If you shoot outdoor portraits and you're not concerned about background areas, take a black cloth and a white cloth in your camera bag. Have someone assist you by holding the cloth behind a subject when you take a portrait photo. You'll find isolating the subject much easier, as well as making tonal and color corrections an easy editing job.

Using Curves Adjustment Layers

We uploaded two Curves adjustment layers to the Wiley companion Web site. (See the Introduction for details about the Web site.) Curves adjustment layers are found on the companion Web site, and you can use the layers provided for increasing and decreasing contrast.

If you want a little more contrast and brightness control, solicit a little help from a Photoshop user. You can request Curves settings to

✐ Darken a photo and increase contrast.

✐ Darken a photo and decrease contrast.

✐ Lighten a photo and increase contrast.

✐ Lighten a photo and decrease contrast.

Here's how to go about it:

1. **Ask a friend who is an accomplished Photoshop user to help you out.**

2. **Request the friend to create the four Curves adjustment layers on four separate low-resolution files.**

   These are basic S curves that accomplished Photoshop users know how to create.

3. **Open a photo in Elements needing one curve adjustment or another and open the respective file with the Curves adjustment layer.**

4. **Drag the adjustment layer to your photo.**

5. **Use the Opacity slider to increase or decrease the amount of Curves adjustment you want to apply to your image.**

For more information about using Curves layers, see Chapter 7.

Shooting in Camera Raw

Not all cameras are capable of shooting camera raw files. When you have the resources, purchase a camera that is capable of shooting in camera raw if your current camera does not support the format.

When shooting your pictures, set the camera to capture both JPEG and camera raw. Don't worry about memory use — media cards are cheap. You'll have a duplicate photo for all your shots. When you need to do some serious editing for tone and color corrections, open the raw files in the raw converter.

Editing 16-Bit Images

If shooting camera raw or scanning photos, keep your photos in 16-bit mode and make all your tone and color adjustments.

In Photoshop Elements, some tools under the Enhance menu are not capable of editing 16-bit images. Ignore these options and use the tools that permit you to edit in 16-bit mode. After editing and sharpening images, reduce the bit level to 8-bit just before printing.

Editing for Content

Not all the content of a photo will always be important to you. You might have areas of a photo that appear overexposed or underexposed that don't detract from the main subject area. This is especially true with photos having overexposed backgrounds. You can target just the important content areas for your tone and color adjustments and reduce the distracting portions of the photo with some simple edits. Try following these steps when you have photos with uneven lighting:

1. **Determine the important part of the photo.**

   If you have a subject in the foreground that's the most important part of the image, focus your edits on that portion of the image.

2. **In Photoshop Elements, open the Levels dialog box and press the Alt/ Option key as you drag the black-and-white sliders to adjust the tones.**

   Disregard the distracting portion of the image and look for the first appearance of black and white only in the content you're interested in to set the black-and-white points for the important content.

3. **Correct color for skin tones or other matter using the Hue/Saturation and Levels tools.**

   Don't worry about the distracting background colors. Just focus on your important subject matter. Chapter 9 covers correcting skin tones in more detail.

4. **Create a selection on the background.**

   It might be easier to first create a selection on the foreground, and then inverse the selection for the background.

5. **Add a slight blur (Filter⇨Blur⇨Gaussian Blur) to the background to diffuse it.**

   The foreground subject appears more prominent in the photo.

Using Filters

Some cameras have lighting controls that help you balance lighting for different white balances, such as fluorescent lighting. Some cameras don't have the settings needed to make the proper adjustments for accurate white points. If you have problems balancing lighting, you can purchase a filter to correct white balance. For an inexpensive solution, follow these steps:

1. **Visit an online photo supplier and look over the filter options they offer you. Find the filter you need to control the white balance for your photo shoots.**

   A number of filters are sold as gels that you can cut and tape over your camera lens. These are much less expensive than glass filters you screw onto the lens.

2. **Cut a piece of the gel and tape it over your flash, as shown in Figure 15-3 — or when shooting outdoors, tape the gel over your lens.**

Figure 15-3: A gel taped over a flash to correct for white balance.

3. **Make several test shoots at different exposures to determine exposure compensation.**

4. **Open the photos in Elements.**

5. **Record the exposure settings that produce the best results and use these when shooting in similar lighting conditions.**

16

Ten Reasons to Upgrade to Photoshop

*I*f you're a serious amateur or professional photographer, you should consider upgrading to Adobe Photoshop. Photoshop does have some additional tools to help you manage color and make color correction much easier and more precise. In this book, we push Photoshop Elements beyond its purpose by creating workarounds and tasks the program wasn't designed to do, just to help you develop some professional methods for color and tone corrections. With Photoshop, you work with a program that was designed to be a professional color correction tool and therefore doesn't require you to create workarounds.

We offer only a preview of what Photoshop can do in this book. For details about working with Photoshop's advanced tools, check out *Photoshop CS2 All-in-One Desk Reference For Dummies,* by Barbara Obermeier (Wiley).

Using the Curves Dialog Box

Photoshop Elements 5 has a new feature for using Curves; however, the Curves commands in Elements are a very simplified version of the Curves tools that appear in Photoshop. In Elements, you're limited to preset Curves adjustments for controlling brightness and contrast. In Photoshop, you have the control that changes tone levels along the 256 distinct grays in an image, in all three channels.

Having the control over the tone points in your images lets you fine-tune adjustments for lightening and darkening an image and adding or reducing image contrast. There's really no substitute for Curves adjustments when you're color correcting images and adjusting tone levels for brightness and contrast adjustments.

You can open Curves by selecting Image➪Adjustments➪Curves or create an adjustment layer in Photoshop and select a Curves adjustment layer. When the Curves dialog box opens, you see the options shown in Figure 16-1.

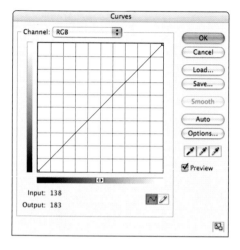

Figure 16-1: The Curves dialog box in Adobe Photoshop.

From the Channel drop-down menu, you can select the RGB channels, as well as the composite RGB channel. Click the curve line to plot points and move those points up, down, left, and right to make tonal adjustments.

Generally, Curves settings are confusing to the most advanced user, but you can easily understand Curves with a little study. You use six primary Curve shapes to make some brightness and contrast adjustments. The six basic shapes include

✔ **Darken:** Note the gradient along the left side of the dialog box where white appears at the top. To darken an image, click the center of the diagonal line and move the point toward the black end of the gradient (down). This move darkens the overall image. (See Figure 16-2.)

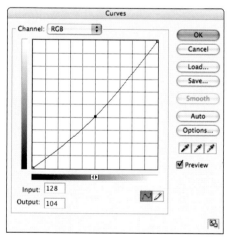

Figure 16-2: Move the center point toward the black end of the gradient to darken the photo.

✔ **Lighten:** To lighten an image, plot a point at the center of the diagonal line and move the point toward white (in the opposite direction you move the point to darken the image). See Figure 16-3.

✔ **Darken with more contrast:** To add more image contrast while darkening a photo, first click to plot a point in the top-right corner to anchor the curve. Then plot a point in the lower-left corner and move that point as shown in Figure 16-4.

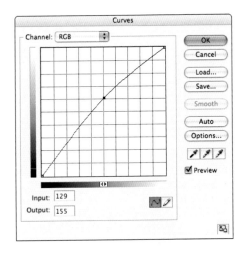

Figure 16-3: Move the center point toward the white end of the gradient to lighten the photo.

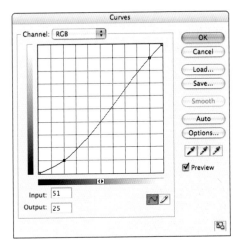

Figure 16-4: This curve darkens a photo while adding more contrast.

- **Lighten with more contrast:** Plot a point in the lower-left corner and move the top-right point left to lighten the photo while adding more contrast, as shown in Figure 16-5.

- **Darken with less contrast:** Plot a point in the lower-left corner and move a point in the top-right corner down to darken the photo while reducing contrast, as shown in Figure 16-6.

- **Lighten with less contrast:** The last basic curve adjustment uses a point plotted in the top-right corner, and the lower-left point is moved up, as shown in Figure 16-7, to lighten the photo while reducing contrast.

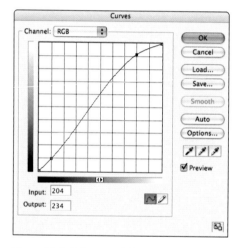

Figure 16-5: This curve lightens a photo while adding more contrast.

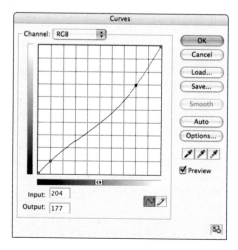

Figure 16-6: This curve darkens a photo while reducing contrast.

You have more options available when you create Curves adjustment layers. You can adjust opacity and choose from different blending modes to further control darkening and lightening photos while adding or reducing contrast.

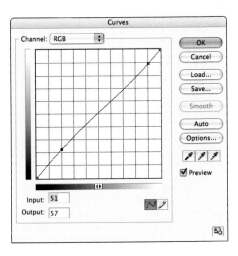

Figure 16-7: This curve lightens a photo while reducing contrast.

Using the Channels Dialog Box

Elements lets you make Levels adjustments in either the composite RGB channel or one of the three individual RGB channels. Unfortunately, Elements doesn't let you see the separate RGB channels, and you can't apply any other type of edit to channel data. In Photoshop, you have a separate Channels palette, where you can

- Apply Curve settings.
- Edit channel data.
- Create gradients and load selections to tweak color and brightness in selected areas of your image, using channels for selections.

In addition to the RGB composite channel, Photoshop permits you to create new channels (called Alpha Channels). In these new channels, you can create channel masks and add gradients to help you create precise selections for targeting the areas of your photos you want to edit.

In Figure 16-8, an Alpha Channel has been added to an RGB color image and painted with a gradient. When you choose Select⇨Load Selection, the selection is loaded as a gradient selection where you can apply image contrast, brightness, and color correction to the selected area.

Figure 16-8: In Photoshop, a Channels palette enables you to edit separate channels and create new channels.

Changing Bit Depth

In Photoshop Elements, you have a single bit-depth conversion option. You can take 16-bits/channel photos opened in camera raw and convert the photo to an 8-bits/channel image by selecting Image➪Mode➪8-bits/channel. Elements, however, doesn't let you convert an 8-bit image to a 16-bit image.

In Photoshop, you can convert 8-bit images to 16-bit images, which enables you to make contrast and brightness adjustments in 16-bit mode. Editing in 16-bit mode helps you prevent data loss and is most often the preferred choice when it comes to brightness and contrast adjustments. (See Chapter 12 for more on 16-bit images and why they are preferred.)

If you have a point-and-shoot camera that takes only JPEG images, the camera always saves your images as 8-bit files. In Photoshop, you can convert the 8-bit images to 16-bit and then perform all your brightness and contrast edits while in 16-bit mode.

To convert an 8-bit image to 16-bit in Photoshop, follow these steps:

1. **Open an 8-bit image in Photoshop.**

2. **Select Image➪Mode➪16-bits/Channel.**

   This command converts the image to 16-bits per channel. But you still need to perform more steps to make your photo a true 16-bit image.

3. **Select Image➪Image Size to open the Image Size dialog box.**

4. **Set the unit of measure to Percent from the Width or Height drop-down menu and type** 50 **in either the Width or Height text box. Be sure that Resample Image is selected, as shown in Figure 16-9, and click OK.**

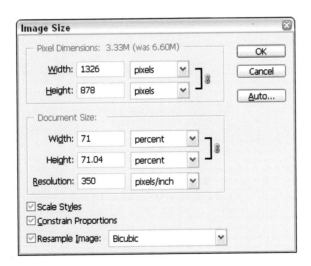

Figure 16-9: Reduce the image 71 percent and select Resample Image.

This step downsamples the photo 71 percent, which reduces the image size by 50 percent.

The end result of your edits is a 16-bit file that you can adjust for brightness and contrast with much less data loss than you'd experience with 8-bit files.

Improving Dynamic Range

The dynamic range of your camera sensor is fixed to capture highlight, shadow, and midtone ranges within defined limits. When light levels fall below or above the dynamic range of your camera sensor, you lose detail in shadows and highlights.

One way to expand the dynamic range of a photo is to use a nifty feature in Photoshop called Merge to HDR. This command enables you to merge several photos taken with different exposures into a composite image that actually produces increased dynamic range. For example, you might use three different exposures of the same image like this:

- Overexpose one photo to capture more detail in shadows.
- Take a second image and intentionally underexpose it to capture as much detail as you can get in the highlights.
- Average a third exposure to obtain all the midtone ranges.

After exposing three or more photos of the same scene, select File➪ Automate➪Merge to HDR. In a dialog box, select your three files with different exposures and merge them into a single photo. You end up with an image that's almost impossible to capture by using a film camera. In Figure 16-10, we changed exposure five times and shot five individual photos. We used the Merge to HDR command to merge the photos, producing the large composite image.

Working with More Color Modes

Photoshop Elements provides you with a limited set of conversion options to convert your photos from one color to another. In Photoshop, you have more options. The most important options for serious amateur or professional work are CMYK color and Lab color.

CMYK (Cyan, Magenta, Yellow, and blacK) are process colors used in offset printing. Before you can print your RGB files on an offset press at a print shop, you need to convert the color from RGB to CMYK.

1 second@F-22 1/4 second@F-22 1/15th second@F-22 1/60th second@F-22 1/250th second@F-22

Figure 16-10: The Merge to HDR command enables you to combine photos with different exposures into a single image.

Photoshop Elements doesn't support CMYK color, but Photoshop does. You can import RGB images in professional layout programs, such as Adobe InDesign, and convert the color at print time from RGB to CMYK. However, if you need to preview color in CMYK to observe any potential color shifts or printing problems, you need Photoshop.

Lab color mode, like RGB color, uses three channels that store your color and brightness values. With Lab color, you have the L, a, and b channels. The a and b channels describe the color information. Half the color spectrum is contained in the a channel and half in the b channel. The L channel contains only image brightness values.

Lab color can help you when you're making brightness corrections to images and converting files from color to grayscale. You can make all your edits and conversions without disturbing the color in your image. When you select Image⊅Mode⊅Lab color and click the L channel in the Channels palette, the image appears, as shown in Figure 16-11. You can adjust Curves and Levels, and perform a mode conversion while the L channel is selected. Your edits are then applied only to the brightness values without changing the color information.

Figure 16-11: Applying edits to the Lightness (L) channel in a Lab color image affects brightness values without disturbing color.

Converting to a Profile

With Photoshop Elements, you need to use a conversion utility to convert color from your workspace to an output profile. In Windows, you might use a utility such as the Dry Creek Color Profile Converter that we discuss in Chapter 4. On a Mac, you might use an AppleScript, also discussed in Chapter 4. In Photoshop, you don't need to exit the program and use an external color profile converter. Here's how it works:

1. **From the Photoshop Edit menu, select Convert to Profile.**

   The Convert to Profile dialog box opens, as you can see in Figure 16-12.

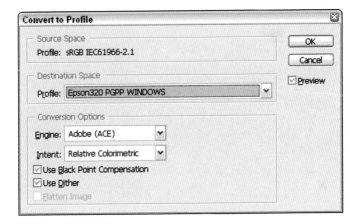

Figure 16-12: Select a printer profile in Photoshop's Convert to Profile dialog box to convert the color.

2. **From the Profile drop-down menu, select the profile you want to use for your output source, and click OK.**

   The color is converted from your working space to your printer profile.

3. **You can then save the file that has the color conversion and send the photo to an imaging center where converted files can be downloaded directly to printing devices.**

Proofing Color

In Photoshop, you can proof color on your monitor without converting the color. A menu command exists specifically for showing you what your image will look like when converted to an output profile without actually converting the color. This command can be helpful if you have several output profiles for several devices and want to preview a color conversion without changing your file.

In Photoshop, select View➪Proof Setup➪Custom. The Customize Proof Condition dialog box opens, as shown in Figure 16-13. From the Device to Simulate drop-down menu, select the color profile you want to proof. Clicking OK in the dialog box doesn't change your image.

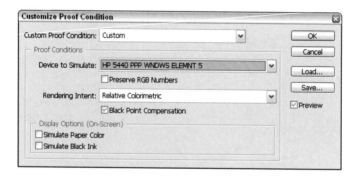

Figure 16-13: Open the Customize Proof Condition dialog box and select a profile to proof color on your monitor.

Embedding Profiles

If you decide to convert your color to an output color profile, you can easily embed the profile in Photoshop. As we explain in Chapter 4, Photoshop Elements affords you only two options for profile embedding — either sRGB or Adobe RGB (1998). In Photoshop, you can embed in the photo any profile you use to convert your color.

After you convert your color, simply select File➪Save As. In the Save As dialog box, your current color profile automatically appears in the ICC Profile section of the dialog box, as shown in Figure 16-14. Click Save to embed the profile in the document.

| File name: | photoCourtneyCostco | ⌄ | Save |
| Format: | TIFF (*.TIF;*.TIFF) | ⌄ | Cancel |

Save Options
Save:
☐ As a Copy   ☐ Annotations
☐ Alpha Channels   ☐ Spot Colors
☐ Layers

Color:
☐ Use Proof Setup: Working CMYK
☑ ICC Profile: Costco-CA-Oxnard-Gls: 14-Apr-2...

Figure 16-14: Saving the file with the ICC Profile checkbox selected embeds the profile in the image.

More Options for Using Camera Raw

Photoshop provides you with many more options when converting camera raw than does Photoshop Elements. Among the additional camera raw conversion options, you can find choices for selecting color space, variable file sizes, a crop and straighten tool, ability to open multiple files in the raw converter, and batch process conversion to DNG, and you also have some additional tab choices for correcting lens distortions, curve settings, and calibration features. (See Figure 16-15.)

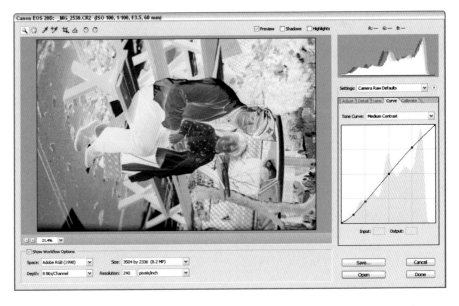

Figure 16-15: Photoshop's raw converter offers many more settings options than does the Photoshop Elements raw converter.

One of our favorite options is the ability to make Curves adjustments. If you use your camera to copy negative film, the file opens in the Camera Raw converter as a negative, as shown in Figure 16-15. It's almost impossible to set the proper white balance and make tone adjustments while viewing a negative image. With just a little adjustment in the Curves tab, you can convert your negative image into a positive right in the raw converter and then make changes for white point and brightness/contrast. In Figure 16-16, we flopped the curve (to convert negative to positive) and moved the points in toward the image data. This file was much easier to edit as a positive.

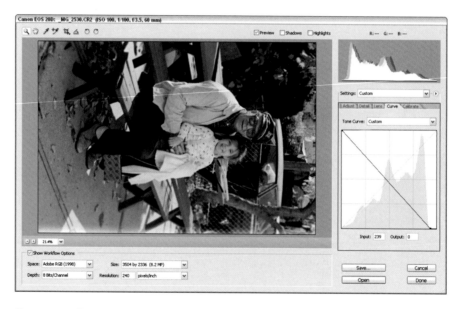

Figure 16-16: The Photoshop raw converter enables you to convert negative images into positives, making tone adjustments much easier.

More Selection Tools

Two tools we find important for creating selections in photos are the Color Range and Quick Mask tools. Having more options for creating selections helps you target areas of a photo that need color and brightness corrections. The Color Range and Quick Mask tools are used for

> ✔ **Color Range:** Makes it easier to target areas, such as flesh tones, that need color adjustments. The Color Range dialog box offers options for making selections based on color samples you make with an eyedropper

tool, as shown in Figure 16-17. You can refine selections by moving a slider (called the Fuzziness slider) in the Color Range dialog box. (The Fuzziness slider works like an opacity slider.)

✔ **Quick Mask:** This tool shows you a selected area with a red overlay color. You can add to a selection or remove from a selection easily by painting or removing paint. This tool helps you precisely target selected areas in a photo, much like the Color Range tool does, where you want to make corrections for color and brightness adjustments.

Figure 16-17: The Color Range dialog box helps you target areas in which you want to color correct and change brightness values.

Index

BUSINESS, CAREERS & PERSONAL FINANCE

0-7645-9847-3

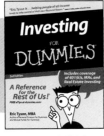

0-7645-2431-3

Also available:
- Business Plans Kit For Dummies
  0-7645-9794-9
- Economics For Dummies
  0-7645-5726-2
- Grant Writing For Dummies
  0-7645-8416-2
- Home Buying For Dummies
  0-7645-5331-3
- Managing For Dummies
  0-7645-1771-6
- Marketing For Dummies
  0-7645-5600-2

- Personal Finance For Dummies
  0-7645-2590-5*
- Resumes For Dummies
  0-7645-5471-9
- Selling For Dummies
  0-7645-5363-1
- Six Sigma For Dummies
  0-7645-6798-5
- Small Business Kit For Dummies
  0-7645-5984-2
- Starting an eBay Business For Dummies
  0-7645-6924-4
- Your Dream Career For Dummies
  0-7645-9795-7

HOME & BUSINESS COMPUTER BASICS

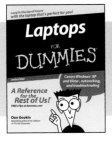

0-470-05432-8

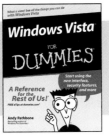

0-471-75421-8

Also available:
- Cleaning Windows Vista For Dummies
  0-471-78293-9
- Excel 2007 For Dummies
  0-470-03737-7
- Mac OS X Tiger For Dummies
  0-7645-7675-5
- MacBook For Dummies
  0-470-04859-X
- Macs For Dummies
  0-470-04849-2
- Office 2007 For Dummies
  0-470-00923-3

- Outlook 2007 For Dummies
  0-470-03830-6
- PCs For Dummies
  0-7645-8958-X
- Salesforce.com For Dummies
  0-470-04893-X
- Upgrading & Fixing Laptops For Dummies
  0-7645-8959-8
- Word 2007 For Dummies
  0-470-03658-3
- Quicken 2007 For Dummies
  0-470-04600-7

FOOD, HOME, GARDEN, HOBBIES, MUSIC & PETS

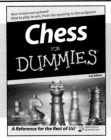

0-7645-8404-9

0-7645-9904-6

Also available:
- Candy Making For Dummies
  0-7645-9734-5
- Card Games For Dummies
  0-7645-9910-0
- Crocheting For Dummies
  0-7645-4151-X
- Dog Training For Dummies
  0-7645-8418-9
- Healthy Carb Cookbook For Dummies
  0-7645-8476-6
- Home Maintenance For Dummies
  0-7645-5215-5

- Horses For Dummies
  0-7645-9797-3
- Jewelry Making & Beading For Dummies
  0-7645-2571-9
- Orchids For Dummies
  0-7645-6759-4
- Puppies For Dummies
  0-7645-5255-4
- Rock Guitar For Dummies
  0-7645-5356-9
- Sewing For Dummies
  0-7645-6847-7
- Singing For Dummies
  0-7645-2475-5

INTERNET & DIGITAL MEDIA

0-470-04529-9

0-470-04894-8

Also available:
- Blogging For Dummies
  0-471-77084-1
- Digital Photography For Dummies
  0-7645-9802-3
- Digital Photography All-in-One Desk Reference For Dummies
  0-470-03743-1
- Digital SLR Cameras and Photography For Dummies
  0-7645-9803-1
- eBay Business All-in-One Desk Reference For Dummies
  0-7645-8438-3
- HDTV For Dummies
  0-470-09673-X

- Home Entertainment PCs For Dummies
  0-470-05523-5
- MySpace For Dummies
  0-470-09529-6
- Search Engine Optimization For Dummies
  0-471-97998-8
- Skype For Dummies
  0-470-04891-3
- The Internet For Dummies
  0-7645-8996-2
- Wiring Your Digital Home For Dummies
  0-471-91830-X

* Separate Canadian edition also available
† Separate U.K. edition also available

Available wherever books are sold. For more information or to order direct: U.S. customers visit www.dummies.com or call 1-877-762-2974.
U.K. customers visit www.wileyeurope.com or call 0800 243407. Canadian customers visit www.wiley.ca or call 1-800-567-4797.

SPORTS, FITNESS, PARENTING, RELIGION & SPIRITUALITY

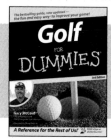

0-471-76871-5

0-7645-7841-3

Also available:

✔ Catholicism For Dummies
0-7645-5391-7

✔ Exercise Balls For Dummies
0-7645-5623-1

✔ Fitness For Dummies
0-7645-7851-0

✔ Football For Dummies
0-7645-3936-1

✔ Judaism For Dummies
0-7645-5299-6

✔ Potty Training For Dummies
0-7645-5417-4

✔ Buddhism For Dummies
0-7645-5359-3

✔ Pregnancy For Dummies
0-7645-4483-7 †

✔ Ten Minute Tone-Ups For Dummies
0-7645-7207-5

✔ NASCAR For Dummies
0-7645-7681-X

✔ Religion For Dummies
0-7645-5264-3

✔ Soccer For Dummies
0-7645-5229-5

✔ Women in the Bible For Dummies
0-7645-8475-8

TRAVEL

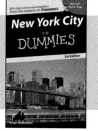

0-7645-7749-2

0-7645-6945-7

Also available:

✔ Alaska For Dummies
0-7645-7746-8

✔ Cruise Vacations For Dummies
0-7645-6941-4

✔ England For Dummies
0-7645-4276-1

✔ Europe For Dummies
0-7645-7529-5

✔ Germany For Dummies
0-7645-7823-5

✔ Hawaii For Dummies
0-7645-7402-7

✔ Italy For Dummies
0-7645-7386-1

✔ Las Vegas For Dummies
0-7645-7382-9

✔ London For Dummies
0-7645-4277-X

✔ Paris For Dummies
0-7645-7630-5

✔ RV Vacations For Dummies
0-7645-4442-X

✔ Walt Disney World & Orlando
For Dummies
0-7645-9660-8

GRAPHICS, DESIGN & WEB DEVELOPMENT

0-7645-8815-X

0-7645-9571-7

Also available:

✔ 3D Game Animation For Dummies
0-7645-8789-7

✔ AutoCAD 2006 For Dummies
0-7645-8925-3

✔ Building a Web Site For Dummies
0-7645-7144-3

✔ Creating Web Pages For Dummies
0-470-08030-2

✔ Creating Web Pages All-in-One Desk
Reference For Dummies
0-7645-4345-8

✔ Dreamweaver 8 For Dummies
0-7645-9649-7

✔ InDesign CS2 For Dummies
0-7645-9572-5

✔ Macromedia Flash 8 For Dummies
0-7645-9691-8

✔ Photoshop CS2 and Digital
Photography For Dummies
0-7645-9580-6

✔ Photoshop Elements 4 For Dummies
0-471-77483-9

✔ Syndicating Web Sites with RSS Feeds
For Dummies
0-7645-8848-6

✔ Yahoo! SiteBuilder For Dummies
0-7645-9800-7

NETWORKING, SECURITY, PROGRAMMING & DATABASES

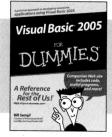

0-7645-7728-X

0-471-74940-0

Also available:

✔ Access 2007 For Dummies
0-470-04612-0

✔ ASP.NET 2 For Dummies
0-7645-7907-X

✔ C# 2005 For Dummies
0-7645-9704-3

✔ Hacking For Dummies
0-470-05235-X

✔ Hacking Wireless Networks
For Dummies
0-7645-9730-2

✔ Java For Dummies
0-470-08716-1

✔ Microsoft SQL Server 2005 For Dummies
0-7645-7755-7

✔ Networking All-in-One Desk Reference
For Dummies
0-7645-9939-9

✔ Preventing Identity Theft For Dummies
0-7645-7336-5

✔ Telecom For Dummies
0-471-77085-X

✔ Visual Studio 2005 All-in-One Desk
Reference For Dummies
0-7645-9775-2

✔ XML For Dummies
0-7645-8845-1

HEALTH & SELF-HELP

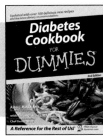

0-7645-8450-2

0-7645-4149-8

Also available:
- Bipolar Disorder For Dummies
  0-7645-8451-0
- Chemotherapy and Radiation
  For Dummies
  0-7645-7832-4
- Controlling Cholesterol For Dummies
  0-7645-5440-9
- Diabetes For Dummies
  0-7645-6820-5* †
- Divorce For Dummies
  0-7645-8417-0 †

- Fibromyalgia For Dummies
  0-7645-5441-7
- Low-Calorie Dieting For Dummies
  0-7645-9905-4
- Meditation For Dummies
  0-471-77774-9
- Osteoporosis For Dummies
  0-7645-7621-6
- Overcoming Anxiety For Dummies
  0-7645-5447-6
- Reiki For Dummies
  0-7645-9907-0
- Stress Management For Dummies
  0-7645-5144-2

EDUCATION, HISTORY, REFERENCE & TEST PREPARATION

0-7645-8381-6

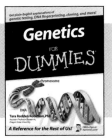

0-7645-9554-7

Also available:
- The ACT For Dummies
  0-7645-9652-7
- Algebra For Dummies
  0-7645-5325-9
- Algebra Workbook For Dummies
  0-7645-8467-7
- Astronomy For Dummies
  0-7645-8465-0
- Calculus For Dummies
  0-7645-2498-4
- Chemistry For Dummies
  0-7645-5430-1
- Forensics For Dummies
  0-7645-5580-4

- Freemasons For Dummies
  0-7645-9796-5
- French For Dummies
  0-7645-5193-0
- Geometry For Dummies
  0-7645-5324-0
- Organic Chemistry I For Dummies
  0-7645-6902-3
- The SAT I For Dummies
  0-7645-7193-1
- Spanish For Dummies
  0-7645-5194-9
- Statistics For Dummies
  0-7645-5423-9

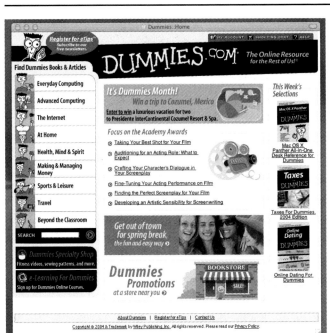

Get smart @ dummies.com®

- **Find a full list of Dummies titles**
- **Look into loads of FREE on-site articles**
- **Sign up for FREE eTips e-mailed to you weekly**
- **See what other products carry the Dummies name**
- **Shop directly from the Dummies bookstore**
- **Enter to win new prizes every month!**

* Separate Canadian edition also available
† Separate U.K. edition also available

Available wherever books are sold. For more information or to order direct: U.S. customers visit www.dummies.com or call 1-877-762-2974.
U.K. customers visit www.wileyeurope.com or call 0800 243407. Canadian customers visit www.wiley.ca or call 1-800-567-4797.

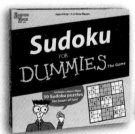